BAILOUT

BAILOUT

An Insider's Account of Bank Failures and Rescues

IRVINE H. SPRAGUE

Basic Books, Inc., Publishers

NEW YORK

Library of Congress Cataloging-in-Publication Data

Sprague, Irvine H.
    Bailout: an insider's account of bank failures and
rescues.

    Bibliographic notes: p. 271.
    Includes index.
    1. Bank failures—United States.   2. Banks and
banking—Government guaranty of deposits.   3. Federal
Deposit Insurance Corporation.   I. Title.
HG2491.S67   1986   332.1'2'0973   85–73883
ISBN   0–465–00577–2   (cloth)
ISBN   0–465–00583–7   (paper)

To Terry and Junie

They would have enjoyed this project

more than anyone else

CONTENTS

PREFACE

FOUR PERSONS met behind closed doors for a few hours in the spring of 1984; they decided to do the largest government bailout in American history—the rescue of Continental Illinois Bank. At the time I thought how different this was from the fishbowl atmosphere at the White House and in Congress where I had participated in less far-reaching decisions. This story is told solely from my perspective; I did not seek advice on whether to proceed from the other three participants—Paul Volcker, Bill Isaac, or Todd Conover.

As I began sifting through my files in preparation for retirement, I decided to write this book to document for the first time how decisions that have enormous impact on the public are made by the bank regulators. Although secrecy is essential at the time of the transactions, it cannot be justified after the fact.

After the decision to write was made, I chose to chronicle the evolution of the essentiality doctrine, which derives from the statutory authority for bank bailouts. Initiated with the rescue of tiny Unity Bank in 1971, the doctrine was developed, expanded, and refined in two subsequent bailouts. Thirteen years later it was used to save giant Continental Illinois. Within this framework, I discuss and describe all of the options considered in every bank failure, large and small. I speak with authority, particularly concerning the rescues. No other principal participated in more than two of the long-term commercial bank bailouts in FDIC history. I worked and voted on all four.

During the latter stages of the Continental crisis, at a particularly frustrating time in the negotiations, I felt the public should know not only the nature of our enormous undertaking, but the conflict of personalities and opinions among the negotiators that made our task unnecessarily difficult. Oftentimes during our deliberations, we debated points that I thought had been decided earlier. I realized that I was subconsciously recalling earlier bailout battles in which I had participated.

Continental was not merely a peak—it was a link in a chain that we had been forging since the 1971 rescue of Unity Bank. Other bailouts, of successively larger institutions, followed in ensuing years; there is no reason to think that the chain has been completed yet. Indeed, new links in this less-than-illustrious progression can form with frightening speed, as experience has demonstrated.

Early in my career the mission of the Federal Deposit Insurance Corporation (FDIC) was to do such a good job protecting depositors that they did not have to know anything about a bank except that it was FDIC-insured. That symbol of confidence on the door means just that. I was proud that the agency to which I devoted a good portion of my working life achieved its objective to a remarkable degree.

Then a new element came into play: the abrupt and steep increase in bank failures in the 1980s. More Americans than ever before were suddenly becoming aware of the presence of FDIC and its handling of bank failures. We were no longer some abstract federal guarantee. Our people were on the scene week in and out, taking over failed banks and taking care of insured depositors. Uninsured depositors, investors, management, stockholders, and delinquent borrowers got another view of FDIC in action. It was very much at our discretion whether and when any person with more than $100,000 in a failed bank would receive any part of it. Delinquent borrowers suddenly found out that they were being pressed for collection. Directors of former banks found themselves sued for damages for neglecting prudent operation of their banks.

Most of all there was a hue and cry over the reality of different treatment between megabanks and small banks. Nowhere was this more apparent than in the Continental case when we announced in May 1984 that everyone who had money in the multibillion-dollar institution would be fully protected, regardless of the amount of insurance coverage. The resulting uproar echoed from one end of the country to the other; it rang in the halls of Congress. Particularly vehement were those newly educated the hard way—those people who had lost uninsured money in small-or medium-sized banks that we had handled without 100 percent protection for all depositors and investors. We were accused of discrimination in favor of large banks in the press, in Congress, and on the scene.

Suddenly the bailout question assumed a vast new relevance. Not only was it a good story, an unknown story, that should be told; it had become important to show that we really had explored all the other options before going to the last resort—bailout. (Although I am now gone from the FDIC, I somewhat automatically interchange the words "we" and "FDIC" throughout the book.) Therefore, my purpose is to illuminate what happened and why it happened. I hope to help a new generation of regulators and bankers learn from the lessons of the past. Even more importantly I hope this book will help raise public awareness of the pitfalls that can keep them from realizing the opportunities of the exotic new financial world of the 1980s.

Although I had long mulled over the idea of this book, my wife, Margery, finally launched this project. I gratefully acknowledge this debt among many others to her. I would not have committed myself to it without her quiet but effective urging, which no doubt stemmed from her desire to find a constructive outlet for the restless energy of a husband entering retirement after nearly thirty active, often hectic, years in public service. I—and perhaps she, too—owe a special thanks to Martin Kessler, my editor and publisher, who first encouraged me to write the book and then was unrelenting in criticism that made the final product better. I wish here to also acknowledge the many persons, within FDIC and without, who shared their recollections and observations with me and verified facts. To each I am indebted. They are too numerous to list individually, but I would like to single out for special mention Alan R. Miller, my top assistant during the first three bailouts; Todd Conover, who generously jogged his memory for recollections of dates, incidents, and conversations; Frank Wille for his memories of how the two of us initiated use of the essentiality doctrine; Stan Silverberg, Mike Hovan, Mark Laverick, Peter Kravitz, Doug Jones, and Roger Watson, who shared with me their recollections; Margery, who excised my split infinitives and made numerous other suggestions regarding grammar and punctuation; Sabrina Soares for her patient, friendly editorial assistance; and for his advice and assistance, Kenneth Fulton.

PART ONE

The Stage Is Set

Chapter I

Bailout

The Thesis Is Introduced

BAILOUT is a bad word. To many it carries connotations of preference and privilege and violation of the free market principle. It sounds almost un-American.

Nevertheless, in recent years our government has participated in eight notorious bailouts. Four were commercial banks declared to be essential and saved by the Federal Deposit Insurance Corporation (FDIC). The other four were assistance transactions for public and private entities enacted by Congress.

This is the story of the four bank bailouts, told in the context of turmoil in the financial arena, a fast-moving deregulatory scene, and increasing concern over the unfairness of the special handling now given to failing larger banks.

Banks are failing in record numbers and will continue to do so for the foreseeable future. The combined 200 failures in 1984 and 1985 exceeded the forty-year total from the beginning of World War II to the onset of the 1980s. It is time to rethink our policies and procedures. The routine solutions of the past no longer suffice.

Megabanks approaching bankruptcy today are given preferred treatment that is denied the smaller banks throughout the nation. This disparity will come into clear focus as the bailouts are discussed.

When bank failures were a rarity it really didn't matter. But today, with the probability of a continuing failure rate exceeding one hundred banks a year, the time is long past when we can ignore the fairness issue.

By focusing on the four bailouts we have a ready framework in which to describe the ways all bank failures are handled, the complex regulatory structure that hampers the effort, the conflicts that arise in stressful situations, and the options for improvement of the process.

The four congressionally approved bailouts were for Chrysler Corporation, Lockheed Corporation, New York City, and Conrail. One, Lockheed Corporation, was approved by a single vote. Each was preceded by extensive public debate.

The four commercial banks declared essential and then saved with long-term FDIC assistance were: the $11.4-million Unity Bank and Trust Company of Boston in 1971, the $1.5-billion Bank of the Commonwealth of Detroit in 1972, the $9.1-billion First Pennsylvania Bank of Philadelphia in 1980, and finally the $41-billion Continental Illinois National Bank and Trust Co. of Chicago in 1984.* All were handled behind closed doors. Penn Square Bank and Seattle First National Bank are also discussed because of their relationship to the bailouts, as are the liquidation procedures used after a bank is either closed or bailed out.

Unity posed a unique problem at a time the nation was wracked by race riots. When Commonwealth, First Pennsylvania, and finally Continental faced the FDIC board, each would have been the largest bank failure in history.

The cost of the bank bailouts far exceeded the congressio-

---

*Bank asset size is shown here at the peak shortly before failure. All had shrunk somewhat by bailout day.

nally approved ones. The contrast between the publicly discussed congressional bailouts and the behind-the-scenes bank rescues by FDIC has generated a debate that seems destined to continue so long as we have megabanks in the nation that might fail.

Chairman Fernand St Germain of the House Banking Committee set the focus in House remarks on July 26, 1984, as he called for hearings a few hours after we announced the Continental bailout:

> The rescue of Continental dwarfs the combined guarantees and outlays of the Federal Government in the Lockheed, Chrysler and New York City bailouts which originated in this Committee. More important is the fact that the Federal Government provided assistance to these entities only after the fullest debate, great gnashing of teeth, the imposition of tough conditions, and ultimately a majority vote of the House and the Senate and the signature of the President of the United States.[1]

The goals of this book are multiple and related as we dissect FDIC's four long-term "essential" commercial bank bailouts and describe the process, the procedures, the conflicts, and the solutions.

1. We will remove the element of mystery and provide an insight as to exactly how bank failures are approached by the regulators, what options are considered, when officials cooperate, and when they resort to confrontation.
2. We will analyze the successes and the failures of the four bank bailouts, describe how the banks got into trouble, and provide a play-by-play account of how the bailouts were accomplished, giving the details of the transactions.
3. We will discuss the public policy question of whether the nation is better or worse off when bank bailouts are consummated. And we will suggest whether or not there will be more.
4. We will provide conclusions as to what changes should be made in terms of attitude, law, or regulation.

This is, of necessity, a personal story since much of what will be told is not on the public record or any record at all in many instances. It is based primarily on my recollections and personal papers. This is not the product of a researcher or reporter attempting to piece together what may have happened. It is not the thesis of a professor opining from remote academia about what should have happened. It is an insider's account of what really did happen. It addresses many questions:

What does the law say? How did the process work? Who made the key decisions? What alternatives were considered? What was the interplay between the bank regulatory agencies and the administration? How did the U.S. Treasury hamper and nearly derail the Continental rescue? What was the behavior of the chiefs of the nation's largest banks? Should the multinational giant banks like Continental continue to enjoy *de facto* 100 percent insurance at bargain basement rates while their smaller brothers have only limited protection?

In short, why and how were four institutions selected to be saved, and only these four? What do these experiences imply for the years ahead? Are bank bailouts a footnote in history, or the wave of the future? Those readers who stay with me will find the answers to all of these questions, and more.

Why am I the one to tell this story? Because I was the only one who was there through all four bailouts. From beginning to end I was involved as either the chairman, or director, as a participant in endless discussions, arguments, meetings, and ultimately the decisions. No other board member was involved with more than two. I worked on the Unity and Commonwealth cases during my first term; after a six-year absence I returned to participate in the handling of First Pennsylvania and Continental. In the first three I provided the decision to proceed for a divided board. The board was unanimous about Continental from the beginning.

A number of other FDIC directors, of course, were deeply involved, making crucial contributions along the way, particularly Frank Wille and Bill Isaac while each was chairman. But none of them benefited from the continuity of working on all four cases.

Who were the people making these far-reaching decisions, subject to no higher review?[2] Bill Camp, from Texas, had been a long-time career bank examiner; Frank Wille and John Heimann had served as New York bank superintendents; Bill Isaac had been a Kentucky bank lawyer; Todd Conover came from a California consulting firm; and Tom DeShazo, a career bank examiner from Virginia, often voted for Comptroller Camp at our board meetings.

Like all the other board members, I had no hands-on experience running a bank. What I brought to the position was a deep insight on how government really works, refined and developed over twenty-nine years in Washington. I served as special assistant to President Lyndon Johnson in the White House, deputy director of finance for California Governor Edmund G. "Pat" Brown, executive director of the House Steering and Policy Committee for Speaker Thomas P. "Tip" O'Neill, and director of the House Whip office for Congressman John McFall.

Wille, Isaac, and Conover are Republicans; Camp, Heimann and myself Democrats; politics, however, played no role in our decisions. FDIC directors are political persons in the sense that the law itself establishes the political participation of the board. The Federal Deposit Insurance (FDI) Act provides that not more than two of the three directors shall be of the same political party. The board elects its chairman, normally to match the party of the president. After that, politics ceases. FDIC is independent in fact as well as on the organizational charts. All directors soon find that the need for safety and soundness of the banking system rises above politics. This is not necessarily true in other agencies of government, such as the U.S. Treasury; these agencies are clearly linked to, and ultimately controlled by, the White House.

Appointed through the political process from widely divergent backgrounds, FDIC board members nonetheless shared many common attributes. All were underpaid, overworked, dedicated, and honest. One was brilliant. One treasured anonymity; one had an insatiable need for personal publicity. All have my respect and friendship.

Washington, D.C., is the ultimate revolving door as people come and go because of ambition, ineptitude, or the changing tides of political fortune. Over the years, many others appeared on the scene while I served on nine different FDIC boards. I served eleven and one-half years—longer than any member since Leo Crowley in the earliest days of the corporation. I observed a wide variety of talents, attitudes, ability, and responses as crises came and went. From this experience I can predict with some confidence generally how any future FDIC board and the other regulators will behave, regardless of who holds the responsibility.

Over the years, I worked with four Federal Reserve chairmen —William McChesney Martin, Jr.; Arthur F. Burns; G. William Miller; and Paul Volcker. Six comptrollers of the currency and nine treasury secretaries overlapped my terms.

From its beginning on January 1, 1934, through April 3, 1986, when I retired, FDIC assisted 908 failed or failing banks. I participated in handling 374, or 42 percent of the fifty-two-year total. In terms of dollar volume of assets I worked on 92 percent.

The Continental bailout is the most recent, the biggest, the most controversial, and the most interesting. I will recount its story last because to understand Continental you need to know the experience we gained and lessons learned in the three previous bailouts. These first crises enabled us to craft the Continental package under enormous pressures with some assurance that what we were doing would work. I will describe the evolution of this thought process in detail in the chapters on the first three "essential" bailouts.

The essentiality doctrine also has been used in two other bank cases not relevant to this account.[3] One bank was deemed "essential" for less than three weeks; the other was a state-owned institution, and the state was considered essential.

The apprenticeship we served in the earlier cases provided me with confidence as we tackled the biggest problem of all. Every single lesson we had learned from previous decisions, good and bad, was incorporated in one way or another into the Continental solution.

The learning years with Unity, Commonwealth, and First Pennsylvania were relatively tranquil. Our board was divided, but never publicly. True, we faced and won a stockholder suit over the warrants in First Pennsylvania, but none of these first three bailouts generated more than nominal public notice. There were minimal congressional hearings. The land was quiet.

Then came Continental.

It was the biggest banking story since President Franklin D. Roosevelt's banking holiday in 1933 and the press played it as such. Serious questions were raised as we grappled for a solution, recurred after the announcement of what we had done, and continue to this day.

Those of us who made the decision were convinced we had no other choice. The Continental rescue, which made available roughly $15.3 billion from several sources,* dwarfed the other seven FDIC and congressional bailouts, which totaled about $6 billion in loan guarantees and grants.

Many believe FDIC should save all failing banks, a concept that is clearly beyond the law. But still, the real world is sometimes hard to accept. The recurring question is, "Why did you save Continental and not my bank?" This is the question I will address.

The following basic changes in the law, technology, and psy-

---

*The Continental use of the rescue package peaked at $13.7 billion on August 13, 1984: $7.6 billion in Fed borrowings, including $3.5 billion later assumed by the FDIC; $4.1 billion in safety net borrowings from other banks; and $2 billion in capital notes from the FDIC and the banks, later reduced to $1 billion from the FDIC. The continuing FDIC investment thus is $4.5 billion.

chology since we embarked on the essentiality trail more than fifteen years ago will certainly color any future decisions.

1. The laws have been amended to permit the interstate sale of a large failed bank.
2. Our technology has been improved and staffing enhanced so the direct payoff of a bank of many billions of dollars is now entirely feasible.
3. The psychology has changed—the public expects bank failures and accepts even big ones. In 1968, my first year on the FDIC board, there were just three small failures all year; on May 27, 1983 we handled six failures in one day and in November of 1985 there were seven failures over a weekend.

What were the real reasons for doing the four bailouts? Simply put, we were afraid not to.

Would an FDIC board be more courageous, or foolhardy, now to allow the collapse of a multinational giant? This question highlights the inequities that abound throughout the system and continue to grow. What we should do about them will be addressed as the bailout stories lead us to a series of inevitable conclusions.

The idea of writing this book came to me as I went through my personal records in preparation for retirement, bundling some to be sent to the National Archives in Washington, D.C., others to the Lyndon B. Johnson Presidential Library in Austin, Texas, and the proposed Jimmy Carter Presidential Library in Atlanta, Georgia.

The exercise focused my attention on the fact that I have a unique perspective gained over a long period of years about how banks are regulated and how failures are handled. All this would be lost if not chronicled now. The stories I tell are based on official records, hearings, and reports that are available to the public, plus personal files and memories, buttressed by postmortem conversations with other participants.

In talking with other past and present regulators, I was encouraged by most to proceed. The time has long since passed when this information might be sensitive, yet it holds historical interest and will be helpful in providing an understanding of the process and in formulating future policy. Other insiders have their own perspective and certainly would tell the story differently, but the basic facts are unchallenged.

Chapter II

The Legal Framework

The Law and the Regulators
Who Interpret It

TO TELL the bailout story adequately we must first describe the incredibly complex mix of overlapping and sometimes conflicting supervisory jurisdictions, and the law under which the regulators labor. In particular, we will show how FDIC operates.

FDIC, the Federal Reserve, the Office of the Comptroller of the Currency, fifty state bank supervisors, the Justice Department, the Securities and Exchange Commission, the Treasury Department, the Federal Home Loan Bank Board, and the National Credit Union Administration, all have roles to play in regulating our financial structure. You will see how these roles often overlap as the bailout stories unfold. The Bush Task Group[1] published the table information shown in figure 2.1. In

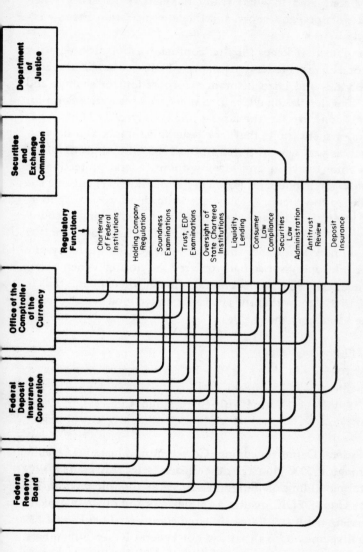

FIGURE 2.1

Functional Analysis of Existing Federal Bank Regulation

NOTE: *Blueprint for Reform: The Report of the Task Group on Regulation of Financial Services (The Bush Report)* (Washington, D.C.: U.S. Government Printing Office, 1984), p. 52.

my opinion this maze of jurisdictional lines is a symbol of clarity compared to what really happens, particularly when state regulators, governors, and the administration become involved.

The glue that keeps all this confusion from disintegrating into total chaos is federal insurance—FDIC for banks, the Federal Savings and Loan Insurance Corporation for savings and loans, and the National Credit Union Share Insurance Fund for credit unions. By far, the largest role is played by FDIC. Customers of institutions that lack federal insurance can be devastated, as was demonstrated in the 1985 Ohio and Maryland crises among savings and loans without federal protection.

Confusion is rampant. When my wife, Margery, tells me she is going to the "bank," I know she is headed for the neighborhood savings and loan where she has her checking account. When the *Wall Street Journal* reports that FDIC has closed another bank, I know that either the Comptroller of the Currency or a state bank supervisor actually ordered the closing. When a congressman asks FDIC to extend farm loans when a bank fails in his district, I know that the law is not understood even by many of the legislators themselves.

The Bank Supervisors

The Federal Deposit Insurance Corporation is headquartered in Washington, D.C., like the other Federals. Its gray granite, seven-story building on Seventeenth Street is a block from the White House. FDIC insures 14,800 banks and of these directly supervises the 8,400 state-chartered commercial banks and 339 mutual savings banks that are not Federal Reserve members. FDIC has the lonely responsibility of deciding how to handle failed or failing banks. Its board makes the bailout decisions.

The home of the Federal Reserve System is on Twentieth Street, a few blocks west of the FDIC offices. Like the FDIC, it is a member of the financial agencies' enclave and somewhat insulated from the political pressures of the White House. The Federal Reserve System—or simply, *"the* Fed," as it is known— is a daily working partner of FDIC, particularly in time of crisis. It supervises the nation's 6,100 bank holding companies and the 1,000 state-chartered banks that have Fed membership.

Even more closely related—although located several blocks farther away, south of Constitution Avenue in L'Enfant Plaza —is the Office of the Comptroller of the Currency (OCC). The comptroller is in the contradictory position of being responsible directly to the secretary of the Treasury for administrative matters and at the same time being a member of the independent FDIC board of directors in the financial enclave. The comptroller supervises 5,000 banks holding national charters. The Treasury Department itself, located two blocks from FDIC on Fifteenth Street, has no direct role in bank supervision, but makes its presence felt. FDIC communication with the administration is through the Treasury, whose head is a senior member of the president's cabinet.

FDIC, the Fed, and OCC share the federal custodianship for the nation's banking system. Each agency employs field examiners who periodically conduct examinations of the institutions under their jurisdiction. These examinations include a review of the loan portfolio and a check on policies and procedures. In addition, the call reports filed with regulators four times a year by each institution are plugged into the agencies' computer systems, which kick out for further analysis any unusual numbers or deviations from industry standards.* The agencies have the power to issue orders prohibiting banks from doing anything the regulators believe is unsafe and unsound. FDIC alone

---

*Call reports constitute a balance sheet of the bank and contain vital statistics on a bank's financial condition and its current operating results.

has authority to institute proceedings for revocation of deposit insurance.

The basic function of the three supervisors is the same. Only the banks are different. Many banks are owned by bank holding companies; most own only one bank, but some own several. Within the same bank holding company banks of all three categories—national, state, and Fed member may exist. This further crosses jurisdiction among the regulators because each bank remains subject to its own supervisor, while the Fed is the supervisor of the holding company itself.

Confusing? The varied and competing supervisory lines already make an unwieldy tangle. It promises to get worse. Interstate banking, which is developing rapidly, means that holding companies may soon own banks not only of different charters but within different states. Thus holding companies may become subject to two or more state supervisors as well as two or more federal supervisors.

The foregoing summary covers only the federal banking agencies. In addition, two doors up the street FDIC has a cousin that takes care of the 3,000 federally chartered savings and loan associations (S&Ls). The Federal Home Loan Bank Board (FHLBB) regulates them and through its Federal Savings and Loan Insurance Corporation (FSLIC) insures them.* S&Ls are distinguished from banks in that they are still primarily home mortgage lenders, but the distinctions are blurring under recent laws that have permitted S&Ls to make loans for other purposes and to offer checking accounts. If FDIC and FSLIC funds are joined together, which I oppose, the distinctions would have to be totally removed over time. Many of the savings and loans are state chartered with no federal connection. Much of the recent savings and loan trouble stems from state laws that allow S&Ls to engage in risky endeavors, compounded by lack of adequate state supervision.

An even more distant cousin is around the corner and down

---

*Confusion is intensified when, under some circumstances, federally chartered banks are insured by FDIC and supervised by FHLBB.

the street from FHLBB. The National Credit Union Administration guides those 18,000 specialized entities that have sprung up in American workplaces across the nation—including FDIC whose employees have long had their own credit union.

These five agencies constitute the financial supervisory establishment of the federal government. Each also has its state counterpart; cooperation with state authorities is an integral part of the supervisory effort.

As charterers, the states and OCC have the sole power to declare any of their banks insolvent. One widespread misconception is that FDIC closes banks. It does not. It has no authority to do so. FDIC's job is to pick up the pieces after the bank has failed and, in rare cases, to save it from closing. As insurer, FDIC immediately handles the claims of insured depositors in a failed bank either through a payoff to depositors or by selling the bank, usually within one or two days or over a weekend. As receiver, FDIC takes over all bank assets with the fiduciary responsibility to liquidate them, that is, to realize as much cash as possible and divide it among all legitimate claimants. In a sale all of the deposits and some of the assets are assumed by the new owner.

How the System Got That Way

It has been said that the federal bank regulatory system is one no sane person would design. That is true, of course, but the system was not put together at a single stroke, by a single person, or even a single group of persons. It is the accumulation of 125 years of lawmaking. Every bit of it has been an uphill struggle against longstanding public distrust of an all-powerful central bank. At no time in that century and beyond would it have been possible to command the political support to enact a comprehensive system of bank and monetary regulation. The system had to be created piecemeal, and each piece had to be wrested from an economic crisis serious enough to muster the support for enactment. Significantly, anticentral bank forces prevailed for thirty years after President Andrew Jackson destroyed the Bank of the United States in 1832. The first element of the modern federal regulatory system could not be forged until the Civil War, which gave President Abraham Lincoln sufficient leverage to win passage of a law creating the Office of the Comptroller of the Currency as a mechanism to finance the Union forces. The comptroller, as the name implies, at first actually controlled the amount of federally authorized currency in circulation.

Fifty years went by before the second regulatory body was established as the legacy of the Panic of 1907. The panic was an especially severe episode of the tight-money crises that periodically seized the nation in the absence of a dependable, properly distributed money supply. A blue-ribbon study group, the National Monetary Commission, was established; on its recommendation Congress passed the Federal Reserve Act in 1913. Even then, concessions to anticentral bank forces made the Fed a decentralized organization of circumscribed authority with a vague mandate to maintain the sufficiency of the circulating medium.

The basis of the sweeping powers the Fed can exercise today did not come until the next economic crisis—the Great Depression. The same set of emergency laws that made the Fed genuinely a central bank also gave birth to the third star in the federal bank regulatory triumvirate—the Federal Deposit Insurance Corporation.

The deposit insurance legislation was not initiated by President Franklin Roosevelt who, in fact, opposed it. He and others were concerned that bank insurance would undermine market discipline and serve as an invitation to banks to speculate freely. The most strenuous opposition came from the American

Bankers Association, which feared federal intrusion into the banking business. Among the most outspoken of the bank opponents of a federal insurance system was Continental. How wrong could they be?

As an accommodation to those who worried that insurance might foster speculation, Senator Carter Glass and other proponents agreed to an insurance limit of $2,500, enough to protect small savers who were the innocent victims of bank failures while still leaving major investors at risk. The insurance provisions were incorporated into the Banking Act of 1933, the banking centerpiece of New Deal legislation that stormed through Congress in the tumult of Roosevelt's Hundred Days. Better known as the Glass-Steagall Act, the landmark law among other things separated the riskier investment banking business from workaday commercial banking. The act also established the framework for the American financial services industry that stands to this day, although on increasingly shaky ground as lawyers seek and find loopholes in the law.

The Glass-Steagall Act inserted the new insurance provisions into the Federal Reserve Act that seemed like a logical repository at the time. They remained there until Congress gave FDIC its own act in 1950 (FDI Act).

FDIC's Independent Financing and Operation

From the first FDIC was designed to operate independently. This meant that funding was independent of general tax monies and management was not beholden to the president or Congress. So FDIC, which opened for business January 1, 1934, was originally funded by a $289 million issue of capital stock subscribed by the Treasury and the Federal Reserve. The 1950 FDI

Act followed by two years the final repurchase of that stock by
FDIC and the severing of all financial ties with the Fed and the
administration.

To this day FDIC uses no tax dollars and is not subject to the
appropriations process in Congress.* It derives its considerable
income from its assessment powers and from interest accruing
on the insurance fund. The law authorizes FDIC to levy an
assessment—in effect to charge banks an insurance premium—
at a base rate of one-twelfth of 1 percent of domestic deposits
each year. In recent years this "domestic" distinction has taken
on vast new importance because it enables banks to escape
assessment on billions of dollars in overseas deposits. It is a
point I will return to with some emphasis later. The law also
provides for refunds to banks of part of their assessments in
years when there is little insurance activity. In the quiescent
decades preceding the 1980s, banks became used to receiving
back more than half their premiums. That has come to an
abrupt halt in these recent years of escalating bank failure rates,
and banks now consider themselves lucky if they receive any
assessment rebate at all. In 1984 the effective insurance assessment was just under one-thirteenth of 1 percent or about dou-
ble the rate of the preceding four decades. For 1985 there was
no rebate for the first time since the rebate mechanism was
established in 1950. There is a $1.1 billion insurance loss carry-
over from 1985, mostly due to Continental, so a rebate for 1986
is unlikely.

The federal deposit insurance fund itself, the financial center-
piece of the agency, is by law invested in U.S. Treasury securities. In 1985 income totaled $3.3 billion, including $1.4 billion
from assessments and $1.9 billion in interest. Insurance losses
and operating expenses totaled $1.95 billion.

---

*This freedom is now threatened with rulings that the FDIC is at least
partially covered by the Gramm-Rudman-Hollings Debt Reduction Act, even
though no tax monies are involved. A further threat, still unresolved, would
take away the last semblance of independence by putting the FDIC into the
congressional appropriation process, and place it under the thumb of the Office
of Management and Budget (OMB).

Despite the enormous drains on the corporation in 1984 and 1985, the fund had grown to $17.9 billion at year-end 1985, up from $11 billion in 1981. When I first joined FDIC in 1968 the fund totaled $3.7 billion.

The FDIC fund has no relevance to the federal budget, but the president's Office of Management and Budget anxiously awaits the figures each year. The profits are used as a cosmetic accounting entry to show a reduction in the federal deficit.

Although FDIC is a full-fledged government entity, its management is separate and self-contained, not subject to direction from any other part of the executive branch. The corporation, as its employees prefer to call it, is run by a three-member Board of Directors. Unlike cabinet officers and certain other federal agency heads, FDIC directors do not serve at the pleasure of the president; each is appointed to a term exceeding that of the president. Two members are appointed to six-year terms by the president with the advice and consent of the Senate. The third director is the comptroller of the currency, an ex officio member appointed for a five-year term; in practice he serves at the pleasure of the president.*

The law specifies that not more than two of the three directors can be of the same political party. Usually, but not always, the chairman is from the president's party. For one example, I served as chairman under President Jimmy Carter, a Democrat, for two years and under President Ronald Reagan, a Republican, for seven months.

To this point, I have described the mishmash of supervision under which the nation's financial institutions must labor. Now it is time to go to the issue of bank failures. Here the picture is clear and simple. FDIC has the lonely responsibility for handling failing banks.

---

*The Comptroller of the Currency is an ex officio member holding the office because of his or her position as comptroller, not as an independently nominated member. In all other respects the comptroller is a fully participating board member.

Dealing with Failure

Life is unfair and this is never more true than when a bank closes or is on the brink of failure. The way FDIC chooses to handle a failed or failing bank can have dramatically different impacts on depositors, customers, and the community. This decision on how to proceed is based on the law, exercised with the discretion and judgment of the board.

The board's three basic choices are: (1) pay off a failed bank, that is, give the insured depositors their money; (2) sell it to a new owner with FDIC assistance; or (3) prevent it from failing —that is, bail it out. Ground rules for the decision are simple. The law is clear. The closed bank must be paid off unless a sale would be less costly to FDIC. The bailout is the rare exception; under certain circumstances, a bank can be prevented from failing regardless of the cost.

In a payoff the insured receive their money promptly; checks in process bounce; the community loses the bank and its services; loan customers must go elsewhere; and uninsured depositors and creditors are at the mercy of the liquidation results. In the sale of a failed bank—or a "purchase and assumption transaction" as it is known at FDIC—all depositors and creditors, insured and uninsured, are fully protected. A new bank or branch replaces the old with no interruption in banking service; the closing of the failed bank goes relatively unnoticed in the community. In either a payoff or sale, FDIC takes over the bad loans of the failed bank for liquidation and advances funds to cover the deposit liabilities. Stockholders in either instance go to the end of the line, receiving some value on their stock only if the liquidation is spectacularly successful and all other valid claims have been paid first.

Granted by a 1935 amendment to the deposit insurance law, the payoff and sale provisions have been the options used in over 99 percent of the failures through the years. True, variations have evolved to meet special circumstances and the law has been tinkered with, but the controlling statutory language is virtually the same and the effect on depositors is unchanged.

Bailout authority was added in 1950 and in 1982 the language was loosened somewhat so that the finding necessary to provide open-bank assistance is easier to make. The only other significant addition to the powers for handling a failed bank also came in 1982—the waiver of the prohibition against out-of-state sales for institutions at least $500 million in size, and a provision allowing for aid to keep a failing bank open if such assistance is cheaper than a payoff.

In a bailout, the bank does not close, and everyone—insured or not—is fully protected, except management which is fired and stockholders who retain only greatly diluted value in their holdings. Such privileged treatment is accorded by FDIC only rarely to an elect few as you shall see as the story unfolds. Of the eighty* cases in 1984 requiring FDIC outlays, sixteen were payoffs, sixty-three were sales, and one was a bailout. In 1985 with 120 cases, twenty-nine were payoffs and ninety-one were sales. By October there were 108 bank failures in 1986. Of these seventy-five were sold, thirty were handled through some variation of a payoff, and three were given open-bank assistance. There were no essentiality bailouts in 1985 or the first nine months of 1986.

The Payoff Procedures

What is now Section 11(f) of the FDI Act provides that "payment of the insured deposits . . . shall be made by the Corporation as soon as possible." This is the basic insurance law and

*I include banks saved with FDIC assistance in the failure totals.

FDIC is under no obligation to use any other procedure. Everything else is optional and discretionary.

Three variations of the payoff have been developed over the years: (1) simply issuing FDIC checks to give to the insured depositors; (2) creating a deposit insurance national bank where the insured can collect their money; or (3) transferring the deposits to another bank that makes the insured money available.

Today, the direct payoff is only used when there is no other option; the deposit transfer is the preferred solution in payoff situations. The payoff by deposit transfer is a hybrid. Not as bad as a direct payoff; not as good as a sale. The insured depositors receive all their money immediately. Some of the loans are transferred to another bank in the community and in most instances an immediate advance payment is made to the uninsured, based on the FDIC estimate of the ultimate liquidation value. Creation of a deposit insurance national bank to do the payoff is a rarely used procedure.

The Purchase and Assumption Procedure

What is now Section 13(c)(2)(A) of the FDI Act states that the corporation may sell the assets and assume the liabilities of the failed bank to facilitate a merger, but only if it is less costly than a payoff.

Initially, the preponderance of bank failures was handled by the payoff procedure. In the 1940s the FDIC board switched to a policy of effectively providing 100 percent insurance by handling all failures through a purchase and assumption transaction without closing the bank, regardless of the law or the circumstances. The deals were called "absorptions" since FDIC absorbed any losses. The new procedures were flagged in FDIC's 1949 annual report that expressed pride in providing

100 percent insurance in every bank failure for a five-year period. This prompted a storm in Congress because it had deliberately set the insurance limits low and contemplated payoffs as the primary tool to be used.

During the 1951 hearings, Senator J. William Fulbright sharply criticized FDIC for providing 100 percent insurance without regard to cost. He showed that in one bank failure FDIC had announced full protection before it could have known what the cost would be. That, he said, was at odds with the law authorizing FDIC assistance only when it would "reduce the risk or avert a threatened loss to the Corporation." He noted that FDIC had consistently provided such swift 100 percent protection in nineteen consecutive bank failures over a six-year span. The question of full protection had also come up the year before at hearings that preceded the passage of the FDI Act of 1950. Senator Paul Douglas suggested that FDIC's actions were creating "a moral obligation upon the Government to protect all deposits and not merely insured deposits."

FDIC took the message to heart and began to hew strictly to the cost test implied in the language "reduce the risk or avert a threatened loss." The result was nothing but direct payoffs for a number of years. Then, gradually, the policy turned to shopping for a merger partner and consummating a purchase and assumption transaction immediately after failure. Bidding was not used; the arrangements were negotiated with a single buyer. The present policy of calling for competitive bids on the purchase of a closed bank started January 12, 1966, with the failure of the Five Points National Bank in Miami, Florida. The effect of this procedural change was to markedly increase the possibility of a purchase and assumption transaction because the premium received by FDIC serves to reduce the cost relative to a payoff.

Language was added in the 1982 Garn-St Germain Act to remove any doubt that the cost test must be used. The new language says: "No assistance shall be provided . . . in excess of that amount which the Corporation determines to be reasonably necessary to save the cost of liquidating, including paying of the insured accounts. . . ."

In a straight purchase and assumption transaction banking organizations or individuals in the same state bid to assume all of the deposit liabilities and the good assets of the failed bank. All customers' funds, insured and uninsured, become available in the new bank and FDIC takes over the bad loans. The vast majority of all purchase and assumption transactions are handled in this manner. Five variations of this purchase and assumption, or sale, procedure have evolved over the past twenty years, designed to meet special circumstances as they arose. All the variations rely on the same provision in the law and have the same effect on bank depositors and creditors.

The variations are: (1) dividing the bank for sale to two parties; (2) sale to a foreign interest; (3) an assisted sale without going through the bidding process; (4) an out-of-state sale; and (5) a delayed sale following a cash infusion by FDIC.

The Interstate Provision

We have seen how the standard sale procedure evolved over many years to the present almost routine system. The interstate sale procedure, by contrast, developed quickly but with considerable acrimony and several false starts. However, the ground rules are now firmly in place.

Early in 1980, faced with the certain failure of one large institution and very possibly others, I began pushing for legislation to allow the interstate sale of a large failed bank. Opposition was ferocious from the American Bankers Association, Independent Bankers Association of America, and the Conference of State Bank Supervisors. Larry Kreider of CSBS told me he was going to beat the bill, but he might reconsider if I could tell him the name of a single big bank in trouble. This, at the height of our struggle to save First Pennsylvania. I declined his offer.

Finally, I enlisted the aid of Treasury Undersecretary Bob Carswell, who set up a working group of Fed Governor Chuck Partee, Comptroller John Heimann, Credit Union Administrator Larry Connell and me. Troublesome issues were: (a) the size cutoff, (b) should it be full interstate or regional, and (c) should there be preferences for same-type or same-state institutions.

We had to balance what we needed with what we could get from the Congress. The compromise we worked out was finally adopted virtually unchanged as part of the Garn-St Germain Act of 1982. Key requirements were that the bank must actually fail, and it must have at least $500 million in assets.

It was not until February 14, 1986, that an interstate sale was actually accomplished when the $593-million Park Bank of St. Petersburg, Florida, was sold to Chase Manhattan Corp. of New York for $62.6 million, the fourth highest bid ever received.* The second interstate transaction followed in just five months when the FDIC board paid First Interstate Bancorp of Los Angeles $73.3 million to take over the failed $1.5 billion First National Bank and Trust Co. of Oklahoma City. Four times previously we had embarked on an interstate sale, but for different reasons, none were accomplished.[2]

The Essentiality Doctrine

What is now Section 13(c)(4)(A) of the FDI Act gives the FDIC board sole discretion to prevent a bank from failing, at whatever cost. The board need only make the finding that the insured bank is in danger of failing and "is essential to provide adequate banking service in its community."

*The five highest bids: Franklin National, New York, 1974, $125 million; U.S. National, San Diego, 1973, $89.5 million; United American Bank, Knoxville, 1983, $67.5 million (estimated); Park Bank, 1986, $62.6 million; First National Bank of Midland, Texas, 1983, $51.1 million.

This essentiality option, the life-or-death bailout authority, is what this book is all about—the Unity, Commonwealth, First Pennsylvania, and Continental syndrome. None of the numerous other applications for bailout have possessed the characteristics that the FDIC board believed would merit an "essentiality" finding.

The law and legislative history of the 1950 act provide no detailed directions on arriving at the essentiality finding. Nor do they define community. The law does list specific kinds of assistance that are permissible to use in preventing a bank from failing. But as to when to employ such aid, there are merely references to the "discretion" of the Board of Directors and the "opinion" of the board. Clearly, however, this authority was not intended for widespread use.

The original draft of the legislation made no mention of essentiality. This prompted concern during Senate hearings that use of the new powers would not be restricted to banks in real distress and that it might conflict with the Fed's powers as lender of last resort. Further, the Senate was aware of and concerned about the prior five-year history when FDIC protected all depositors and creditors by refusing to do a single payoff. Following the hearings, the Senate Banking Committee added the requirements that an assisted bank "is in danger of closing," and that an essentiality finding must be made. The House accepted the Senate language that became law.

It really boils down to a judgment call by the FDIC board; the courts have always upheld an agency's discretionary authority.[3] The record shows this discretion has not been abused. In each instance careful, factual analysis preceded the action, formally adopted guidelines were followed, and no challenge has been successful. So there you have it. A bank can be bailed out if two of the three FDIC board members determine it should be. In practice, the bailout decisions do not come easily and FDIC boards have been reluctant to make an essentiality finding unless they perceive a clear and present danger to the nation's financial system. Unity Bank of Boston is the exception. Although it did not threaten the nation's financial system, it posed other threats.

As the story unfolds you will see that the bailout option is taken only after all other avenues have been explored and exhausted: merger with another institution, foreign or domestic; or sale to anyone interested and capable, be it a bank or individual. When the other options disappear the choice then lies between a payoff and a bailout. The bailout results differ in one significant respect from a payoff, sale, or merger. Of necessity, in a bailout there is some protection for stockholders and creditors. If the bank is not allowed to fail, it is impossible to structure a transaction that does not provide at least the possibility of some residual value to stockholders and creditors of the failing institution.

The FDIC Bank Failure Routine

Armed with the array of options and faced with an avalanche of failures in the 1980s, FDIC evolved a bank failure routine designed to let the staff operate with little board oversight in the ordinary cases, but to permit the board to become intensely involved in the large or complicated ones.

At the end of the FDIC regular board meeting,* a "probable fail" list is read aloud by the chairman. There is only one copy. It is kept under lock and key.

The list is updated weekly and contains the banks that have a high probability of failure over the next ninety days. Banks go on the list based on reports by OCC, the Federal Reserve, a state supervisor, or FDIC's Division of Bank Supervision. The complicated prospective failures trigger a lengthy sequence of

*The regular meeting, which had been held each Monday afternoon was switched in mid-1986 to every other Tuesday.

analysis, meetings, and discussions on the best way to handle each case. On occasion, the failure of a bank comes with lightning speed when a run develops as in Continental's case or when fraud or shady operations are discovered as in Penn Square's case. Then the bank barely makes the list before it fails.

After discussion of the ninety-day list, the Division of Bank Supervision is asked for a report on the expected failures during the current week. In each case, two questions are always asked: First, can we sell the bank? Selling the bank is the preferred solution because it causes the least disruption in the community. And second, when must the board members be available for the special meeting on disposal of the bank?

By this time preparations for a sale have been well underway. They begin as soon as a bank goes on the ninety-day list. Examiners go into the bank to prepare a bid package containing such information as the size, type, and duration of the deposit base; the volatile deposits that may run off; contingencies, such as standby letters of credit and other off-balance-sheet items; leases or loans on the bank buildings; pending or anticipated lawsuits; and anything else that is needed for a bidder to make an informed decision on possible acquisition of the bank. An important part of the investigation is determining whether a sale will be cheaper than a payoff and thus permissible under the law. If the examiners discover fraud or suspect hidden liabilities, or anything else that would make a sale more costly than a payoff, FDIC goes directly into a payoff mode. In all other cases, FDIC proceeds to a sale. Sometimes this eventually leads to a payoff anyway when the conditions for a sale cannot be met.

What is offered for sale is all deposit liabilities, insured and uninsured, together with the good assets of the bank, usually including the bank building itself and certain performing loans in the bank. As part of the transaction, FDIC will advance enough cash to the successful bidder to balance deposits against assets. What bidders offer is a premium for the franchise. FDIC calculates the minimum it must receive in a premium to reduce the outlay below the payoff cost. The bidders are not told what it is.

Then FDIC draws up a list of qualified bidders. The ground rules set by the board call for inviting bids from well-regarded individual investors or banks located in the area served by the failed bank. The institutions must be well managed, approximately twice as large as the bank to be acquired, and have adequate capital. Further, FDIC checks to be sure that the purchaser will not be acquiring a monopolistic hold on the community. Individual investors must satisfy similar criteria. A few days before the bid meeting Paul Ramey, in our special unit that handles failed banks, goes over the options with the FDIC board, which then gives Ramey the go-ahead on how to proceed.

The proposed list of bidders is circulated to the three board members, the Federal Reserve, and the state supervisor. Any of these can remove a prospective bidder for cause. The day before the anticipated failure those on the approved bid list are called to a meeting with the FDIC regional director. They are given the bid package; a draft of the sale agreement; and instructions on the regulatory approvals needed, capital requirements that must be maintained after acquisition, and the rules of the bidding process. Bidders are permitted to ask any clarifying questions, but only in the presence of all the other bidders so all have the same information.

Sealed bids are due at the regional office at the hour of the anticipated closing. After the bids are opened, the top bid is checked to see if it meets the minimum dollar figure, conforms in every respect to the guidelines, and if all necessary regulatory approvals have been received. If all is in order, the board can approve the sale in a matter of minutes. The regional director phones in with the bid information; the FDIC board convenes in a special meeting and promptly acts.

Those are the easy ones. When there are no bidders, or no qualified bidders, or if the offer is too low to comply with the cost test, FDIC scrambles to decide what to do.

One approach is to ask the high bidder to increase the bid. If the high bidder declines, he then is asked if he is interested in a deposit transfer, that is, a payoff of insured deposits using the bidding bank as agent. If he again declines FDIC goes to the last resort—straight FDIC payoff.

Complications arise and board participation intensifies in the unusual cases: The bailout candidates, for example. Or when a payoff is indicated for a very large bank. Or when another bank has a big stock investment in the failing institution and wants to negotiate to take it over without competitive bidding. Other instances requiring concentrated attention and innovative decisions include: Working out solutions to the problems of giant mutual savings banks. Deciding what to do when multiple failures in a state have made the qualified bid list too small to be meaningful. Determining how to handle large failures when the sale process will not work because of anticompetitive problems or lack of a large enough suitor. Resolving what to do about chain and related banks, such as the Butcher banks in Tennessee or the Parsons chain in Michigan. The special cases seem to grow.

The pendulum has swung once again toward 100 percent protection of depositors and creditors. Despite the fact that Congress made it clear in the 1950 Act that FDIC was not created to insure all deposits in all banks, in the years since Congress has gradually increased the insured amount to $100,-000. In addition, the regulators have devised solutions that protect even the uninsured in the preponderance of cases. The exceptions, where no such solution can be devised, produce the unfairness factor.

Now you know the law, who the regulators are, and the ground rules under which they operate. Next: How is the law implemented?

PART TWO

The First Three Bailouts

Chapter III

Unity Bank

The Essentiality Doctrine Is Established

THE BAILOUT of a small bank in 1971 was the first application of the essentiality doctrine; it happened only after weeks of agonizing deliberations by a divided FDIC board. The essentiality law had been on the books for twenty-one years, but it never had been used; there were serious questions about whether it should now be instituted as an operating policy.

Unity Bank of Boston was not the best case to embark on untested waters, but we did. The trail that eventually led to the Commonwealth, First Pennsylvania, and Continental bailouts began with the impending failure of Unity Bank. This $11.4-million institution in the Roxbury section of Boston was minority owned and served the black community.

At the time, I was in my third year on FDIC's Board of Directors. Frank Wille had recently replaced Kay Randall as the chairman. Our third board member was Bill Camp, comptroller of the currency.

From its start, Unity had been a special case: a minority bank that opened its doors in 1968 in a deteriorated urban core. The year was more noted for inner-city rioting and destruction than any positive development such as starting a bank. Yet, Unity was launched in south Boston despite the atmosphere of uncertainty and fear that generally prevailed in big cities throughout the United States that year.

The new bank had a dynamic organizer in thirty-seven-year-old Don Sneed, whose background was in real-estate brokerage and door-to-door selling. He turned out to be an effective promoter. Sneed went on television to urge the formation of the bank, appealing to the black and white populations of the Boston area to unite behind the effort. Many people saw the bank as a symbol of regeneration flowering in a season of strife. Money came in from widely scattered sources, from companies and individuals who wanted to show their good will and their sympathy with the effort. The 120,000 shares of common stock sold readily at $10 a share. The bank had some 3,200 stockholders, most owning small amounts. When House Speaker Tip O'Neill asked me to come to his office to fill him in on the situation, he smiled and said that as a $10 stockholder he had a real interest in the bank. What he really cared about, of course, was the community.

Depositors responded enthusiastically to the new bank opening in the neighborhood; deposit growth during the first years exceeded expectations. Much of it was due to Sneed, whose strong points were public relations and bringing in business. "I really thought the bank had a chance to make it," FDIC Regional Director Mark Laverick told me years later, "considering all the support the bank was drawing. I had to hand it to Don Sneed. Nobody thought he could do it. Nobody believed you could raise money at that time to start a black bank. In many ways, Sneed was a very capable fellow."

But Laverick knew that it would still be tough going. When a bank is launched even under the best of conditions, it will take at least two or three years before it shows its first profit.

Unity, in less than three years of operation, found itself badly in the red. The problem was partly location. The bank's single office was in a shabby old downtown area with many empty buildings. There was very little commercial activity; not enough of an economic base to support a bank.

The real problems were lack of management, lack of trained staff, and lack of experience. By this time Unity had few competent and experienced bank officers. Raising money on that early wave of euphoria had been relatively easy. The problem was knowing what to do with the money after they got it. Unity needed someone with banking experience to make the loans— someone who would know when to say, "No," and who could recognize creditworthy loan customers.

Laverick recalled that they'd

> do things like make a really risky $100,000 loan to a small business and think they were all right because the loan was 90 percent guaranteed by the Small Business Administration. Well, that still cost the bank $10,000.
>
> They didn't realize how close to the brink they were. They made the same mistake I've seen with a lot of businesses; they thought that if you have cash on hand, you must be doing all right. Well, in a bank, you always have cash on hand. Don Sneed couldn't understand how the bank could be losing money.

John Regan, the assistant regional director, recalls that personnel was a problem from the start. FDIC vetoed one person for a key bank officer position the day before the bank opened because in FDIC's opinion the individual utterly lacked qualifications. Regan remembered that the bank opened without a door for the vault, and a security guard was needed for several days until the door was delivered. He saw the bank as the product of the times. "It was part of that social era," he said.

More than 90 percent of Unity's depositors were black. Unity was the only minority owned bank in Boston, or, for that matter, in all of New England. It was one of only twenty-nine minority owned and operated banks in the nation.

In 1971 no one could be sure that the failure of a black bank in a rundown urban center would not touch off a new round of 1960s-style rioting. The Watts; Washington, D.C.; and Detroit race riots were not long behind us. These and other riots of the era in New York City, Rochester, Jersey City, Patterson, Elizabeth, Chicago, and Philadelphia came very readily to mind when we thought about Unity.

Early in the year, State Banking Commissioner Freyda Koplow told me she was worried about the situation. She was approaching the point where she would have to revoke the bank's charter. A new examination was underway and it seemed certain to show that Unity was broke. The major Boston banks that had put money into Unity for good will purposes were concerned. They felt they had a moral commitment as well; and they were rallying around Dick Hill, First Boston Bank president, who was trying to put together a private assistance package.

The Search for a Creative Solution

In early March the Boston banks were considering an assistance plan that basically called for them to lend Unity $400,000 and provide management assistance. Two minority oriented groups would provide certain guarantees and purchase $300,000 in certificates of deposit which would be held in custodian accounts. By midmonth, the Boston banks had turned to discussing a plan for issuing $500,000 in capital notes and a $500,000 stock sale.

FDIC initiated a new examination of Unity and simultaneously made plans for handling the bank if it closed. A closed-bank transaction was all the agency had ever done: Wait until the bank fails; then act. That was perceived as FDIC's statutory mandate at that time. The big question was whether we could arrange a closed-bank merger. It was going to be very difficult to find a buyer for a minority bank in that undesirable location. Without a buyer, we could not keep a bank in the community. We would simply pay off depositors, and the people would once again be without an independent neighborhood bank.

By March 24 when Wille and I went to Boston to meet with Koplow and the bankers, it was clear to them that none of the plans they were exploring were sufficient to save Unity. Something new and dramatic and different would be required.

Neither Wille nor I had any trouble viewing the problem in its broader social context. We were willing to look for a creative solution. But we also knew the law provided us with few options.

Before meeting with the bankers, Koplow, Wille, and I were briefed by the bank examiners on the current situation. They told us, not surprisingly, that Unity's capital was depleted; most of its loans were bad; its loan collection practices were weak; its personnel situation combined the worst of two worlds: overstaffing and inexperience. Laverick told me that there were two persons for every job, and neither one had been taught the job.

The city's four largest banks had all sent members of their top management to the meeting as evidence of their concern. Wille emphasized to the bankers that we were in Boston on a fact-finding mission and that our meeting with them was not a commitment. They said they understood.

Hill described the bankers' efforts to put together a private rescue package. He said that as the banks got more deeply into the matter, they discovered that Unity's financial and personnel problems were far worse than they had dreamed. Based on these findings, the bankers argued that control should be taken

out of the hands of the present board and officers and vested
in a state-appointed conservator—an extreme and rarely used
power.

Koplow at first suggested that FDIC be the conservator. We
turned that down promptly and flatly. We were not going to
run the bank. After some discussion, the group agreed that any
conservator appointed should come from outside, should be full
time, and should supplant current management entirely. They
were concerned that ousting local management might be seen
as a power play that would invite severe repercussions in the
community. We agreed, therefore, that the conservator had to
be black and had to be a leader. But the conservator did not
necessarily have to be a banker.

Now FDIC and the local bankers understood that $500,000
was woefully inadequate: A capital infusion in the range of $1
million to $1.5 million or more would be necessary. The bankers
wanted someone to put the money in before they would make
their own loans to Unity. They looked straight at Wille and me.
They made the point that the situation—a failing minority bank
in a black neighborhood—could be repeated elsewhere in the
nation. It was, therefore, not simply a local Boston matter, the
bankers argued. They said it was really a national policy issue
with broad social implications; and, therefore, FDIC should be
involved with a substantial financial commitment.

An Unprecedented Proposal—Bailout

We listened. What they asked was unprecedented. Whenever
FDIC had put money into a bank, it was to merge the bank out
of existence or to pay off its depositors. But to preserve a failing
bank in its present corporate existence? It had never been done.

Wille summarized FDIC's position to the bankers. First, he said, there was no question of the seriousness of Unity's financial condition. Second, he pointed out that national policy implications or not, any action FDIC might take still had to be governed by law. If, for example, we would consider making a capital infusion, we would have to be able to make the finding that the bank was essential to provide adequate banking services in the community. That, in turn, implied that whatever aid we would render must afford a reasonable chance for the long-term survival of the bank. It had to continue providing banking services to the community; otherwise, it could not be regarded as "essential."

This aspect was particularly troubling to our staff, even insurmountable to many who could divine no trace of hope in the cold figures of the examination report. Under the law Unity had to have legitimate prospects for recovery as a result of the aid before we could provide it. That would hinge on whether capable management could be obtained. I hoped that the replacement of Unity's management by a conservator might be the key to that dilemma.

Beyond that, staff operations would have to be vastly improved. We told the banks we considered their offer to provide staff support and training as critical to the success of any assistance plan—far more important than their $500,000 in loans. Unity's staff badly needed fundamental instruction in lending procedure, credit documentation, loan administration, and other daily operations. Without that there was no way to create even the possibility of a viable bank.

That still left the question of our willingness to assist a failing bank. Such a radical departure from our traditional function, Wille said, would set a precedent and no one knew where it would lead. Would our aid to Unity be seen as guaranteeing the survival of all minority banks? Would not white-owned banks have the right to ask us to bail them out, too?

How about the unintended reprieve for stockholders? If mar-

ket discipline means anything, stockholders should be wiped
out when a bank fails. Our assistance would have the side effect
—most undesirable from our point of view—of keeping the
stockholders alive at government expense. This question
proved to be a recurring and particularly thorny one, confront-
ing us again in the Commonwealth, First Pennsylvania, and
Continental cases.

When the meeting broke up, Wille and I said we would study
the banks' plan. We said we had to wait until the bank examination was finished. We already knew what that would tell us.
We were really waiting for the results of a searching analysis
by our Legal Division of that untried essentiality provision
embodied in Section 13(c) of our law. And for time to do some
deep inner searching within ourselves.

The enigmatic "essentiality" test posed intriguing questions.
What are "adequate" banking services? What was the community? Could we legitimately stretch the law to its outer limits
in this special case? Where would it lead us in other bank
failures? Was setting this precedent too high a price to pay in
order to save Unity?

Some fifteen years after the fact, over lunch at the Union
League Club in New York, Wille and I reminisced about how
we had triggered use of the essentiality law at Unity. Wille
recalled that at the time we were considering how to handle
Unity, we also were looking ahead to Commonwealth which
was in deep trouble. Both served minority communities. He was
right. I returned to my files and found a memorandum to Wille
and me from our general counsel, Bill Murane, who traced the
legislative history of the essentiality law and discussed its ap-
plicability to both Unity and Commonwealth.[1] There was a
relationship. If we said "yes" to Unity, then it would be more
difficult to say "no" to the much larger Commonwealth.

Murane's April 27, 1971, memo was a well-researched and
footnoted document, but it did not shed much light on any
ground rules we should follow. The memo reported that the
purpose and the moving force for including 13(c) in the 1950

FDI Act were not clear. It might have been an effort to preserve banking franchises in small towns, but maybe not. The testimony of FDIC Chairman Maple T. Harl said little about the provision other than that he favored it.

Our legal analysis of the language and legislative history two decades after the fact told us at least two things: First, Congress had given us broad, even sweeping, discretion in determining when to aid a failing bank and in setting the terms and conditions of such aid. Second, Congress had not defined the word "community," leaving it open to our interpretation under the times and circumstances. The authority to do bailouts was clear; the ground rules were left to FDIC.

Congress may have had geographical communities in mind when it passed the law, but by 1971 the word "community" had begun to take on a broader meaning. Groups or constituencies scattered throughout the nation were being recognized as "communities" in their own right; for example, the black community, the Hispanic community, or any ethnic community. Court cases and some recent enactments of Congress supported the interpretation. Our Legal Division gave us its opinion that the facts would support a decision to assist Unity because it was a biracial bank located in and serving the community of Roxbury. And no other black or biracial bank served that community.

Neither Wille nor I had any problem with the definition of "community" that we finally came up with. As far as I know, no one on the FDIC staff had any problem either, and that staff had been analyzing "communities" for bank merger and acquisition purposes for a long time. It was clear to us that the black interests in Roxbury constituted a distinct and valid community.

That was a threshold finding. Next we would have to make the finding that the bank was "essential" to its community within the meaning of the law. That was harder since other banks had branches in Roxbury not far from Unity.

I decided to go to Boston again to have an on-the-scene look at the patient. My assistant, Alan Miller, went with me. Our driver, John Quinn, was a bank examiner who had grown up in Roxbury when it was an Irish Catholic enclave. Quinn had been with FDIC since April 1934, four months after the corporation opened for business. We drove through Quinn's old neighborhood to the street where the bank was supposed to be and could not find it. We drove up and down the street three times and still could not find it. So we parked the car where the street numbers indicated the bank should be; only then did we spot it, directly across the street. The building was painted green and purple. It had once been an automobile repair garage, and we could see where the overhead door had been. Our examiners were still inside, monitoring Unity on a daily basis, as we do when a bank is on its last legs. I watched the customer traffic and observed the location of nearby branches of other banks and then returned to Washington for decision time.

Structuring the Rescue Package

Looking into our crystal ball, Wille and I determined that it would take $2 million to keep Unity going. The big Boston banks said they were ready with their $500,000; this meant that FDIC would have to come up with $1.5 million. Actually, the large banks' risks were minimal; they were relying on loan guarantees through a unit of the federal Office of Economic Opportunity and the Interracial Council for Business Opportunity Fund, Inc. The four biggest banks—First National Bank of Boston, Shawmut Bank of Boston, New England Merchants, and State Street Bank and Trust Company—were going to put up $100,000 each, and another $100,000 was to come from a group of other banks. Ultimately, the loan by the banks totaled $485,000. And buying into it got to be so popular that sixty-seven additional banks, besides the big four, had a piece of the loan, mostly in small amounts ranging from $250 to $1,000.

Our assistance agreement provided for a purchase of capital notes in the bank. It would be subordinated debt.* At first the major banks wanted their subordinated notes to be senior to ours, so that they would be paid off before we were. We rejected their proposal. Instead we worked out an arrangement by which the banks would be repaid in three equal annual installments beginning after four years; FDIC would be repaid in a lump sum after five-and-a-half years. Our portion of the infusion carried a 5.25 percent interest rate, which was more than reasonable even for those days.

We had included a formula for earlier, partial repayments whenever Unity's annual earnings exceeded $100,000. That was pie in the sky; we knew it would be a long time before Unity reached that level of earnings, if ever. In fact, we expected our repayment to come from recapitalization, rather than earnings. If the bank could grow into an acquisition target and be purchased by a private investor, we might expect lump-sum repayment. But it would take time to train Unity's staff, improve its management, and upgrade its operations; the bank would need all its resources during the growing period. So we opted for a single payment at the end of the term in 1976, with the idea that we would review the bank's progress and the status of our note at that time.[2]

Meanwhile, Koplow had settled on Richard L. Banks to be appointed conservator. A prominent black attorney, Banks took a leave from his job as director of the Boston Lawyers for Housing, an activity sponsored by the American and Boston bar associations. Banks had no background in banking; with Koplow's concurrence, he appointed Arthur B. Dimmitt as chief operating officer. Dimmitt was a white banker recently retired as senior vice-president of Manufacturers National Bank of Bristol County in Mansfield, Massachusetts. He had been in

---

*Subordinated debt would mean that certain other existing debt in the bank would be paid off first if the bank failed and its assets were liquidated.

banking almost forty years and had a reputation as a stern lending officer.

One by one the pieces of a rescue fell into place. The mechanism would be ready. The question still remained: Would the FDIC board trigger it?

Bill Camp, the third member of our board, had not participated in the discussions but I kept him informed. He told me he was dead set against assistance from the outset, a position he maintained later in our Bank of the Commonwealth deliberations. Camp believed that bailouts were bad public policy and doing the first one would lead to many more, possibly an uncontrollable flood. In those days OCC had offices in the ornate Treasury building which has occupied the same site since the earliest days of the nation. I always enjoyed visiting Camp to learn from his lifelong experiences as a bank examiner and to listen to his stories about deer hunting in Texas.

If Camp would not vote, that meant that Wille and I had to agree on a deal or there would not be one. With Wille ready to vote "Yes," and Camp abstaining, I was left to cast the deciding vote. Wille remembers it a little differently—he cannot recall Camp's opposition. I will stick with my recollections and the official FDIC minutes which show that Camp did not vote for the essentiality finding at Unity.[3] Later on July 30, our full board ratified the transfer of the $1.5 million, with DeShazo voting in place of Camp.

The Trigger for the Decision

More than just bank safety was on my mind as we approached decision time. Increasingly, my thoughts revolved around public safety. I found myself harkening back to the violent scenes of our riot-torn cities not many years before. Watts, in particu-

lar, haunted me. The eruption in that black section of Los Angeles was the first major big city riot in the country, and the
ordeal of those harrowing days was—and remains—vividly
alive in my mind.

When the rioting broke out on a hot August afternoon in
1965, Governor Pat Brown was in Greece. I was the state's
deputy director of finance stationed in Washington. Hearing
the riot news, the governor had cut short his trip and was
already on his way home when Counsel to the President Lee
White telephoned me to say the White House needed decisions
urgently: How many troops or guard units would we need?
What units should be mobilized? Where should they be de-
ployed? What kind of relief efforts needed to be undertaken?
What detention facilities should be used? A thousand things
that only the governor could decide.

White said there would not be time for the governor to go
back to California. We decided to intercept him in New York.
Flown there in a White House plane that afternoon, White and
I met the governor's flight from Europe at JFK Airport. We took
him quickly to a command post that we had set up at the airport
in a stark and windowless room. It was utterly secure. The only
furniture was a desk, two chairs, and a telephone. There we
stayed for hours, working through an open telephone line, receiving reports, conferring with the White House, and making
the decisions. As the governor called the shots, we relayed the
word to Sacramento and got back information on how things
were going. It was an explosive situation, leaping ahead of us
like a California range fire. When it was over, the toll was 34
dead, 1,032 wounded, 3,952 arrested, and $40 million in prop-
erty damage. The agonizing hours we spent in that grim and
airless room made an indelible mark on me.

We did not know then that the ordeal would persist throughout the remainder of the decade. Two summers after Watts, I
was serving in the White House during the flaming tragedy that
was Detroit in 1967. I remember hearing the reports of the
terrible events happening there from Deputy Attorney General

Warren Christopher, who had been dispatched by the president
to lead the Detroit task force. I remember how dreadfully familiar it all sounded—the violence in the streets, the burning, and
the chaos. Anything seemed to touch it off, and then it would
spread from city to city. At times it seemed unstoppable.

These still raw experiences became the background against
which I considered Unity, the tiny black bank in the run-down
inner city of Boston in 1971. No one knew what repercussions
might flow from its closing. We knew that besides Unity's
internal problems, the bank had suffered somewhat from white
borrowers who had taken advantage of the inexperienced black
lending officers. But our main concern was simply the specter
of a black bank failing in a big city in those times.

In retrospect, my vote to make the "essentiality" finding and
thus save the little bank was probably foreordained, an inevitable legacy of Watts. And since mine was the deciding vote, it
may not be too much to say that the Watts riots ultimately
triggered the essentiality doctrine.

Early in July I told Wille I would support the bailout. The
only remaining question was when. Koplow called us the
week of July 19 and notified us that she would act the next
week.

Wille and I flew to Boston Tuesday afternoon, July 22. With
us were Miller and Murane. At the banking commissioner's
office, we witnessed while Koplow officially placed Unity into
conservatorship and appointed Richard Banks conservator.
Then we convened our FDIC board meeting with Murane acting as secretary. It was over in two minutes. We voted two to
zero to render the first 13(c) essentiality assistance in FDIC's
history.

The precedent-setting session unintentionally included another innovation: that of voting bailout deals in the field, standing up beside a desk in a small cluttered office, as we later did
in the Continental case. But the important precedent was, of
course, the irreversible turn we had taken with Unity, away

from our historic narrow role of acting only after the bank had failed, and then merely to dispose of the remains through a payoff or sale. Now we were in the bailout business, how deeply no one could then tell.

Neither Wille nor I thought about making history. We did it because we believed it was the right thing to do at that time in that situation. We certainly had no idea we were setting the precedent that would lead to the Continental solution thirteen years later.

The Unity deal caused comment in banking circles where the nature of the transaction was well understood. It also brought in some congressional mail asking for explanations. A protest came from an individual who denounced "this brand of civil rights" and threatened a class-action suit. The trade paper, the *American Banker*, tracked me down in Houston where I had gone on other FDIC business. The reporter asked if he could take the Unity solution to be the first of more to come in cases of troubled banks. I told him it was hard to see how, because I could not visualize other cases like Unity's. I said Unity was a unique case, one of a kind.[4] At that point I was not focusing on Commonwealth. Wille was.

All told, our historic act and its implications went relatively unnoticed. However, H. Erich Heinemann of the *New York Times* saw through to the heart of the matter and wrote a perceptive analysis of our action.[5] He described the saving of Unity as an example of "one of the thornier questions American society has to face these days—how to resolve the often apparently irreconcilable between responsibility to the community and responsibility to self." He suggested we were on thin legal ice for making the use we did of a section of the law "that Congress had in mind for small, isolated rural communities" and then stretching the essentiality requirement in a situation where large Boston banks, including those that participated in the loan to Unity, had branches near the little bank. Heinemann wrote:

> The fundamental question raised by the F.D.I.C.'s action, though, is the precedent that it sets. . . . Some bankers are asking whether the F.D.I.C. has any business using its insurance fund —built up by the contributions of 13,500 banks for the protection of millions of depositors—to bail out the stockholders of any bank, no matter how important the social value that bank might have in its local area.

Heinemann was thirteen years ahead of the times in initiating the public policy debate about bailouts; that debate did not really explode across the land until Continental.

The deal went into effect July 27, 1971. From the start, the new arrangement had rough sledding. Although the conservatorship status automatically took all control away from the board of directors and vested it in the conservator, the board was retained as an advisory committee. It continued to agitate for a greater voice in the direction of the bank. Sneed often found his way to his old desk in the bank until we insisted he stay away.

The training provided by the major Boston banks, moreover, proved to be less of a success than we had hoped. The banks sent their personnel on a rotating basis, which precluded continuity. Most of the personnel were white and were concerned about their personal safety in the rough neighborhood served by the bank. They worked short tours, one or two weeks, and then would not want to come back when their bank's turn at the rotation came around again. So the bank would send other staff to help out at Unity.

Unity's own personnel, from the teller level to operating management, went through constant turnover. Our personnel reported that books were not kept properly, bills were not paid on time, loans were not worked to the extent they should be, and operations in general continued as slipshod and haphazard as ever. There was even turnover in the conservator's position. A second, and then a third, conservator was appointed.

Unity met its first payment of $90,000 on the notes due the

banks in 1975. Well before FDIC's $1.5 million note was due at the end of the next year it was apparent that the bank would not be able to pay off the debt. In 1976 the Board of Directors that succeeded us at FDIC voted to extend the note for five-and-a-half years until June 30, 1982. The Boston banks also extended their notes to the same date.[6]

Unity Fails Again

When I returned to the FDIC board as chairman in 1979, Unity was still there and as much of a problem as ever. A branch had been opened in an effort to generate deposits but had been unsuccessful. Other efforts to help had been of no avail. Talk of buyouts had produced no firm offers.

FDIC had received $200,000 in principal reduction on its note but was still owed $1.3 million. The Boston banks had been receiving installment payments and their collective debt was reduced to $280,000 from the original $485,000. There was no prospect of further repayment. As the due date approached, our board—Bill Isaac, Todd Conover, and I—decided we could not renew the note again even though it would force the closing of Unity.

So when June 30, 1982, arrived State Banking Commissioner Gerald T. Mulligan took away its charter, and FDIC had the bank again, this time as receiver. We did a conventional closed-bank merger and in the process lost most of our stake from the original bailout. The winning bidder was an investor group that had been trying for a year to raise enough cash to buy the live bank. We sold the deposits, some other liabilities, the good loans, and other sound assets. The bad ones we retained for liquidation. In early 1986 our FDIC Board established a $4,-

463,000 reserve for loss on the Unity failure. The investors obtained a state charter for their new bank, named the Boston Bank of Commerce, and opened a new main office in the downtown Boston business district. The old Unity Bank facility was retained as the Roxbury branch. Appropriately, the new bank is minority controlled. The new bank struggled but by year-end 1985 it had grown to $25 million in assets and showed a $250,-000 profit for the year.

The bailout gate had been opened. Would it become a floodgate?

Chapter IV

Bank of the Commonwealth

The First Bailout of
a Billion-Dollar Bank

NOTHING was preordained about my vote to bail out the Bank of the Commonwealth in Detroit. The first billion-dollar institution ever to face certain failure unless the government intervened was ten times the size of Public Bank, the largest previous failure. Ironically, that bank was also in Detroit; FDIC sold it to Commonwealth in 1966.

FDIC Chairman Frank Wille and Federal Reserve Chairman Arthur F. Burns favored a bailout. Burns feared the domino effect that could be started by failure of this large bank with its extensive commercial loan business and its relationships with scores of other banks. Wille was concerned about the impact on municipalities and special districts throughout Michigan since Commonwealth was the leader in the municipal bond business.

Comptroller Bill Camp was opposed. Burns did not have a vote on our board, but he made his desires known. I did not know what to do, and it took me months to decide.

Ultimately, I provided the deciding bailout vote, but not without serious reservations. Coming so quickly on the heels of the Unity rescue, it made me feel that Camp's argument that we were escalating the precedents had considerable merit.

When it was rescued in 1972, Commonwealth had $1.2 billion in assets and $960 million in deposits. At its peak in the late 1960s Commonwealth had reached $1.5 billion in assets, after tripling in size in just six years and becoming the forty-seventh largest bank in the nation. The bank operated fifty-seven branches throughout the Detroit area and was heavily represented in the urban core. In 1969 Commonwealth had a gross income at an all-time high of $103.5 million and paid out $7 million in dividends, nearly 50 percent more than in the preceding year. It also landed on our problem bank list in March of that year shortly after I joined the FDIC board.

As a state-chartered member of the Federal Reserve System, Commonwealth was under the direct supervision of the Fed and the state. FDIC's role was solely that of insurer at Commonwealth, but we had supervisory jurisdiction over a number of related institutions.

State Banking Commissioner Bob Briggs and I had worked well together on a pair of Michigan failures: the $2.3-million Morrice State Bank in 1969 and the $11-million Peoples State Savings Bank of Auburn in 1970. This set the stage for our cooperative efforts on what we called "the Parsons problem" that was headed our way. The state and FDIC both supervised eight Michigan banks related to Commonwealth: Birmingham-Bloomfield Bank in Birmingham, State Bank of Michigan in Coopersville, Oceana County Savings Bank in Hart, Industrial State Bank & Trust Company in Kalamazoo, Monroe Bank & Trust in Monroe, the Muskegon Bank & Trust Company in Muskegon, Peoples Bank of Port Huron, and Presque Isle Bank in Rogers City.

All were problems; most were considered by the supervisors to be serious problems. All were part of the mushrooming banking empire put together around the Commonwealth flagship by Donald Parsons and a group of business associates.

Parsons had broken into banking in 1960 as a thirty-year-old lawyer with the law firm retained by Detroit Bank and Trust Company, the city's second largest bank. C. Allen Harlan, a Detroit businessman, invited Parsons to become one of five incorporators and a member of the board of a new bank Harlan was establishing in Birmingham, Michigan, the Birmingham-Bloomfield Bank. Two years later Parsons was elected chairman of the board. The new board put out a $600,000 issue of convertible debentures,* but it sold only $50,000 at public offering. Parsons and his associates then formed an investment company under the Small Business Act and bought the rest. Through that maneuver, Parsons could obtain enough stock to take over ownership control from Harlan whenever the debentures reached the convertible price. Harlan sold out to Parsons in December 1965.

Even before that coup was completed, Parsons spotted a much larger prize. In 1964 rumors circulated that the Bank of the Commonwealth might be for sale and that the chief bidder was the Atlas Credit Corporation from Philadelphia. Parsons and two associates, James C. Holmes and George B. Kilborne, formed the Parsons Investment Company; these general partners had eight limited partners. They borrowed $8.25 million from Chase Manhattan Bank in New York. Thus bankrolled, they acquired a stake in the bank and launched a proxy fight accompanied by a publicity campaign for the votes and support of the shareholders. They set themselves up as a "local ownership committee," pledged to keep the bank out of the hands of "eastern interests." The story circulated that Howard Parshall, Commonwealth's chief executive officer who had long dominated bank policy, was soliciting proxies on Atlas's behalf. The

---

*A form of debt that may be converted into stock ownership when the stock price reaches a certain level.

other shareholders' angry reaction was to sweep Parsons and his associates into office, displacing eight of the eleven members of the board of directors.

Parsons, himself, took the Commonwealth chairmanship. To solidify their controlling interest, the three associates formed a second, larger partnership—the BOC Investment Company with forty-nine general partners—and turned to Chase again for more loans to purchase additional Commonwealth stock. Chase Manhattan Bank ultimately loaned the two partnerships combined more than $20 million that enabled the investors to acquire a 47 percent controlling stake in Commonwealth. In 1966 after the Fed had recommended that Commonwealth increase its capital base, Chase served as trustee for a twenty-five-year capital note issue that raised $15 million for Commonwealth. During Commonwealth's period of rapid growth, Chase was fueling the fire.

Flushed with triumph, Parsons and his associates set off on a rampage of acquisition; in five brief years they controlled sixteen additional banks in the United States and interests in two small banks in Zurich, Switzerland. Parsons and his group parlayed a small financial stake and a lot of borrowed money into a $3-billion banking empire.

The Parsons Partnerships

The partnerships that had worked so well with Commonwealth became the group's trademark. Michigan law at that time prohibited the establishment of bank holding companies and sharply restricted bank branching. Consequently, Parsons and his associates created a network of overlapping partnerships to serve as a vehicle for multibank ownership.

Parsons spawned partnerships. We ultimately counted 128, including nonbanking companies. In congressional testimony Parsons estimated that more than 150 individuals were involved in his bank partnerships. He underestimated. We later determined there were more than 250.[1] Parsons argued that partnerships held less potential for abuse than corporations because partner involvement served as an effective restraint. However, most of his partners were limited. They merely invested their money, were liable only to that amount and had no say in management. Only eighteen general partners actually ran the operations, and these were members of the Parsons group —or close to it. It was as thorough an interlock as any group of like-minded corporations could aspire to.

The arrangement successfully circumvented Michigan's single bank ownership statute and the state's restrictive branching law. But the partnership network could not match the facility and unity of a holding company for exercising strong central command of the entire banking empire.

To accomplish that, in 1967 the Parsons insiders created yet another partnership. This time there were eleven general partners. They called it COMAC. The acronym stood for Comprehensive Oriented Management Activities Company; and the name was just as murky as COMAC's exact role in the Parsons banks.

COMAC presented itself as a management consulting firm. The Parsons banks were simply "clients" that retained COMAC under generous contracts approved by bank boards controlled by COMAC partners. COMAC was to formulate investment advice and operating plans. It was simply a circuitous scheme to centralize the management of the institutions.

In addition, the COMAC partners were often at the loan windows of the "client" banks. The partners, as bank officers, approved large and not always good quality loans for each other's outside business interests. At its high point, COMAC-related borrowing reached $67 million. The banks were being tapped from both directions: the partners were receiving consulting fees at one end and loans at the other.

The COMAC partners prided themselves on being "different" from traditional bankers. And they were. Parsons and David L. Tennent were lawyers in the same law firm. James C. Holmes had been involved in real-estate and property management. Stephen C. Miller was a Birmingham businessman. Thomas G. Gies was a professor of finance at the University of Michigan and formulated much of the investment advice. George B. Kilborne, after working at a New York textile firm, had become an investor and started his own business research firm. Thomas H. Wagner was an investor and early associate of Parsons. Herbert Fisher was a lawyer in Birmingham. Bernard C. White was a Birmingham businessman. Gordon L. Walker was with Ford Motor Company, as was the eleventh COMAC general partner, Don K. Learned. The names of the first ten appeared again and again on the boards of the Parsons group banks, often in the key positions of chairman and vice-chairman. Each sat on the boards of at least two banks; Parsons, Wagner, Holmes, and Kilborne sat on six boards apiece. Yet none had significant banking experience.

Undaunted, they described themselves to advantage:

> The backgrounds of COMAC's ten active partners bear witness to the various kinds of expertise that can be brought to bear on banking practices: Two attorneys, two former operators of medium-sized businesses, a mortgage banker, a real estate management expert, a university professor, a former corporate specialist in personnel and organization, an advertising executive and a former corporate controller: the various inputs from these men insure that new concepts will be drawn from many other realms of successful business activity—and especially from the industrial area.[2]

Besides the COMAC partners, two other associates, Frederick C. Matthaei, Jr., and G. Bretnell Williams, were insiders and part of the Parsons core group. Both served on the boards of

Commonwealth and two other banks. Williams, president and director of Cunningham-Limp & Company, an engineering and construction company, was a substantial Parsons investor. He was one of three directors (including Parsons and Wagner) who resigned from the Birmingham-Bloomfield Bank in 1968 under pressure from the Fed because of conflict with their simultaneous service on the Commonwealth board.[3]

COMAC's "challenge to business as usual" turned out to be a disproportionate and pernicious emphasis on government securities and tax policy. Instead of tending to the loans which are a bank's bread and butter, COMAC tried to manipulate the government securities portfolio into a windfall profits scheme. Commonwealth's pattern, which was repeated at other banks, was to sell off the safe, steady, and staggered federal securities in the bank's portfolio and load up on low-grade, long-term municipal securities that bore higher interest rates. After almost a decade at low relatively stable levels, interest rates had been drifting upward in the late 1960s, and COMAC was trying to lock them in. COMAC believed the rise was cyclical and that rates were ready to fall. If that happened, all those high-yielding municipals in the 5 percent tax-free range would surge in value and the client banks could sell them at a princely profit. In their headlong rush to buy up municipals before rates fell, the COMAC principals ignored the time-honored banking policies of diversification of risk, laddering of maturities for a continual turnover of securities, and picking quality issues. They steadily bled away the bank's liquidity.

As early as January 1968, representatives of the Chicago Fed met with Commonwealth's board and expressed concern to the directors about the course bank management was following. Parsons, as Commonwealth chairman, strongly defended their policy, saying it would produce vast capital gains for the bank. He said the projections of Dr. Gies showed that a downturn in interest rates would occur between July 1, 1968, and July 1, 1969.

Instead of changing course, Parsons and COMAC were so

sure they were going to make a killing that they reoriented their tax policy to shelter the anticipated gain. They began pushing tax deductible expenses into future years rather than claiming them in the year in which they normally would have occurred. Most of it was interest, which was paid on January 1 instead of December 31. Such practices increased taxes for the current year; but the Parsons group planned to get the taxes and more back by rolling up a backlog of deductions to be taken when interest rates went down and Commonwealth sold its municipal securities at a high profit.

In anticipation of that gleaming payday in the beguiling future, the COMAC managers entered the sheer promise on their books as a bona fide asset, took it into income and paid dividends on it. It was money the bank did not have and would not have until the municipals could be sold at a high profit. That would occur, of course, as soon as interest rates went down.

What actually happened in 1969 was that the nation entered a tight money period. Interest rates not only continued up— they began to soar. The prime reached 8.5 percent. The hoard of municipals earning 5 percent tax-free, far from turning into a treasure trove, suddenly became low-yielding as well as long-term and low-quality. The securities' value in the marketplace plunged. The banks were losing money just holding onto them, but the banks would go broke if they sold those securities and took the market losses. The banks were squeezed in, illiquid, inflexible, and capital deficient.

The carefully concocted tax policy had backfired along with the rest of the scheme. Instead of a tax shelter, it had generated potential losses that in themselves were large enough to threaten the bank's solvency.

That was the situation the regulators were trying to correct by supervisory nudging. The COMAC principals were not only resisting—they were still buying banks. They added their last six in 1969, and they were not even giving banks full-time attention. They had too many other irons in the fire. Real-estate partnerships, industrial equities investments, and a small business investment company kept them occupied. They were trying to get into aircraft chartering, oil field equipment, Australian land, and international ventures through their holdings in Swiss banks. Parsons bought a share of the Pittsburgh Penguins hockey club. It is hard to understand how they could have time for banking. As a matter of record, the chairmen were instructed not to spend more than two days a month in their banks and the vice-chairmen not more than four, although they were to be the major contact with the bank on day-to-day matters.

The Regulators' Response

By 1969 the regulators had formed a working partnership to cope with COMAC. Since the Parsons empire had banks of all three classes, that is, state-chartered Federal Reserve members, state-chartered nonmembers, and national banks, they were supervised by the three federal agencies—the Fed, FDIC, and OCC—plus the state. We orchestrated simultaneous examinations of all the Parsons banks and pooled our findings. Previously we had been sharing information only on a case-by-case basis. The combined findings of the examinations showed imminent disaster. We toughened our supervisory prodding.

The largest bank under direct FDIC supervision, the Birmingham-Bloomfield Bank, simply would not respond to our pressure for remedy. So at the end of 1969, when all else had failed, our board took the ultimate step of initiating proceedings to revoke the bank's deposit insurance, a process that takes months of procedural maneuvering.

The problems of the Parsons banking empire still were being

handled behind closed doors. Nothing had broken through to the public view. Then in March 1970 the Fed denied Commonwealth's application for an office in Nassau in the Bahamas. In its desperate search for funding, the bank wanted to try the Eurodollar market.

Branch applications generally receive easy approval. The rare denials are routine matters that get almost no coverage in the press. But the Fed used this one as a general public rebuke to the Bank of the Commonwealth. The Fed's public statement said, "it is the Board's considered judgment that, by any reasonable standards, a serious deterioration has occurred in the financial condition of your bank." There has been "an inadequate regard for liquidity," and capital has been "disquietingly low in relation to the character and condition of its assets. . . . the general character of management and the bank's financial history and condition, including its liquidity and capital positions, militate against approval." The Fed went so far as to say that approval "would be contrary to the public interest."

What happened after that was prompt and predictable. The money lenders in the markets quit renewing their notes. Credit dried up. It was an ironic and bitter refutation of one of the "modern" banking principles formulated by the COMAC managers. Gies had told the board of the Birmingham-Bloomfield Bank in April 1969 that "frequently borrowed funds" were far more stable than large corporate deposits. Corporations could and would pull their funds and move them elsewhere in search of higher yields. "Frequently borrowed funds," of course, are absolutely volatile, particularly in 1969 when interest rates were moving up. It was a serious blow for Commonwealth which had come to rely heavily on short-term borrowings to fund its expanding asset portfolio.

In May 1970, two months after the branch denial, Commonwealth started borrowing from the Fed. The draws started at $140 million and kept going up throughout the summer, peaking at $335 million. Now the Fed was wearing two hats: lender of last resort as well as supervisor. But it was still the Fed handling Commonwealth single-handedly.

In July the Fed moved against another Parsons bank, the Bank of Lansing in Michigan's capital city. The $160-million institution was also a Fed member bank and it was in almost as bad shape as Commonwealth. The Fed issued a cease and desist order against Lansing on July 21, 1970.

The next day Fed Governor J. L. "Robbie" Robertson called a meeting of the regulators and the Commonwealth principals. FDIC had staff there as did OCC. The Michigan Banking Commissioner attended and the Federal Reserve Banks of both Chicago and New York were represented. Parsons was there with John Thompson, the newly named president of Commonwealth.

Governor Robertson told Parsons and Thompson that both Commonwealth and Birmingham-Bloomfield probably could not survive without Fed loans. If they wanted the money they had to meet three conditions:

1. Parsons, Wagner, Gies, and Fisher had to resign not only as bank officers but as directors.
2. Birmingham-Bloomfield had to take the corrective measures specified in FDIC's termination of insurance proceeding.
3. Commonwealth had to consent to the issuance of a cease and desist order by the Federal Reserve.

The cease and desist order had three main thrusts: get rid of COMAC, shrink the bank's asset portfolio, and suspend the payment of dividends. Commonwealth was also to stop lending to COMAC partners and start collecting on outstanding COMAC loans or take over collateral. The purpose of reducing assets by a stipulated $45 million per quarter was to ease the liquidity strain, reduce the bank's borrowing needs, and give it a little slack in which to begin restructuring itself.

The ultimatum left no course for the Parsons organization except retreat and finally rout. Within three weeks Parsons,

Wagner, Gies, and Fisher had resigned from the Commonwealth board leaving the bank in the hands of Thompson. The
president had never been a partner, investor, or a member of the
Parsons inner circle. He was in his middle thirties and had
worked for the Bank of the Commonwealth since 1964. In 1969
the Parsons principals had asked him to become president of
Birmingham-Bloomfield Bank; a year later he had been moved
to the same spot at Commonwealth. He took over working
control of the bank and was in charge of taking the corrective
actions in the Fed's cease and desist order.

The Parsons principals spent the next several months dis-
mantling their empire and liquidating their holdings to pay
their debts. First to go was the National Bank of Royal Oak, a
$33-million institution sold in August 1970 to a hometown
group that included some of the bank's local directors. In five
months eight more banks were gone. They included the serious
problem Bank of Lansing that was sold under pressure from
Continental Illinois, holder of a $4-million acquisition loan dat-
ing to 1966. A $5.3-million bank stock loan to the Monroe Bank
& Trust in Monroe, Michigan, was foreclosed by Franklin National Bank of New York, which resold the bank to a group of
local investors. The other banks were sold to local interests,
sometimes back to former owners.

Chase Manhattan Pulls the Plug

Then in January 1971 it became the turn of the troubled Bank
of the Commonwealth itself. Chase pulled the plug by calling
its notes. Although Parsons had been forced off the Commonwealth board by the Fed in 1970, his two partnerships were still
the bank's principal stockholders. They were more than a year
in arrears on their loan payments when Chase foreclosed.

Chairman David Rockefeller announced that Chase "is taking immediate steps to reduce to ownership" its collateral interest in 39 percent of Commonwealth's common stock securing $20 million in Chase loans to the partnerships. A press account said that Chase had demanded payment several months earlier; when it was not received, Chase went looking for buyers for the bank among Detroit businessmen, including two former executives of General Motors Corporation. The quest was unsuccessful, and Chase itself then took over Commonwealth. Under federal law, Chase could maintain ownership no longer than two years.

After noting that the Federal Reserve Board had "led a regulatory campaign against Mr. Parsons that has succeeded in driving him out of big-time banking," the *Wall Street Journal* quoted an enthusiastic Governor Robertson: "I heartily applaud Chase Manhattan's initiative in moving into this situation."

Rockefeller said that Chase was installing one of its senior lending officers, John A. Hooper, as chairman and chief executive officer of Commonwealth. Hooper remained a senior vice-president of Chase. His job was to get Commonwealth in shape to sell as rapidly as possible.[4]

Three weeks after the Chase foreclosure on Commonwealth, the Birmingham-Bloomfield Bank became the next Parsons casualty. It was the only out-and-out failure in the whole tottering empire. Birmingham-Bloomfield was a case study in Parsons-style operations.

In five years the associates had pushed it from a $13 million to a $123 million bank. Its deposits and other stable funding sources had not kept pace with its burgeoning loan volume, and the bank was borrowing heavily to carry its assets. Loans, especially COMAC loans, continued to go bad. Other bank lenders began to cut off credit. Emergency loans from the Fed were arranged with Commonwealth as the conduit.* Birmingham-

---

*At that time the Fed did not lend directly to state nonmember banks. The law has since been changed.

Bloomfield was losing money rapidly and steadily, but it was still paying large dividends.

FDIC had examined the bank seven times in five years. Wally Ryen, our regional director in Madison, Wisconsin, administered periodic tongue-lashings to bank management beginning in 1966. In retrospect we should have been more aggressive earlier, rather than waiting until 1969 when we had to resort to our ultimate weapon, insurance removal. We could have instituted a formal cease and desist action to order remedial measures. This was another instance of a law being on the books, but unused. Such orders had never been put in place by FDIC. The bank continued its errant way until collapse became inevitable. That experience led Wille and me to inaugurate the use of cease and desist orders by FDIC on June 17, 1971, on another troubled Parsons bank, the Peoples Bank of Port Huron, Michigan. The Fed had shown the way the year before with its order against the Lansing bank. These orders are used routinely today as a supervisory tool by all the regulatory agencies.

State Banking Commissioner Briggs finally declared Birmingham-Bloomfield insolvent on February 11, 1971. As the receiver, we immediately sold it to a new bank organized by local investors.

In Detroit meanwhile, Chase was losing no time in taking charge of its new not-so-welcome acquisition. Hooper brought with him two Chase vice-presidents. All three remained on the Chase payroll while they were running the Detroit bank. They held John Thompson over as president. A special team was flown from New York to make an analysis of Commonwealth's condition. Chase's next step was to approach the government.

In March barely six weeks into its stewardship, Chase solicited a meeting with the Fed in Washington. Significantly, FDIC was invited. It was our first direct involvement with Commonwealth although we had observers at the earlier meeting when Governor Robertson laid down his ultimatum to the Parsons group. John Flannery, our director of bank supervision, sat in for us. Governor Robertson chaired the meeting. Other supervisors present were Fred Solomon, Jack Ryan and Jim Morrison from the Fed, and Briggs. Hooper and John Thompson had come from Detroit. Two Chase officers and a Chase lawyer, Roy Haberkern of Milbank, Tweed, Hadley & McCloy had flown down from New York.

Chase officers did the talking. Flannery reported to us that Hooper started out discussing the loan portfolio, which was salvageable, and then turned to the real problem, the municipal securities. They were yielding about 5 percent, or two to three points less than prevailing interest rates. That meant the securities could not be sold without discounting them steeply from face value. Chase estimated that the loss from such discounting would amount to $40 million on the portfolio of $309 million. Flannery said Hooper complained that "every time you try to do anything you come back to the municipals—you have to get this monkey off our backs or it won't fly."

Chase officers made it clear they wanted to get rid of the securities. They then suggested that Commonwealth was a public interest problem that the governmental agencies should resolve. That unsubtle hint was the way Chase phrased its request for a bailout by the government. Governor Robertson noted that a number of difficult questions had to be resolved, among them—who does it and how? One of the Chase officers suggested that his bank did not want to make a killing out of any federal aid, that the bank would settle for recouping its investment and expenses.

In responding, the Fed staffers said they believed they had no specific statutory authority to buy the municipal portfolio. Haberkern agreed, but he said he thought the Fed had "implied powers." FDIC, Haberkern said, had "broad authority."

It was then Flannery's turn. He gave the group a brief lecture on Section 13(c) essentiality law and the findings we would have to make before we could consider assistance. A lot of faces fell. Governor Robertson, nevertheless, asked Flannery to con-

vey the tenor of the meeting to the FDIC board. All the participants were well aware of the Unity precedent we had set
shortly before.[5]

Very clearly, FDIC was now right in the middle of the Commonwealth crisis. The Fed's concern was that the failure of a billion dollar bank like Commonwealth would have severe repercussions for the nation's economy—the domino theory we still
have not tested in the real world. Robertson invited Wille over to
the Fed and proposed we buy the municipal securities at book value. Of course, we had no intention of buying all that depreciation.

From the start I believed Chase had a responsibility. Chase,
after all, had financed Parsons from the beginning. I have always felt that those responsible for a bank's problems or its
failure should pay. After all, they are the ones who make the
profits when things go right. I was not enchanted with the
Chase people's attitude that all they wanted was their money
back, plus expenses. Their proposal would come down to bailing out the shareholders, the largest of which was Chase. Neither Wille nor I were about to agree to that.

After the March meeting we embarked on a round of study
and analysis that went on for months. Instead of continuing to
rely on the Fed for financial information about Commonwealth,
Flannery told Ryen to start collecting our own. Wille and I went
to interminable meetings at the Fed with Governor Robertson
and Commonwealth officials. Camp never attended, but I kept
him informed. As at Unity, first we had to determine whether
there was a legal basis for aiding Commonwealth. Second, if
there was, should we do it? Finally, if we agreed we should,
what was the best way to structure it?

We did not do it all in the office. Again, as at Unity, I went out
to get firsthand information on the community so I could see
what I was voting on. I decided to visit all fifty-seven of the
Commonwealth branch offices. Ryen reluctantly "volunteered"
to conduct the tour. My deputy, Alan Miller, came along. It was
summer; it was hot and we drove and drove. I went to every

branch. I stood in the lobby in many of them and watched the customer traffic. I did not know what I expected to find; I just watched and thought. I told myself I was analyzing the community service of Commonwealth. Actually, I was stalling until I could figure out the right thing to do. Some of the branches were in big fancy buildings, some were in shopping centers, some in burned-out ghettos, and one was in a cornfield. To find it, we passed a huge field of yellow crookneck squash. Around a bend in the road was a tiny trailer in the middle of the field. Squatter-like, it was holding a place for a possible future full-scale branch. Michigan then had very restrictive branching laws.

Wille was focusing on another aspect of the problem: Detroit's concentrated banking market. He knew the law prohibited excessive concentration so that consumers and loan customers would not be left at the mercy of a few big banks. In a series of two to one votes, Wille and I consistently had turned down proposed mergers that would have produced far less concentration than we already had in Detroit. The Phillipsburg decision was fresh in our minds.*

One of the pleasures in working with Wille was his attitude of trying to determine what the law said and then acting accordingly. Of the nine different FDIC boards I served on, the time with Wille was the most educational and rewarding for me. He was not burdened with ideological hangups, just the law.

Commonwealth, the fourth largest bank in Detroit, had only 10 percent of the deposits. The three largest banks in the city had 77 percent. The entire city of 1.5 million people had only seven banks altogether. Since out-of-state acquisitions were prohibited, any merger would have to be with one of the big three, increasing the concentration to an intolerable 87 percent of deposits in three banks. Neither Wille nor I could support that.

---

*In 1970 the Supreme Court ruled in *United States* v. *Phillipsburg National Bank & Trust Co.* that commercial banking was the relevant product market and that the relatively small local area "to which the purchaser can practicably turn for supplies" was the relevant geographic market.

Much later Wille told me we probably would have avoided the bailout if Michigan had allowed statewide branching.

Chase finally made its formal proposal for assistance on June 30, 1971, in another meeting at the Fed. Flannery and other FDIC staff members attended for us. After six months of running Commonwealth, Chase said that if it did not get assistance, it would have to walk away. That would mean the failure of Commonwealth. In prepared written remarks Hooper's pitch was that Commonwealth had a "moral obligation" to continue operations in its "retail-oriented inner-city branches which predominantly serve black customers." In eight areas of the inner city, Commonwealth maintains the only banking office within the radius of one mile, he said. "Without help," Hooper said, "I feel that Commonwealth's financial position will rapidly deteriorate to a point where it can no longer carry on despite all the efforts we are making."

Chase wanted the Fed or FDIC to buy the entire municipal portfolio—then reduced to $280 million—without loss to the bank. Chase also wanted one of us to underwrite a $30-million stock offering to inject new equity into the bank. Chase asked that the Fed suspend Regulation F covering the reserve for loan losses at Commonwealth in 1971 and 1972, with the proviso that BOC reserve these amounts from the proceeds of its proposed equity sales.* Finally, the "future income tax benefit," that now amounted to a $13.6 million potential loss, was to be spread over the next ten years instead of being charged off immediately.[6]

None of the specific points would really fly, and I still felt uncomfortable with the whole idea of the bailout proposal. My thoughts kept coming back to Chase having that big stake. So I just stalled for time until I could find a way to deal with it. I knew that eventually I would. There were real pressures. Arthur Burns called me several times to insist that I acquiesce. "We need your vote," he said. Nobody wanted to face up to the biggest bank failure in history, particularly the Fed.

*Regulation F is an 194-page Federal Reserve Regulation that requires detailed disclosure of a bank's condition to the public when a stock offering is made.

This was my first opportunity to compare working styles of Fed chairmen. I was used to dealing with Bill Martin on Regulation Q matters as the federal regulators set ceilings on the interest paid on deposits in financial institutions. His tactic was to sit back and listen to all the discussion and then gently nudge us to a consensus.

Here was an abrupt change. The Burns style was to say here is what must be done, and then ask how soon we could do it. Later I observed that Bill Miller wanted all the facts but was impatient with economists' philosophizing. Still later I found the Paul Volcker style was more akin to the Bill Martin approach, with Volcker far more aggressive than Martin. I worked more closely and for a longer time with Volcker than any of the others. Over the years we faced crisis after crisis together and he many more alone. It never ceased to amaze me how strong and unruffled he was. I imagine we have never before had such a selfless public servant. It was dismaying to watch as administration economists, far less qualified than he, sniped from the sidelines—anonymously, but for publication—as he took all the tough steps necessary to stop inflation in its tracks and put the economy on the mend.

As the Commonwealth meetings continued, I kept telling them all that I could not see the essentiality of the bank. I wanted Chase to take a real hit if we put in government money. Wille also wanted that outcome. The meetings and analysis went on. The pressure increased as the bank's condition continued to deteriorate. I just let it build. Whenever "essentiality" would come up, I would shake my head. They were not going anywhere without that essentiality finding. The bank produced charts, graphs, and arguments about how essential Commonwealth was to the community.

Finally, after one of those long sessions, when the meeting had broken up and we were all on our way out, Haberkern caught up with me in the hallway. He asked me how it would strike me if Chase took some kind of hit. I told him it might put things in a different light.

Rescue Plan That Sets Precedents

With no further discussion of this issue tl
changed and in December the process shi
about generalities to drafting specifics. It wa
Chase would be taking a hit in whatever deal
Murane, and Flannery were working on va
asked Alan Miller to add to the discussion hi:
instead of providing a windfall to the stock
brunt on them. Under Miller's plan, FDIC would buy the
nicipal portfolio, but at its discounted market value, not book
value. The bank would have to take the loss on the sale. FDIC
would also agree to make a short-term loan provided the stockholders agreed to a major dilution of their ownership. All common stock and surplus and most of the preferred stock would
be used to absorb the $40-million loss on the sale of the munici-
pal securities and $18 million in loan losses. The bank would
then seek to sell new capital stock within sixty to ninety days,
using the proceeds to pay off the FDIC loan and get us out of
the transaction. The plan would need the shareholders' approval; Miller proposed that as an inducement we give present
stockholders preference in purchasing the new stock.[7]

The spirit and the major elements of Miller's plan blended
well into the other ideas we were considering. They were to
survive all the drafts and revisions of our working proposal and
to emerge in the final contract adopted by the board. Finally, as
the plan gained general acceptance I told Wille I was prepared
to vote for essentiality.

Our general counsel, Bill Murane, provided an analysis and o-
pinion that there was legal basis for making an essentiality finding. The conclusion was based on two points: Commonwealth's
service to the black community of Detroit and concentration.

Wille was the principal architect but the Fed and the Michigan Banking Commissioner also were involved in fine tuning

the final plan in negotiations with Chase. The mechanics of the deal worked like this: The bank would reduce the par value of all outstanding stock from $45.5 million to $7.9 million. The $37.6 million surplus thus created would be transferred to undivided profits to be used in absorbing losses on the sale of municipal securities and bad loans. The effect was to throw the loss onto the stockholders, of which Chase was the largest.

To replenish the bank's capital as the securities and loans were sold and the losses taken, FDIC would lend the bank up to $60 million. The loan would be in the form of capital notes maturing April 1, 1977—a five-year plan. The FDIC loan would bear interest at 5.5 percent per annum, which was two-tenths of a percentage point higher than what FDIC earned on the deposit insurance fund invested in U.S. Treasury securities. Commonwealth also would pay FDIC a $300,000 loan commitment fee. The FDIC notes had to be repaid before any dividends could be declared on Commonwealth stock or before any of the preferred stock could be redeemed. The notes were subordinate to claims of depositors and general creditors, but they were senior to the existing capital notes.[8]

The rehabilitation plan specified how the federal assistance could be used and gave FDIC a final review and approval before funds were disbursed. Our agreement with the bank gave us a veto over the appointment, retention, and compensation of the bank's top management. All of these major features of the plan were to reappear years later in the First Pennsylvania and Continental bailouts.

Wille, Deputy Comptroller Tom DeShazo, and I voted unanimously to adopt our first big bank bailout plan on January 17, 1972.* Camp told me at the time that he felt a little better about the bailout after the Chase windfall was eliminated. Years later,

---

*Unlike the two appointive members of the FDIC board, the comptroller is allowed to delegate his vote to an acting comptroller at board meetings. The FDIC chairman and director must personally participate. At the time of Unity and Commonwealth, the voting members had to be physically together. On March 2, 1972, our board changed the bylaws to permit official meetings by telephone conference call.

at my retirement reception, DeShazo recalled Camp's adamant opposition to a stockholder bailout. "Camp and I talked, of course, but the vote was mine," he said. The plan was then approved by the board of the Bank of the Commonwealth.

We put out a detailed, ten-page press release that hinted at 100 percent insurance protection. The specific language was: "depositors and general creditors of the bank now have, and under the plan will continue to have, the protection of FDIC deposit insurance."[9]

Everything would have to be submitted to the shareholders and capital noteholders for approval. The noteholders had to agree to an override of an indenture on the bank's existing $15-million note issue. The indenture prohibited the bank from issuing new debt that would be senior to the capital notes. But we insisted that our cash injection be senior to the notes. The Fed added a little encouragement for a "yes" vote by issuing an order that prohibited payment of principal and interest on the notes until the FDIC plan was approved by the stockholders.[10]

Not surprisingly, the consent of the shareholders and capital noteholders was readily obtained at the annual shareholders' meeting on February 28. Shareholders also reelected the entire nine-member Commonwealth board. Most were long-time directors, three dating from before the Parsons takeover. The notable newcomers were Chase's Hooper, who was chairman of the board and chief operating officer, and Thompson, who had become a director when he assumed the bank presidency in February 1970.

The plan went into effect and within a matter of days, Commonwealth presented us with an application for its first draw. Four more draws followed, the last on December 29, 1972. All told, the bank borrowed $35.5 million under its agreement with FDIC.

I would like to be able to report that the package we adopted was a good and final cure, that the rehabilitation plan rehabilitated, and that the bank lived happily ever after. It did not work out that way: The bank never grew.

One vital ingredient was lacking in the assisted bank: confidence. That was the biggest mistake we made—thinking we could cure the bank simply by putting enough money into it. The fact was that government money seemed to have made the bank suspect in the eyes of depositors and private investors. Rather than restoring confidence among the public, the federal assistance by itself seemed to have had the opposite effect. It was a lesson we took to heart several years later when we were dealing with the much larger problems of First Pennsylvania and Continental. In both those instances we made certain that our packages contained joint federal and private assistance to show that the private banking sector also had confidence that the problem bank would recover and that the other banks had a real stake in the recovery.

Several months before the statutory 1973 deadline when Chase would have to divest Commonwealth, the New York bank arranged a sale that at the time seemed a good match. The buyers were James T. Barnes, Sr., and his son, James, Jr., members of a prominent and prosperous Detroit family whose principal business interests were real-estate investment and mortgage banking. Commonwealth was a major mortgage lender in the Detroit area. Neither Barnes had any background in banking, but they were highly visible in Detroit and its business community. Wille and I investigated the Barneses and we hoped that their local ownership takeover would help restore public confidence in Commonwealth. Shortly after I left the board for a six-year hiatus, the new FDIC board voted to approve the sale.

Commonwealth Problems Resurface

When I returned as chairman in February 1979, I found Commonwealth still limping along. The bank had exchanged one set of problems for another; ownership had again changed hands and an extension had been granted on the FDIC loan, all without much effect on the fortunes of the bank. Commonwealth had continued to stagnate throughout the 1970s. Deposits had continued to trickle away, and the bank's market share shrank.

The new owner was First Arabian Corporation, a Luxembourg corporation headquartered in Paris. The principal negotiator on behalf of the buyer was Ghaith Pharaon, a Saudi Arabian businessman. The purchase had been contingent on FDIC extension of the loan and approval of the transaction, to both of which the FDIC board agreed in early 1977 provided that the new owners would inject $10 million capital into the bank and meet other regulatory conditions. Repayment of the principal began in 1980 and was to continue in seven annual payments. By 1983 $8.5 million had been paid, leaving an outstanding balance of $27 million. By this time, First Arabian was in serious negotiations for a sale to Comerica, Inc.—as Detroit Bank & Trust, the city's second largest, had renamed itself. Comerica asked FDIC for another extension of the note and as inducement offered to guarantee repayment. After several months of negotiations, the FDIC board approved a restructuring on September 30, 1983. Repayment of the principal is scheduled in six equal annual installments from 1990 through 1995. The new interest rate is tied to the U.S. Treasury fifty-two-week bill rate and is payable quarterly.

When the purchase was consummated December 31, 1983, Commonwealth had about $900 million in assets, $300 million less than when FDIC did the original assistance transaction almost twelve years earlier. Comerica had grown to a $7.3 billion institution. All of our efforts to keep Commonwealth from adding to the banking concentration in Detroit had been frustrated.

The Commonwealth name vanished. The bank's identity was submerged into Comerica. The problems, our loan—and the opportunity for Comerica—remain.

Our second bailout took care of the immediate problem, but it has to be classified as something less than a long-term success.

Chapter V

First Pennsylvania Bank

The Prototype Is Created
for Megabank Bailouts

IF the Unity and Commonwealth cases were prolonged, dragged out affairs, First Pennsylvania was like a whirlwind. The crisis developed, came to a head, and was resolved all within five tumultuous weeks in the spring of 1980.

First Pennsylvania Bank in Philadelphia is the nation's oldest and at that time was the nation's twenty-third largest bank with assets of more than $9 billion. It was 9 times the size of Commonwealth—nine hundred times larger than Unity.

Soon after I returned to FDIC as chairman in February 1979, I learned that the Fed and OCC were monitoring the big bank as a problem institution. We were told, however, that the problems probably were manageable.

So I turned my attention to a major crisis brewing within

FDIC's own supervisory bailiwick—the mutual savings bank industry. Centered in New York City and the northeast, the industry's stock in trade was taking deposits from small savers and lending them out to people who wanted to buy homes. This policy, to me, has always been one of banking's noblest purposes. The trouble was that short-term interest rates were soaring at the end of the 1970s and the mutuals had committed most of their money to long-term mortgages. When the mutuals could find new funding, they had to pay double-digit interest rates to get it. Meanwhile, the mutuals' own income was limited to 5, 6, and 7 percent returns on their long-term mortgages. As the months wore on, the strain seemed to threaten even the largest of the mutuals, a group that never before had given FDIC any concern whatsoever. Now we were monitoring them closely.

I began meeting with savings bank officials to see what, if anything, they could do to help themselves. Their desperation came through clearly as I met with all the chief executives in two mass meetings, first in New York, then in Boston. Next, I asked Bill Isaac, then an FDIC director, to set up a task force to analyze the mutual situation, explore all our options, and lay out plans for dealing with the crisis we were certain to face. I knew that bailout was not an option. With a savings bank on every corner in New York City, there was no way we could declare one of them essential. We had to find alternatives. The project took nine months, but when it was finished, the task force had laid out game plans for whatever we might have to face. When the mutuals began to fail, beginning with New York's Greenwich Savings Bank in November 1981, we were ready. We handled them without a ripple, merging the weaker institutions into stronger mutuals or selling them to new owners with heavy FDIC subsidies. In each case the bank's top management was removed, but mutuals, as their name implies, are depositor owned and have no stockholders to take a loss. No depositor lost a penny.

Three mutuals failed in 1981 and eight more in 1982. The prospects were for the trend to escalate as the interest rate squeeze continued relentlessly. Then in September of 1982, Congress chose to paper over the problem by enacting a three-year net worth certificate program that authorized us to exchange notes with the banks and allow them to call. it capital. It was just funny money, but it did stem the tide to some extent. In late 1985 Congress extended the net worth certificate program temporarily to April of 1986.* With or without the certificate program, the problems of the mutuals persist and no doubt will face future FDIC boards. By year-end 1985, we had handled seventeen savings banks that required FDIC outlays.† The estimated FDIC loss from the mutuals was then estimated to exceed $1.5 billion.

The savings bank problems, in addition to eating up our time and our energy, complicated our deliberations about First Pennsylvania. How could we save a big stockholder-owned commercial bank at the same time we were planning for the failure of all these mutual savings banks?

Thus troubled mutuals were uppermost on my mind at the end of our regular Monday afternoon FDIC board meeting on March 24, 1980. Then Comptroller John Heimann quietly asked if Isaac and I could stay late. He had something else he wanted to talk about. After the staff filed out and the doors were closed, Heimann told us that one of the nation's largest banks was on the brink of failure.

That was enough to catch my attention. Every now and then during the past year I had received status reports on First Pennsylvania. All had said that the bank was continuing to have a rocky go of it, but none rose to the level of an alert. What had gone wrong?

---

*The net worth program, given short-term extensions several times in 1986, was allowed to die, the victim of a House-Senate dispute over other banking legislation in the closing hours of the 99th Congress.

†These have been consolidated into the list of the one hundred largest failures in the appendix.

A series of recent developments, Heimann said, had compounded the old problems; and the bank's chronic liquidity deficiency was tightening into a choke hold. Worse, confidence in the bank was crumbling fast.

I immediately called an interagency emergency meeting. We gathered in the FDIC conference room on Wednesday, March 26—my deputy Alan Miller; Isaac and his chief assistant, Pete Burr; and representatives from our Legal Division and our Division of Bank Supervision. From the Fed came my old friend and neighbor, Governor Chuck Partee, who brought along Jack Ryan, the Fed's top bank supervisor. Heimann invited his top officials from OCC—Paul Homan, chief of bank supervision; John Shockey, general counsel; and Bill Martin, deputy comptroller for surveillance.

Heimann gave us a grim situation report. In short, he said that First Pennsylvania was headed for certain failure unless FDIC intervened with a massive rescue package.

The bank was going to report a $6.4 million loss for the quarter then ending, on top of a $1.8 million loss in the fourth quarter of 1979. The announcement would deliver a sharp blow to whatever confidence in the bank remained in the financial community. The bank's market for its certificates of deposit had nearly disappeared, and the Eurodollar financing might well follow suit. Bank borrowings from private sources exceeded $3 billion; in addition, First Pennsylvania was borrowing $340 million from the Fed, a constantly escalating figure that was to exceed $700 million on bailout day.

John Bunting was the chief executive officer of First Pennsylvania during the 1970s when the bank embarked on a period of fast expansion and growth. Bunting had resigned as bank president under regulatory pressure in July 1979, and then he stepped down as holding company chairman in December. The resignations had spotlighted the bank's problems.

Regional banks that did regular business with First Pennsylvania, and even some of the larger banks, were taking their business elsewhere. So were the brokers, and, of course, the

brokers' customers. The downstream banks were beginning to
stir.

Street Rumors Escalate the Problem

Rumors circulated that the bank was seeking a merger partner
or that the Fed was arranging a takeover by another holding
company. The talk had remained largely within the financial
community until Friday, March 21. On that day a New York
money market research firm, McCarthy, Ried, Crisanti &
Maffei, Inc., reduced its ratings of First Pennsylvania's borrowings to "speculative," the firm's lowest rating.[1] On Saturday the
first stories appeared in the Philadelphia press. On Monday, the
day that Heimann brought the matter formally before FDIC,
the *Wall Street Journal* carried a story buried inside, that was
headed: "First Pennsylvania Is Finding It Harder to Fight Rumors, Erosion of Confidence."[2] The bank's stock price dipped
below $5 that day, continuing a slide from the $12 to $15 range
where it had been through most of 1979.

Embarrassingly, FDIC had inadvertently contributed to the
problem. Word got out that FDIC had people in the bank and
the rumors were that they were measuring our exposure in case
the bank failed. Regional Director Jim Sexton in Philadelphia
promptly denied it. These were not examiners nor liquidators;
they were assessment auditors who had been there at least a
month auditing deposits to make sure the big bank was paying
its proper assessment, or premium, for deposit insurance. It was
a routine, long scheduled, periodic function of FDIC's financial
office, but the timing was unfortunate. We got the assessment
auditors out that day. Bank confidence is a fragile reed, and a
troubled bank is damaged by any rumors, true or not.

Desperate for cash First Pennsylvania had announced in October 1979 that it had agreed to sell to Manufacturers Hanover Corporation most of its consumer finance subsidiaries for $82 million and part of its mortgage banking subsidiary, PEN-NAMCO, Inc., for $24.5 million. But even that $106 million one-time injection of cash was insignificant in light of First Pennsylvania's needs. Besides its funding requirements, the bank was carrying $328 million in questionable loans. That was $16 million more than the bank's entire equity capital.

Heimann told us it was time for the regulators to step in. He said we faced three choices: First, we could shore the bank up with FDIC money. Second, we could let it die slowly, as had New York City's $3.7 billion Franklin National Bank in 1974, the nation's largest bank failure to that date. Or, third, we could close First Pennsylvania quickly and merge it, as we had done at San Diego's U.S. National in 1973.

Heimann pressed for option one. He said he would flesh out a detailed proposal in a few days. My instinct went immediately to the third choice—handle the problem quickly before it turned into a confidence crisis in the entire banking system, and get it out of the way. Isaac agreed with me as did most of our top staff.

But who was big enough to take it? We were immediately handicapped by antitrust considerations. Only one other bank in Pennsylvania—Mellon Bank in Pittsburgh—was big enough to absorb a $9-billion institution overnight, or ever. But such a megamerger would concentrate much of the banking resources of the state in one gigantic institution. We could not look elsewhere because there was no statutory authority for an interstate merger.

I was, at the time, lobbying for just such an interstate bill.* While at the Greenbrier American Bankers Association conference in April, I had lunch with Jim Higgins, chairman of the

---

*The bankers were adamantly opposed to the interstate bill we had drafted under the leadership of Treasury Undersecretary Bob Carswell in a series of Monday night meetings at the Fed. It finally was enacted two years later when Congress belatedly recognized the enormity of the problems we faced.

Mellon Bank. Mellon badly wanted to take over First Pennsylvania and had made a proposal to FDIC. I told Higgins frankly that I did not want to deal with him because of antitrust considerations, but I said I might have to if all else failed. Would he still be interested? He told me he would be interested at any time of the day or night. I never had to go back to him.

Heimann said that he had had confidential discussions with some of the nation's major banks. Bank of America, Citibank, and Chase Manhattan—the top three—were unanimous in the opinion that no private solution was possible. We must have massive government support, they said.

Heimann then unfolded the details of his rescue plan. His office, as the chartering agency and supervisor, would issue a statement saying the bank was solvent. The Fed would say that the discount window was open to the bank to meet its liquidity funding needs. And FDIC would either buy the bank's entire government securities portfolio at a book value of about $1 billion and include a $300 million loss, or FDIC would put in a subordinated capital note for $300 million.

The major banks—twenty-five of the nation's largest—for their part would subordinate a fairly long-term note; say, $200 million for one or two years at a market rate of interest. They would also agree to keep in their Fed funds, or overnight loans between banks.* This would save First Pennsylvania from having to find new sources to replace these funds also.

Substantial as the assistance was, Heimann said one bank still had doubts about whether it would be sufficient. Mellon had told Heimann that the plan would not prevent further operating losses nor the loss of the bank's Eurodollar and large certificate of deposit support. Mellon was a suitor for First Pennsylvania, but still Mellon's points were well taken.

There were other concerns: That very month the Fed had put credit controls on the economy at the behest of the president

---

*Banks are required to keep some money with the Federal Reserve. At the close of business each day some have excess money at the Fed and this is borrowed by other banks that have a shortfall.

to fight runaway interest rates and inflation. The stock market was in disarray. The financial markets were, if anything, in a greater state of chaos with the near collapse of the silver market after the Hunt brothers' speculation.

Given that context and the fact that First Pennsylvania was so much larger than Commonwealth, the old foreboding about the consequences of the fall of a major banking house loomed larger than ever. Is there really a "domino effect"? What would it do to the nation's economy?

With the experience of Commonwealth and Unity behind us, we knew what questions to ask and what alternatives to consider as we began our First Pennsylvania investigation. The first step was to review the bank's problems in depth. How had it gotten itself into such a mess?

What Went Wrong at First Pennsylvania

In the early 1960s, First Pennsylvania was a very ordinary bank. It grew at a modest 7 percent a year; its return on assets was about .08 percent. The bank was healthy but humdrum.

The coming of John Bunting created a transformation. Bunting joined First Pennsylvania in 1964 and was made chief executive officer in 1968. He had previously been an economist with the Federal Reserve Bank of Philadelphia for fourteen years. He was an aggressive, outspoken, and articulate individual.

Bunting felt that the economy of the Philadelphia region was basically stagnant and that First Pennsylvania would have to seek business outside the region if it wished to enjoy more than modest growth. His goal was to transform First Pennsylvania into one of the nation's major financial institutions.

Bunting sought to increase the bank's loan volume at a more rapid pace than the growth in the bank's core deposits would sustain, funding the new loans with purchased liabilities. He was also willing to accept greater risks. The higher risk loans facilitated rapid growth and at first contributed to earnings due to both volume and higher rates charged on loans.

From 1967 through 1974, First Pennsylvania tripled in size, going from $2.1 billion in assets to over $6 billion. Return on assets improved slightly to the .85 percent range, and return on equity climbed sharply to a high of 17.9 percent in 1972. Bunting's fame spread in financial circles and he became a leader in banking's "go-go" era. He was highly regarded by his board of directors, which was content to let him lead. His attitudes and philosophies permeated the entire organization; officers who could not adjust to the new order of things were pushed aside.

But the new First Pennsylvania was built on a very weak foundation, and the depression of 1974–75 made that abundantly clear. Loan quality was poor—problem loans rose from 10 percent of capital funds in 1967, to 32 percent in 1969, and 156 percent in 1976. Leverage was excessive as equity declined from 7.3 percent of assets in 1966 to a low of 3 percent in 1978. The Fed in 1969 and subsequent years became increasingly critical of management and the condition of the bank. We assumed that an attempt to escape such criticism motivated the bank in 1974 to convert to a national charter which meant that it would be examined and supervised by OCC rather than the Fed, which would continue to supervise the holding company.

As the bank became increasingly strapped for cash, it embarked on the policy that had brought it to its present pass. In 1976 First Pennsy began to buy long-term U.S. Treasury securities when their interest rates began nosing up through the 7 and 8 percent levels. Here, the bank reasoned, was a way to stabilize secure income at a high level. So the bank bought bonds in massive amounts; it held more than $1-billion worth by 1979. About half the Treasury portfolio would not mature for more than ten years; some thirty-year bonds would not be due until 2007, paying rates of 7.6 to 7.9 percent a year. To fund these long-term instruments, First Pennsylvania continued to rely on short-term borrowings. It was a strategy that would work only if interest rates went down. As short-term rates continued to

climb beyond the yield on the Treasury bonds, those obligations became a drain instead of a boon. Further, their resale
value had plunged by 1980 to $300 million below their face
value. First Pennsylvania, like Commonwealth eight years before, had lost its gamble on interest rates.

Complicating the bank's difficulties were the nonbanking activities which fragmented the organization's energies and attention. The holding company also had a government securities
subsidiary, as well as the mortgage banking subsidiary. In addition, foreign banking operations amounting to $2 billion were
more than a fifth of the organization's consolidated assets.

Despite its difficulties, the bank continued to grow, instead
of retrenching to contain its problems. The bank's assets increased by 20 percent in 1977 and almost 12 percent more in
1978. It grew from a $6.8-billion organization at the end of 1976
to $9.1 billion at year end 1978. Earnings for 1979 plummeted
to .18 percent of assets. Finally, in July under pressure from
both OCC and the Fed, the bank's board asked for Bunting's
resignation, ending his eleven-year reign.

For new leadership the board turned to a career employee of
the bank, George A. Butler, who had been with the bank since
1950. He had become president in 1977. The board promoted
him to chairman, president, and chief operating officer of the
bank and its holding company.

Should We Do Another Bailout?

In the spring of 1980 the surge in interest rates that began in
October 1979 and other events drove First Pennsylvania first to
the Fed and then to FDIC. Once again I was faced with the
prospect of the nation's largest bank failure, this time as FDIC

chairman. The first questions, of course, were: Should we prevent it? Was this bank "essential to its community" under the same tests we had applied to Unity and Commonwealth? Could we once more step outside our role as insurer of deposits and become a rescuer of a troubled bank? Did those who wrote the law contemplate this type of situation?

First Pennsylvania hired the Wall Street investment banking firm of Morgan Stanley & Co. Inc. to put together a proposal for FDIC assistance. At the same time the firm undertook a worldwide search for a white knight to take over the ailing bank. No one was interested.

Ted Dunn, a Morgan Stanley partner, presented an outline of a rescue plan for review by OCC on Monday, April 2. In essence, the plan called for a $400-million, ten-year loan from FDIC at a concessionary interest rate tied to bank earnings. Repayment of principal would not begin for five years and then it would be in 10 percent increments with a lump sum payment due in 1990. The loan was to rank on a level with other capital notes of the bank and be subordinated to all other creditors. For "additional compensation," as the bank called it, First Pennsylvania would offer us 5 million warrants to purchase common stock. For its part, the holding company would omit payment of dividends to shareholders for two years.

The bank said it understood that the regulators might impose certain limits on its operations, but insisted that it not be unduly hampered by these restrictions.

The regulators were to use their best efforts to help the bank obtain $1 billion in lines of credit and term deposits from major banks. There was no mention of a real investment in First Pennsylvania by the other banks. For its part, the bank was to sell its depreciated and debilitating government securities and use its loan from FDIC to cover the loss. A general retrenchment would be undertaken to shrink the bank and return it to a quality regional institution, less dependent on money market sources of funding.[3]

When the plan was formally presented to the FDIC board the next day by Butler and John Brine, his chief financial officer, the loan request had been reduced to $300 million, the amount of the depreciation in the government securities portfolio which by then had climbed to $1.2 billion.

First Pennsylvania had a shareholders' meeting scheduled for April 29—four weeks away—at which it would have to disclose its first-quarter loss. The management wanted to announce a rescue plan at the same time as a *fait accompli*.

We were not about to be stampeded. I created a task force within FDIC to evaluate the bank's proposal and set in motion several separate studies. For the main undertaking I asked Bob Shumway, our chief of bank supervision, to choose whatever staff he wanted and take whatever resources he needed to come up with an analysis of the proposal and a response as rapidly as he prudently could.

Shumway was told to examine all our alternatives—merging the bank, either on an open- or a failed-bank basis, or even breaking it into pieces that could be acquired and digested by several different purchasers in the Philadelphia area. He was also to include in his study the last resort bailout option.

Our Legal Division, under General Counsel Frank Skillern, Jr., had the task of evaluating the essentiality question, the crucial threshold if we were to assist. Skillern also set up a separate legal task force to prepare for a closed-bank merger, which was very much a possibility at that time. Finally, our Division of Liquidation was directed to make detailed plans for paying off the bank, if that became necessary.

We were far from a decision on how to proceed. There was strong pressure from the beginning not to let the bank fail. Besides hearing from the bank itself, the other large banks, and the comptroller, we heard frequently from the Fed. I recall at one session, Fred Schultz, the Fed deputy chairman, argued in an ever rising voice, that there were no alternatives—we had to save the bank. He said, "Quit wasting time talking about anything else!" Paul Homan of the comptroller's office was equally intense as he argued for any solution but a failure. The domino theory dominated the discussion—if First Pennsylvania went down, its business connections with other banks would entangle them also and touch off a crisis in confidence that would snowball into other bank failures here and abroad. It would culminate in an international financial crisis. The theory had never been tested. I was not sure I wanted it to be just then. My preference was any solution but a bailout after the unsatisfactory results at Commonwealth. Isaac and most of the staff continued to oppose a rescue.

The Fed's role as lender of last resort first generated contention between the Fed and FDIC during this period. The Fed was lending heavily to First Pennsylvania, fully secured, and Fed Chairman Paul Volcker said he planned to continue funding indefinitely until we could work out a merger or a bailout to save the bank. Our position was clear. The Fed refuses to lend without impeccable collateral, so it is always protected. FDIC, however, is exposed. Beyond that, if Fed funding keeps an institution open longer than it should be, then uninsured depositors who withdraw their funds during this period receive a preference, and the ultimate bank failure is more costly to FDIC.

First Pennsylvania's hand-tailored rescue plan did not stand up well under our scrutiny. First, the mega banks were not being asked to make any real commitment to the rescue. My objection involved more than just throwing the entire burden on us. We had learned from Commonwealth that government funds alone would not restore public confidence in a problem bank. Bank peers had to demonstrate their confidence in a troubled member by committing their own funds to its recovery. Otherwise, no other private investor would believe in the bank.

Second, the bank's plan gave us no hold on management, that is, the power to hire, fire, set pay, and oversee both long-range plans and daily operations.

Third, the proposal included no operating plan that would get the bank back in shape to stand on its own.

Fourth, and very importantly, the bank's proposal was far too generous to the stockholders. The only cost in the proposal for them was a two-year omission of dividends and the issuance to the rescuers of five million warrants for the purchase of stock. The warrants would represent a potential dilution of stock value. All in all, the stockholders would come out of it pretty well and with a chance for full recoupment in future years. What usually happens to stockholders in a bank failure is that they end up with nothing. And this clearly was going to be a bank failure if the government did not intervene.

Another aspect about which we had major doubts was the sufficiency of the aid request. Was the $300 million the bank was asking enough? The bank had focused heavily on the depreciation in its government securities and made too little allowance for its possible loan losses. I believed that if we did decide to go through with this, we should put in enough money to do the job right. The worst thing that could happen would be if we put in $300 million and the amount fell short of the bank's needs so that it would continue to founder.

We embarked on lengthy discussions with First Pennsylvania. Their officers protested our invasion of their business prerogatives and our interference in their affairs. They rejected the idea that they were supplicants, proprietors of a bank headed for certain failure. Finally, using the same tactic I had used in Commonwealth, I reminded them that the FDIC board had not yet made an essentiality finding. No finding, no deal. They were told that the negotiations while the essentiality investigation was still in progress were simply to save time. Ultimately, I said, as they persisted, they should be happy we were negotiating at all instead of dictating terms.

The essentiality question posed the familiar problem—why this bank among all others? If a big commercial bank like First Pennsylvania were to be saved by government intervention, there had to be a compelling reason to set it apart from the troubled mutuals that had far fewer powers and recourse than a commercial bank. Skillern was embarked on an exacting and exhaustive investigation of First Pennsylvania's claim to a unique eligibility. The studies and the negotiations, the meetings and the analyses, and the telephone calls and the pressure went on throughout April until Skillern formally advised us that the FDIC board would be able to make the finding of essentiality under the law, if the board wanted to.[4] But should we? Isaac initially pushed hard for allowing the bank to fail. "How else do you maintain discipline in the marketplace?" he said. But if the bank was in fact essential to its community, should it not be saved? And if it were to be saved, how could we do it without providing shareholders with a windfall in the process? I believed from the beginning that if we were to agree to a plan, it would have to treat the shareholders as much like a bank failure as possible. We were not impressed that the plunge in the bank's stock price had already wiped out more than two-thirds of the shareholders' investment. That was not enough of a hit.

We began to consider the idea of the warrants to purchase stock as first proposed by the bank. We could not buy common stock itself in a bank. That would be inappropriate for us both as a federal government agency and as a bank supervisor. It also would be illegal. But the irrevocable right to purchase was something else. We could take the warrants and later sell them. It seemed to pose as substantial a threat to stockholders' interest as the stock itself. Of course, the bank's warrant proposal was far too meager. A token, really. We would have to do some work on that.

Other decisions were how to treat the bank's board of directors and management in particular. We decided these questions could be put off until later. We were running out of time. Besides, the board had already undergone significant turnover with the shake-up in top management after Bunting left eight months before. We simply let it be known that if we went into the deal, there were going to be changes in the board and possibly with management.

Little by little our intensive analysis convinced us that in this case intervention was the proper course. There was no specific moment when the balance shifted; it evolved over the course of the month, as one by one the alternatives proved not feasible. At some point I decided to do a bailout and we found ourselves talking about how to do the deal, not whether to do it. I let Heimann know we would declare the bank essential and save it. But it would be our deal, not the bank's.

The Rescue Plan Is Structured

The assistance itself was simply the straightforward infusion of $500 million, a figure that we hoped was the right amount. The package we structured called for the assisting banks to put in $175 million of it, which was the portion Dunn figured he could raise from that source. The money had to be a legitimate, at risk investment from the banking industry. Further, we agreed that $25 million had to come from the Philadelphia area. All this was to demonstrate banking industry support locally and nation-wide for a giant troubled institution and faith in its prospects for recovery.

Needless to say, the banks did not rush forth, fighting to get into the pool. What had been a drafting and negotiating process for several weeks suddenly was transformed into a fund raiser. Dunn canvassed the industry, working closely with Ed Palmer of Citibank. His hand was immeasurably strengthened by the fact that a group of banks had $50 million in term loans to First Pennsylvania that they stood to lose if the bank closed.

One hurdle which proved more controversial than I had expected was the issue of disclosure and stockholders' approval. First Pennsylvania's outside counsel, Winston Churchill of Saul, Ewing, Remick & Saul assured us that the bank board had authority to accept and implement this package.

"What about the shareholders?" I asked. There was no need for shareholders' approval, he responded. "Maybe there is no need, legally," I said, "but there is going to be a shareholders' vote on the plan. It's their bank."

Dunn also argued that there was no need for a shareholders' meeting and he observed that it would entail a dangerous delay between the time of announcing the deal and its implementation. Heimann sided with their view. This was an emergency, he said; the bank was in imminent danger of failing. He did not believe we had time to wait six or seven weeks for a shareholders' vote; the board has full power, he said; we should go ahead.

I heard them out, and then said: "There will be a shareholders' meeting." That triggered clamoring and raised voices. I just sat it out.

Isaac was with me on it all the way. He agreed that although it may not have been legally required—and both of us were persuaded that it was not—the only fair thing to do was to give the shareholders a vote on the plan. They were going to take the hit if we put the plan into effect. Beyond fairness, we both knew that full public disclosure and a shareholders' vote was the best defense against any possible lawsuit. In addition to the shareholders, there were also the holders of subordinated debt to think about. A stockholder vote would protect us against any challenge.

Early on Skillern said that the bank probably was right; there was no necessity under law for a shareholders' meeting. But he wanted to do his own research before giving me a final opinion. I never asked him to. I trusted my instinct on this issue; and so far as I was concerned, a stockholders' vote was the right thing to do. I did not need any legal research to tell me that.

As we were working on the details, Skillern came to know Churchill quite well. He said: "Every time my secretary would tell me that Winston Churchill was on the phone for me, I'd have to think, just that extra tenth of a second before I realized who it was."

Paul Volcker, too, was seriously concerned about what would happen during the weeks between our announcement of a deal and the stockholders' meeting and voiced his worry repeatedly. The night of our last regulator meeting, the week before the scheduled stockholders' meeting, when we signed off on the package that would go to our board the next Monday, the tension escalated. Both Dunn and Heimann again asked me to back off. Volcker was in New York that evening and called me twice, asking me to reconsider. He was clearly worried.

Isaac saw the pressures build. Late in the evening, he called me aside and said: "I just wanted you to know that you're right; but if you want to change, I'll support you."

"I ain't gonna change, Bill," I said immediately.

"Okay," he said. "I just wanted you to know."

That last Sunday session was a long and stressful one. Bob Miailovich, who headed our failing bank section, later gave me his notes listing all of the participants and their time of arrival beginning before 10 A.M. His final notation: "Day ended 11:30 P.M."

Finally, we were all set to make an announcement. All three federal bank regulators stood together in supporting this trans-action—FDIC, the Fed, and OCC. Our board voted the deal unanimously at our regular meeting on Monday, April 28, 1980. Fed Governor Partee then joined us as we gave details of the assistance package at a lengthy press conference.

The essence of the bailout package was the $500 million in FDIC-bank loans—$325 million from FDIC, $175 million from the banks. The loans were to shore up the bank's capital while it sold off the debilitating government securities. We required the bank to immediately sell a first installment large enough to cause a $75 million loss. That would reduce the severe interest drain on the bank.

The FDIC loan was for five years, interest-free for the first year and for the last four years at 125 percent of the average return on FDIC's investment portfolio. The early documents called for a simple matching of FDIC interest income the last four years, but in the final week Partee called me to suggest a revision for cosmetic and equity reasons. He asked, "Why not 125 percent for the last four years to compensate in part for the first year subsidy?" I worked over the figures with our staff and concluded Partee was right, so we put it in the contract. At one of our final meetings with the bank officers I told them of the change, and it was accepted without a murmur. They no doubt wondered why we had not proposed the change sooner.

Our then-current portfolio rate was 8.54 percent, a bargain, about half the going rate in the overheated markets of that time. The prime rate had just topped 20 percent. So we were affording the bank a significant subsidy from what the market would charge if, indeed, the market would have provided any money at all to a bank whose troubles were as widely known as First Pennsylvania's. The true benefit of that first interest-free year can never be accurately computed—first, because dollars get cheaper in terms of purchasing power as the years go on. Second, and more important, because of the incalculable benefit to First Pennsylvania of having the money right then, when it was a matter of life or death.

The interest rate charged by the banks on their loans was the Citibank one-year certificate of deposit rate adjusted annually. The banks' loans were made senior to all other subordinated debt; the FDIC loan was senior to all other subordinated debt except the banks'.

In terms of auxiliary funding, the banks had announced a $1 billion line of credit. The Fed said its discount window would be available as appropriate.

The warrants, as we finally constituted them, had taken on

a potent new twist. They were lightly regarded by the participating banks at the time, but over the ensuing five years they developed a life of their own and proved most controversial.

Essentially we reduced the exercise price from what the bank had proposed, increased the volume, and trimmed the length of their term.* Instead of 5 million warrants, there were 20 million. Since there were 15.6 million shares of common stock then outstanding, the warrants would represent a strong controlling majority, not a mere dilution of existing ownership. The warrants were to be granted in proportion to the loans of FDIC and participating banks. That meant FDIC would get 13 million warrants, and the rest would be distributed among twenty-seven banks. The warrants would be exercisable at $3 apiece— a price that was based on the bank's average stock price over the thirty days preceding our negotiations. The bank originally had proposed a $6 exercise price. The warrants would be good for a term of seven years instead of ten. We required that First Pennsylvania must invest proceeds from any exercise of warrants into equity capital of the bank.

Further, we required that the holding company also invest $55 million in proceeds from the sale and liquidation of its finance and mortgage company subsidiaries into bank capital. And we added other conditions: The corporation had to dispose of or reconstitute the affairs of its securities dealer subsidiary. Neither the corporation nor the bank could pay dividends without the approval of FDIC. The bank had to provide us with its long-range operating plans, particularly its specific plans for curing its problems and returning to a healthy state. It had to make progress reports. Directors and principal officers of the bank and the holding company could not serve if FDIC objected and their compensation was subject to FDIC approval. All in all it was a tough, tight package.[5]

The plan was to be submitted to shareholders of the First

---

*The exercise price was the price at which the warrants could be used to purchase stock at a given date.

Pennsylvania Corporation for their approval or rejection. The annual meeting, set for April 29, was converted into an informational meeting. The actual voting was done at a special meeting May 28. It came off "without hysteria," as one British newspaper dryly observed. Despite some vocalizing about the terms, the result was overwhelming approval. About 68 percent of the 15.6 million shares were voted, and the final count was 10 million yea, 523,000 nay, for 94 percent approval. A motion to table drew only 49,000 votes.

We had successfully carried off a megabank rescue that was to be the prototype for the Continental transaction. John Heimann, in a January 1986 *Bankers Magazine* interview, observed:

> Looking at the design of the package for Continental Illinois, it very closely parallels the basic concepts of First Pennsylvania's. It was a different situation, the bank was a different size, and it was a different time, so it is not exactly parallel. But, once again, the basic principles apply: The shareholders bore the financial burden of the depositors; management suffered the penalty for the mistakes they made; and the board of directors, for the same reason, also suffered for the mistakes the members made. The structures were different, but every banking situation is somewhat different.[6]

The Closing of the Transaction

I drove up to Philadelphia the next day to sign the agreement and deliver the money. I had it in my pocket—a plain, green government punch card check issued by the Treasury for $325 million. It awaited only my signature. I had taken a fancy to the idea of signing one check for the full amount. I had more trouble getting it than I expected.

I had sent Jim Davis, FDIC controller, over to the Treasury Department to get the check. He came back to report he could get four checks. Apparently, none of the Treasury's check-writing machines had more than ten digits on them. They could not write checks for any more than $99,999,999.99. I told Davis to try again. He did and was told again that the Treasury did not have any machine capable of cutting a $325,000,000 check.

I asked him if they could do it by hand then, just type it out. Davis said they told him no, it would mess up their bookkeeping. So I called Treasury Undersecretary Bob Carswell. I figured if he could work out a major piece of interstate legislation to deal with the interstate sale of multibillion-dollar failing banks, he could surely get me a little thing like a $325 million check. Carswell said he would see.

A little later Bob called me back. He said the Treasury did not have machines with enough digits to write $325,000,000.00. But they would be happy to get me four checks totaling. . . .

I said, "Bob, I know that. I've already tried. Can't you just this one time, make an exception and write out a check—one check—for $325 million?"

Bob said, "Irv, is this something you really want to do?" An electronic transfer of the funds, of course, would have been much simpler.

I said, "Bob, I really want to do it."

He said okay. I do not know what he did, but the next day somebody at Treasury had the check for me.

So I took it up to Philadelphia with me. I cannot tell you how many times I patted my coat pocket on the way to Philadelphia —just to make sure I still had the check.

The closing was going to take a while; it was not a simple— or even a single—stroke of a pen. There were mounds of documents: credit agreement and subordinated note, warrant agreement, certificates of incumbency, consents from various parties, legal opinions, and other items. They overwhelmed a large conference table and spilled onto the floor. Butler and I were supposed to go around reviewing and signing what was necessary. They included some pretty thick and foreboding sheafs of documents, all done in rather formidable legalese.

I wanted my lawyer to have one last look at them. I also wanted assurance that the state had signed the necessary approvals. Skillern was not there. I said I was not signing anything until he told me I could. This set off a great stir and consternation among the First Pennsylvania folk. They were anxious to get that check deposited in the Fed that afternoon so they could collect that day's interest on it. One day's interest on $325 million amounted to something like $150,000.

Skillern should have been there by then. I suspected—and rightly as it turned out—that it had taken a little more time than we had allowed to clear up some final details with State Banking Commissioner Ben McEnteer in Harrisburg, more than one hundred miles away.

That same Thursday morning, Skillern, who had come up to Philadelphia for the signing, rose early and drove to the state capital. He was to meet the state's legal counsel at 7 A.M., and McEnteer at 9 A.M. The commissioner wanted a full-dress discussion of the proposal and the rescue plan. McEnteer did not sign on until shortly after eleven o'clock.

We figured it would take Skillern more than two hours to drive to Philadelphia. The signing itself would take at least another two hours. That would put us past three o'clock and not leave First Pennsylvania time enough to get the check to the Fed and be credited with that day's interest.

Skillern had just started onto the Pennsylvania Turnpike when he pulled off at the first exit and called me at the bank. He said he would be late. Butler said: "We'll send a helicopter."

Flying is not Skillern's favorite pastime, and he had never flown in a helicopter. But he said all right. He was told to get back on the turnpike and drive to the next exit where there was a small airfield.

He told me later: "Hell, it wasn't even an airport. Just a little, itty-bitty landing strip probably for farmers to land on. There was just a wooden shack there, something to get in out of the rain, and it was right next to a cornfield." He said there was a farmer out plowing with horses, and he stopped to watch when he saw Skillern's car pull off the dirt road to the landing strip. Sure enough, the helicopter came. Skillern just left his car, swallowed hard, and climbed on.

Once back in the board room, Skillern was his lawyerly self; and we moved through that mountain of closing documents with dispatch. Most of the documents had been drafted in-house by the FDIC Legal Division under Skillern, assisted by Doug Jones, Dan Persinger, and many others. Skillern was proud that we had not needed to hire an expensive outside law firm to do that work for us. He trusted his staff and was willing to rely on them.

First Pennsylvania made it to the Fed on time with the check. Pictures were taken at the signing. A few weeks later when I was in Philadelphia to give Butler the hard news about trimming his board, I found my picture hung in the entryway to his restroom. The symbolism escaped me.

That same day Butler promised me he would select a president within six months. We felt strongly that turning First Pennsylvania around was not a one-man job. He needed help.

This turned into one of the major irritants of the entire transaction. We wanted Butler to have top flight support, but if he brought in really talented assistance at the upper levels of the corporation it could pose a threat to him. In any event, the president's job went unfilled. Butler did bring in Fred Leary, a retired Bankers Trust Company officer, as a member of the board and chairman of the Loan Committee. That helped some, but it did not address the central question of a full-time president. Finally, two years later, we had to call the bank's Board of Directors compensation committee to Washington and tell them that no more pay raises or bonuses would be allowed until a president was hired. Frank Reed from Morgan Guaranty joined the bank as president and chief operating officer in May of 1984.

It had taken us at least the first summer to consummate the marriage with First Pennsylvania. The bank bridled at the conditions that went along with the money, and the newlyweds quarreled. We had to get to know each other, particularly since First Pennsylvania was not a bank we supervised, and we did not have an examiner's familiarity with it.

We had decided to retain Butler as our best hope to turn the bank around but postponed a decision on the board. I asked Isaac to take charge of the board question. He analyzed the board makeup, committee structure and operations, and the participation and performance of each director. He went to Philadelphia to get firsthand information. He even sat in on First Pennsylvania's board meetings and later had meetings with top management officials. Altogether it was an extraordinary intervention in corporate affairs. At first our inclination had been to fire the entire board. They had served as directors while policies were followed that led to the bank's failure. We concluded eventually that the prudent course was to keep a few for the sake of continuity.

One by one we went over Isaac's list, winnowing by qualifications and contribution to the bank's operation. The board we inherited had already undergone radical change since the departure of Bunting in mid-1979. Six insiders were among those who left as the board membership dropped to seventeen. Finally, Partee, Isaac, and I sat in my office for a final review; and we decided to replace three more members of the board, making a turnover of ten. There were no public objections from those deposed. Since we did not want more disruption at that delicate stage of the bank's recovery, we permitted the outgoing directors to stay on until the next election by the stockholders seven months later in April 1981. We were to follow a similar approach with the Continental board later.

Bunting had negotiated a severance contract that would pay

him his $222,600 annual salary for another six months, where-
upon he would receive a $100,000 lump sum payment and his
$4,833 monthly retirement benefit would then begin, five years
early. He also retained some stock options.[7] This was just before
they started calling these arrangements "golden parachutes." At
the time the contract was negotiated and accepted by the First
Pennsylvania board, the members were concerned that a public
fight over the terms might unsettle First Pennsylvania's funding
sources further; so they paid dearly.

The contract was in effect when FDIC entered the picture.
None of us liked it, but our lawyers said we had no legal
grounds to revoke the contract.

The Warrants

We soon were in court on another matter—the warrants. Almost
three months after the deal was concluded, the action was filed
in August 1980 by Philip Zinman, a stockholder who held 1.8
percent of the First Pennsylvania shares. It was a class-action
lawsuit that disputed our right to acquire, hold, and exercise
warrants representing potential ownership of the bank. The
Zinman suit contended that the law gave us no such authority.
The suit also contended that the deal took the property of the
stockholders without just compensation or due process because
the warrants potentially dilute shareholders' ownership.

Skillern said: "I was just glad all over again we had had the
shareholders' vote approving the deal." Our defense was that
the Section 13(c) bailout provision gave us sweeping powers to
render assistance "upon such terms and conditions as the Board
of Directors may prescribe." The warrants were simply a term
or condition of our assistance.

Disposition of the case took much longer than we had expected. The depositions were as grueling as any courtroom cross-examination, but I just kept repeating that the warrants were an integral part of the deal; without our assistance the bank was certain to fail and the stock would then be worthless. "The warrants were not separable," I said. Three years later the case was still pending, and by that time it presented an additional problem—this one to the bank. By 1983 First Pennsylvania had recovered strength and was making plans to buy out the assistance agreement two years before its maturity and to go into the capital markets. I had no doubt that one strong motive of bank management was to free itself from federal oversight. The bank was chafing under our review of its operations; on our part, we were not comfortable with our role as a combination Big Brother and Godfather.

However, so long as the validity of the warrants—and perhaps the entire assistance agreement—was in question, the market for the bank's stock would also be uncertain. By mid-1983, First Pennsylvania was as anxious as we were to dispose of the case.

It came to a happy termination at the end of June when Federal Judge Norma L. Shapiro ruled in our favor. She held that FDIC did indeed have authority under the broad grant of the law to shape the First Pennsylvania deal as we had. Her opinion was an important exposition of Section 13(c) essentiality powers. She reaffirmed congressional intent that the assistance powers of Section 13(c) be liberally construed. Other key findings included the following: FDIC has no obligation to bail out a bank to protect its shareholders, and acquisition of the warrants represents a legitimate regulatory effort by FDIC to minimize a windfall gain to shareholders from government assistance. It is a decision that will serve as a valuable precedent.[8]

Five weeks before the court ruling First Pennsylvania had repaid $150 million of the $500 million loan. The action was announced at the annual shareholders' meeting the next day, April 26, 1983. While the news was not as welcome as a dividend, which the bank had not paid since 1980, the repayment signaled a new vitality that the bank hoped would help restore market confidence. FDIC's pro rata portion of the repayment was $97.5 million, with the remaining $52.5 million divided among the assisting banks.

The bank continued to press FDIC for reductions in the interest rate on our $227.5 million outstanding. Our first year of interest-free money was a gift of about $35 million. Thereafter, the floating rate formula had produced an 11.8 percent rate for the nine months ending March 31, 1982, and 13.6 percent for the year ending March 31, 1983. We refused to budge. Now they wanted an additional donation after we had bailed them out. The bank had eagerly agreed to the contract terms. Our loan had brought the bank back to life.

The prepayment on the loan had been a preliminary for a new preferred stock offering. Now their investment banker, Lehman Brothers Kuhn Loeb Inc., had advised First Pennsylvania that the potential dilutive effect of the 20 million warrants would make the new stock too unattractive for a successful sale. The bank wanted to buy back at least half of the warrants. The key was settling on a price. The assisting banks had agreed on $1.65 per warrant. First Pennsylvania offered us the same for half of our 13-million warrant holding. Besides the $10.7 million we would receive, the real bait was an offer to pay off the loan. First Pennsylvania planned to use the proceeds of the stock sale as part of a lump sum repayment of the remaining balance on the loans from FDIC and the banks.

Our consideration of the offer contained a built-in conflict: On one hand, we were glad to see the revival in the bank and especially gratified to see the bank going into the equity market for new capital. That was what we had wanted it to do. We were concerned about the effect of a $350 million payout on the resources of the bank, and we wanted to do our own analysis to assure ourselves that the bank could tolerate it. On the other hand, we wanted to make sure the bank was paying us a fair price for our warrants.

The other intangible was the benefit of getting FDIC out of the bank so that First Pennsylvania could be perceived by the market once again as a wholly private institution being run without government involvement. We would be off their back. I was sorely mindful of what our lingering involvement with Commonwealth had cost us in terms of dollars and cost the bank in terms of confidence. If there was a curse attached to government money in a private institution, it would be well to remove that stigma as soon as possible.

The discussions were brief—and turbulent. First Pennsylvania said our counteroffer of $2.50 a warrant was—to use a polite word—exorbitant. Within a few days we settled on a price of $2. Morgan Stanley gave us an opinion that this was a fair, market-oriented price.

Our board voted to sell the warrants on October 10, 1983. The sale was consummated on November 15. First Pennsylvania paid off its loans with the proceeds of its $150 million stock offering, a new $75 million loan from the assisting banks, and with liquidity. The bank's projections showed that it would save money because of the net reduction in interest expense and could even return the bank to profitability within the next year or so.

The paying off of the FDIC loan was celebrated at a dinner hosted by Lew Glucksman at Lehman Brothers' New York office. I toasted the "bailout" and received heavy applause. I am not sure whether it was for my bailing out First Pennsylvania in the first instance or for Butler bailing me out of the deal by repaying the loan.

Our involvement was reduced to the remaining 6.5 million warrants. Their life had been extended seven years to 1994, rather than two as the bank had proposed; but the duration became academic when First Pennsylvania returned in early 1985 with another proposal. We had been toying with the idea of selling our warrants on the open market; First Pennsylvania wanted to acquire them all but pay for them with proceeds from a stock offering. Our big concern was that the funds come from some source other than First Pennsylvania's own capital or liquidity. So, after considering that underwriters' bids at a public sale would have to reflect commissions and expenses, and that the sale would involve legal and other costs, we decided to go with First Pennsylvania's new proposal.

We agreed to base the price of the warrants on the related market offerings of First Pennsylvania stock, but with a $4 minimum, or $26 million for the block. First Pennsylvania posted a forfeitable, interest-bearing $2-million surety up front.

Our board voted to approve the transaction on April 30, 1985, and on May 29, First Pennsylvania gave us the final payment of $30,062,500. It was five years from the day when I went to Philadelphia to deliver the bailout check.

FDIC is out of it completely now; it is their bank once again as we had planned. At this writing, First Pennsylvania stands as the only certified successful bailout in history.

PART THREE

Two Potential Bailouts That Never Happened

Chapter VI

Penn Square

*A Small Oklahoma City Bank
Triggers a Crisis*

PENN SQUARE BANK permanently altered the public's perception of banker infallibility and the shape of banking and bank regulation in the United States. It should have happened sooner.

Until the long Fourth of July weekend in 1982 when Penn Square went down, these myths distorted the thinking of banks, regulators, and the public:

- No bank with deposits in excess of $100 million would ever be paid off. It would be too difficult, too disruptive.
- Managers of the giant multinational banks were much more talented, brilliant, and experienced than their small-town brothers. No big bank could ever fail.

Penn Square proved the first myth wrong to the surprise of most and consternation of many. Later Continental Illinois National Bank, as an outgrowth of Penn Square, disproved the second.

The genie was out of the bottle, never to return. The public now knows the myths were never true. The regulators have substantially adjusted their perception, their oversight of major banks, and their approach to all bank failures.

By the time Penn Square became notorious, Ronald Reagan had been elected president and Bill Isaac and I had exchanged jobs. Isaac was chairman and I was director of FDIC. Todd Conover was the new Reagan comptroller and Donald Regan was Treasury secretary.

Penn Square had been in the news for weeks, but to FDIC it seemed the stories should have been on the entertainment pages. Bill Patterson, the bank's vice-president in charge of energy lending, titillated big city bankers by drinking champagne out of his boot in an Oklahoma City bar and by wearing a Mickey Mouse hat to business meetings. Patterson was also doing a lot of business with the money center banks, funneling huge sums of their depositors' money through Penn Square Bank to Oklahoma oil men.

It was an extraordinary operation as we later learned. FDIC was counting on OCC, as supervisor of national banks, to keep watch on things and let us know if there were serious problems that would involve us. We were indeed notified, as the bank was on the way to the mortician. Late Tuesday afternoon, June 29, Paul Homan, OCC's chief of bank supervision, called FDIC to request an urgent meeting on Penn Square. The bank lived just four operating days after Homan's call—Wednesday through Saturday. It was hardly enough advance notice to enable FDIC to prepare for the most complicated bank failure in history.

On Tuesday Homan told us Penn Square was under examination, headed for certain failure, and its web had ensnared at least five of the nation's largest banks. We were stunned. Jim Sexton, our chief of bank supervision, and Roy Jackson, our Dallas regional director, were told to put together whatever information they could on the bank. Jim Davis, our liquidation chief, was told to plan for the failure.

That same day OCC began alerting the involved banks that they had a problem. They, too, were taken by surprise. Conover recalls that when Bill Martin, his international banking supervisor, called Chairman Roger Anderson at Continental, he found that Anderson did not even recognize the Penn Square name. For many, the first reaction on hearing about Penn Square was, "This must be some bank in Pennsylvania."

Wednesday morning we began a six-day marathon of meetings. Our board and the staffs from FDIC, OCC, and the Fed gathered in our sixth-floor conference room. The bankers assembled at the comptroller's office. Conover moved back and forth; in between he visited with Don Regan at Treasury and Paul Volcker at the Fed.

Homan opened the Wednesday session with an outline of the Penn Square problem: Penn Square was plunging other banks' money into the risky oil and gas exploration business. Its mode of operation was to make large, high-priced but chancy loans to drillers and then to sell the loans, in whole or in part, to other banks while pocketing a fee for the service. Such loan sales are called "participations" and are a common practice in banking. Penn Square, however, transformed the practice into a species of wheeling and dealing. The bank used the proceeds of its participations to fund more oil and gas loans; it would then turn around and sell these as new participations to other banks to obtain proceeds to finance still more loans.

A lot of things could go wrong with this dangerous merry-go-round and most of them did. Not only did much of the drilling fail to find oil and gas, so that the prospectors began missing payments on their loans, but also oil and gas prices finally began to falter and decline after rampaging through the 1970s. The uncertain economy and the run-up in interest rates in the early 1980s compounded the problems; the entire confection that had no genuine base of solid, performing loans began to crumble.

OCC had been watching Penn Square for some time and had an enforcement memorandum in place. The problem was that neither the examiners, nor anyone else for that matter, had identified the extent to which the bottom had fallen out of the oil business. Drilling rigs used to secure loans had been worth millions. Now their worth added up to only dollars.

Dick Mitchell of OCC's Washington office recalls being sent out to accompany OCC Regional Director Cliff Poole to meet with Penn Square directors in 1981. The message Mitchell carried was that the escalating participations were dangerous and Penn Square needed new management. Bank Chairman Bill Jennings and Vice-President Patterson denied they had any hidden agreements to take back participated loans that went sour. They also reported they had new management. Eldon Beller, a long-time Oklahoma banker, was the new president. Later FDIC learned that Beller was given authority over everything except the root of the problem—Patterson and his energy loans.

Penn Square was in terminal trouble when we met. The large participating banks were exposed, embarrassed, and threatened. Buying loan participations in enormous amounts were some of the country's leading, and supposedly, most sophisticated institutions. They seemed to have been ready, even eager, victims. They had let the lure of the fast buck get the better of their business judgment. Their transactions with Penn Square violated all tenets of sound banking. They were buying loans out of their geographical territory for risky oil and gas drilling projects secured with doubtful or, in some cases, no collateral at all. The acquiring banks neglected to undertake their own credit analyses. They were content to rely on someone else's faulty and fragmentary loan documentation. Now they were exposed to massive and potentially fatal losses.

During its heyday Penn Square had grown pathologically from a $62-million institution in 1977 to a roughly $520-million bank by mid-1982. But it was still deceptively small beside its damage potential. It had set afloat more than four times its asset base—more than $2 billion in oil and gas participations—on other banks' books.

A shocking $1 billion was held by one bank, Continental Illinois National Bank. The remainder was divided largely among four other major institutions: Chase Manhattan Bank, Michigan National Bank, Seattle First National Bank, and the Northern Trust Company.

Before it was over, Seattle First was sold to avoid failure; Michigan National lost its management and had to fight a take-over effort; Chase Manhattan had big losses and greater embarrassment; and Continental was bailed out. Northern Trust Company of Chicago, one of the last to join the Penn Square round-robin, escaped with somewhat less damage than the others.

Immediately following Homan's Wednesday briefing, we sent ten examiners to Penn Square to get the facts on the bank's condition for ourselves. They had instructions to be unobtrusive. We did not want our presence to trigger a run. Our examiners were to pass as part of the large examination force OCC had in the bank. The next day, Thursday, we dispatched fifty liquidators. They were to begin preparations for either a sale of the bank or a payoff of insured depositors.

Our ploy did not work. Unobtrusive or not, the FDIC people were spotted and reported in the press. We stepped up our preparations. In Washington thirty additional staffers began what would be virtually a nonstop effort through the long weekend to back up our Oklahoma City team and to prepare for every possible contingency in handling the failure.

Jim Sexton, who was our chief of bank supervision, told us that Penn Square was a textbook case for a payoff. "If we don't do a payoff in this case where it is so obvious, then this will mean 100 percent insurance for the entire system—forever."

We all were looking at the fraudulent loan participations and unfunded loan commitments. The numbers were uncertain, but a $2 billion or more exposure to loss for the FDIC fund was not out of the question.

Close on the heels of OCC's Wednesday afternoon briefing came devastating stories in the *American Banker* and the *Wall Street Journal* on Thursday. *American Banker* reporter Phil Zweig had been following Penn Square closely and his Thursday story related significant activities.[1]

The key development was that the bank chairman, Jennings, had stripped Patterson of his oil and gas lending authority, cutting the wings off the bank's main line of business. Zweig also reported that (1) the bank was seeking to sell stock to shore up its capital base; (2) disenchanted investors in oil and gas drilling promotions had obtained injunctions in five states to prevent Penn Square from calling their standby letters of credit; and (3) Penn Square and Longhorn Oil and Gas Company of Oklahoma City, the promoter of several drilling programs, were to be in court that day in San Francisco defending lawsuits accusing them of fraud and misrepresentation.

On Thursday the interagency planning sessions became heated. OCC's Homan argued vehemently that the bank should be sold through a purchase and assumption transaction or assisted in any other way to avoid a payoff. He believed that a payoff would create such uncertainty in the markets about the stability of the major participating banks that it would precipitate an international banking crisis. Mike Bradfield, the Fed general counsel, also insisted in his renowned confrontational style that we had to find some answer other than a payoff. Isaac saw no other solution as being feasible. No one argued that the bank should not be closed.

The arguments between Isaac on the one side and Bradfield and Homan on the other became so heated that Conover apologized to Bradfield after the meeting on behalf of our board. Homan was wrong in arguing against a payoff. It was the only legal solution. But he certainly was right in his predictions about the havoc a Penn Square failure would cause with the large participating banks and he called it accurately in naming those who would be hurt the most.

Friday was a waiting day as the regulators and the banks continued to develop information on the magnitude of the problem at Penn Square and debated means of coping with it. The run had not started in any significant amount. OCC's examination proceeded on an expedited basis. Policy decisions were again deferred.

On Saturday, July 3, things took a decided turn for the worse. The bank had Saturday business hours; almost as soon as it opened, the run began in earnest. Long depositor lines formed with extensive television and press coverage. The bank did not have sufficient cash on hand to meet depositors' demands and resorted to issuing $1.8 million in cashier's checks. There was some confusion as to why cash was not available. Bank officers said the Federal Reserve vault was not open on Saturdays, but the Fed said it had told the bank it would make cash available on request. We never did sort out the facts on this one.

The Long Weekend Begins for the Regulators

I look back on Penn Square as my most memorable birthday present. The Fourth of July is always special to me because that happens to be my birthday. My wife and I like to have our children and grandchildren over for a barbecue and to watch the fireworks. The weatherman said that particular weekend in 1982 was going to be especially nice. It turned out to be the hardest five days I have ever worked.

In Washington we began a round of top level crisis meetings that continued throughout the holiday weekend. Saturday

morning Conover called and asked us to come to a meeting at
the Fed about the "problem." A small group assembled in Paul
Volcker's cramped office: FDIC's three board members;
Volcker; Fed Vice-Chairman Preston Martin; Jack Ryan, the
Fed's chief bank supervisor; and Homan.

We listened while Conover and Homan gave us an update on
the bank's troubles. It was much worse than they first had
thought. After hearing a hair-raising description of the bank's
dealings and its enormous contingent liabilities, it became increasingly clear to me that the bank would have to be closed
and paid out. One by one we discussed the options available to
us, given the sketchy circumstances as we knew them then.

Our preference is always for a closed-bank merger because
it causes the least disruption to the community. FDIC takes out
the bad loans, funds the deposits, and sells the bank. We also
indemnify the new owner against loss from contingent liabilities—that is, unknown claims. In most cases these prove to be
minimal. In Penn Square they would be a bottomless pit. To
begin with, $2.1 billion in loan participations had been sold to
other banks. If these involved large losses, as OCC told us, the
participating banks might well sue us to repurchase the loans
or otherwise to provide recovery. Additionally, OCC had found
loan commitments and letters of credit totaling somewhere between $500 million and $900 million. (Like all the other information on Penn Square at that time, this was an ever changing
figure.) If these commitments were not funded, the holders also
would likely sue and claim consequential, as well as actual,
damages. We had reason to believe that fraud was involved,
and that could produce more money claims as well as criminal
prosecution.

In short, we had to conclude that the potential liability could
not be calculated. It certainly would be enormous. Knowing the
magnitude of the risk, no bank would want to assume it, nor
would we want any bank to. The risk involved prevented us
from making the statutory finding that a closed-bank sale was

clearly cheaper to FDIC than a payoff of insured depositors. Without that finding it would be illegal to do anything with the closed bank but pay it off. There is no indemnity in a payoff.

We turned to the live-bank option—bailout. Here there was no cost test; we could put in as much as we felt necessary—provided, of course, that we could make the finding that the bank was essential in its community. With thirty-six banks in Oklahoma City and more in the suburbs, there was no way we could make such a finding.

That brought us down to the statutory bottom line in bank failures: pay off the insured depositors. On the basis of the meager information we had as we entered the long weekend, we estimated $465 million was deposited in 27,000 accounts, with some $270 million insured.* The dollars far exceeded our largest previous payoff—the $78.9 million Sharpstown State Bank in Houston, Texas, in 1971—although the number of Penn Square accounts was similar to Sharpstown's 27,300.

We made a rough estimate of what we could expect to recover on Penn Square's assets, and we projected a net loss to the insurance fund of about $140 million—give or take scores of millions—if we paid off the bank. It was a big number, but it was minimal beside the contingent liabilities that we then placed at $2.5 billion to $2.9 billion.

Volcker wanted to discuss every option that would avoid a payoff and insisted, hour after hour, that we explore every alternative. We even considered such fantasies as the Fed guaranteeing our exposure on the contingencies. The major banks had declined to do so, nor should they have. We talked of foreign purchasers, deposit transfers, assisted mergers, and all sorts of complicated variations. None stood up under scrutiny.

The Fed worried that a payoff would have "ripple effects" on the financial markets. The Fed also feared a possible domino effect because of Penn Square's involvement with the major

---

*We later determined there were actually 24,534 accounts with $218 million of insured deposits at the time of closing.

money-center banks. No one knew what would happen. No bank even remotely approaching this size had ever been paid off.

Unlike the relatively short sessions we had at the start of the First Pennsylvania and later the Continental crisis, our deliberations continued through the day on Saturday. During a lull, Isaac and I went off into a corner of Volcker's office and talked it over. Our instincts were the same; the risk was too great. We could not legally expose our fund simply to avoid a payoff. Conover agreed. We said so to the group.

Volcker then asked about the extent of wrongdoing involved. Was it more than just the economy, the energy business, and some bad judgment? The answer was an emphatic affirmative. It was at this point that Volcker said he supported a payoff.

Conover, who had made plans to take his family to Connecticut for the holiday weekend, had sent them on ahead. He kept calling his wife, Sally, to tell her it would be a few hours longer before he could leave to join them. Finally, he told her to have a good time; there was no way he could leave.

We broke up Saturday night with nothing resolved. In Oklahoma City Penn Square gratefully closed for the weekend after its hectic Saturday business. It was still an operating bank, scheduled to reopen Tuesday morning after the Monday holiday. We were certain there would be massive withdrawals at that time. OCC's examiners continued at their labors. Each report from them was more disquieting. The comptroller still gave no indication of when he would close the bank. Conover had been on the job just 199 days. This was his first big crisis. He was under heavy pressure. He had received a call during the weekend from Continental Chairman Roger Anderson, who had rapidly educated himself on Penn Square and Continental's involvement, in the wake of Martin's warning call a few days earlier. Anderson pleaded with Conover to at least avoid a payoff. Anderson knew Continental's involvement would come to light and put a real strain on the bank. I am sure at that point he was not contemplating the ultimate failure of Continental, just embarrassment. The other participating banks also became hyperactive toward the end of the week, checking on their loan documentation and lobbying against a payoff. Their top officials assembled in Washington.

The same regulators' group met early the next morning, Sunday, July 4, again at the Fed. It soon became apparent our stalemate would continue; Volcker decided that Treasury Secretary Don Regan should be in on the meeting. Conover said he had kept Regan briefed on a regular basis as the crisis unfolded.

Volcker called for him. Regan came over in sports clothes and took a seat on a couch at the side of the room. He listened while Conover and Homan repeated their presentation of the bank's problems and prognosis. We went over our options again. Then Regan asked several very pointed questions. They were all the right questions; they went straight to the heart of the situation. Apparently it was as obvious to him as it was to us that the only legal solution was to close the bank and pay it off.

Regan, who clearly did not want to be part of the decision process, rose from the couch, smiled at us and said: "Well, I'm sure you gentlemen will do the right thing." Then he left.

We all had a laugh out of it. It broke the tension. Then Isaac said to Conover: "Well, Todd, I guess that was an order to close the bank."

"I guess it was," Conover agreed, adding that he would not act before he was ready. FDIC wanted to get started. We preferred to work over the long weekend, rather than waiting for the inevitable failure on Tuesday.

Recalling the tense drama more than three years later, Conover told me: "I was new on the job. I was under a lot of pressure to close Penn Square. I kept asking people in the agency to tell me what it took to make a finding of insolvency." He was told there is nothing in the law that defines insolvency.* The law just says the comptroller shall close the bank

---

*The National Bank Act (12 USC 191) states: "Whenever the Comptroller shall become satisfied of the insolvency of a national banking association, he

whenever it becomes insolvent, "or something nondescript like that," Conover added. So he kept waiting for the examiners to get him the necessary evidence of insolvency. The examination was still going on. "Finally," Conover recalled, "I made it pretty clear to a lot of people to get off my back: I'd close it when it was insolvent."

Throughout the weekend, Conover maintained his position that he would not act until his examiners could furnish definitive figures showing insolvency. Sexton, who later left FDIC to become banking commissioner of Texas, empathized with his fellow charterer. "He was right, too," Sexton said. "He had to have the facts."

Sexton pointed out that Penn Square was the first energy bank failure. "It was a new area. The examiners were not really familiar with it and, especially, they did not know the oil rigs and drilling equipment had depreciated so badly in value. What finally happened was, after they got a specialist in there, he found out that all the collateral was nearly worthless, and so the bank actually had long since passed the point of insolvency."

Conover's examiners were discovering that a large number of savings and loan associations and credit unions had money in Penn Square. However, neither the Federal Home Loan Bank Board (FHLBB) nor the National Credit Union Administration (NCUA) had been notified for fear that word might leak out to the affected S&Ls and credit unions. If they withdrew their money, they would be receiving a preference over other depositors. Conover recalled: "Later that night at home in the kitchen, I got to thinking—this is crazy! They're the government, and we're the government. This is the government saying it can't trust the government. I thought how ridiculous we were. I decided they had to be told." Conover could not reach Ed Gray, the FHLBB chairman. He finally reached one of his senior peo-

---

may, after due examination of its affairs . . . appoint a receiver, who shall proceed to close up such association."

ple and told him Penn Square was on the verge of failure. He also notified NCUA officials.

"There was never any argument that the bank had to be closed," Conover said later. "The argument was what to do after Penn Square was closed."

A bank can be book insolvent, its liabilities exceeding its assets; or it can be liquidity insolvent, not having sufficient cash to meet its obligations. Conover was looking at book insolvency. The Fed also could have closed the bank by pulling its loan to Penn Square from the Kansas City Fed, making the bank liquidity insolvent. Meanwhile, we continued talking on Sunday and Monday, but now it was mostly about how to do the payoff with the least possible disruption to the community. Usually it takes two to five days to get the first checks into depositors' hands. It had taken more than a week at Sharpstown, a relatively simple task compared with Penn Square. No one could tolerate that kind of a delay. Penn Square would have to be handled expeditiously if we were to prove that payoff of a large bank was a genuinely viable option. We decided to resurrect a rarely used power in the FDI Act—our authority to establish a deposit insurance national bank. In the 1930s Congress envisioned that a DINB—as we called it—would be set up and used to pay off depositors in every bank failure. Although it had proved too cumbersome for the small bank failures of the 1930s, it would make an appropriate vehicle to facilitate the payoff of a bank the size of Penn Square. A DINB has no loan authority. Its sole function is to pay off the insured depositors.

We resolved that if Conover made his insolvency finding by Monday night, the bank facilities would reopen at 9:00 A.M. Tuesday, as scheduled, but no longer as Penn Square Bank. Instead the Deposit Insurance National Bank of Oklahoma City, with its proprietor, FDIC, would be ready for its first day of business.

Penn Square Is Turned Over to FDIC

Still another day slipped away before Conover had the evidence to do the inevitable. Shortly after 8:00 P.M., Monday, the Independence Day holiday, Conover closed Penn Square Bank and named FDIC receiver. Now it was our baby.

Our liquidators had been in Oklahoma City since Friday, anxious to get into the bank and get to work. Now they could. We put Mike Newton, a supervisor in the Washington office, in charge of the DINB. Newton was one of the very few FDIC employees who had ever handled a DINB. He had worked at the last two, Swope Parkway National Bank in Kansas City and Peoples Bank of the Virgin Islands, seven years before. We purchased additional computers and shipped them to Oklahoma City. We rounded up more liquidators and examiners from their posts throughout the country and dispatched them to Penn Square. Everything possible was done to ensure a smooth transfer of the accounts, but it was a massive, nearly impossible job. We could not postpone the opening for a week, or even for a day, or an hour. Tomorrow was Tuesday and our bank had to be open at 9:00 A.M.

At one point bringing the bank's books up to date for the payoff was the hangup. An outside computer firm handled Penn Square's work; its programmers were off for the long holiday weekend. Jim Davis, then our new liquidation chief, despaired of working out the problem.

Isaac asked me if I would support a large payment—a bribe I guess you would call it—to get the programmers back to work. I said, "Sure." Isaac called in the staff and said, "Let's get their attention. You can offer a $100,000 bonus if they get the job done." I had agreed to a "large" bonus but was somewhat startled when Isaac offered $100,000. In the end they did the work for their regular fee, plus overtime. The bonus was never offered and did not have to be paid, but it surely caught the attention of our FDIC staffers who saw that the board was determined to do this job right and on time.

We put out a "Notice to Depositors" Monday evening explaining how the DINB would work. The important thing was that checking accounts, that are usually stopped dead in a payoff, would remain operational through the DINB. We wanted account holders to know they did not have to stampede to the bank to get cash for living expenses. We thought that would help hold down the crowds.

For the same reason, we decided to continue paying interest for up to ninety days to give depositors time to move their savings accounts. Interest usually stops at the moment of a bank's closing. Similarly, we told checking account holders to transfer to other banks as soon as it was convenient, either by writing a Penn Square check for the balance of their accounts or coming to the bank to be paid by government check.

The automatic teller machines were available as before, and the DINB provided a check-cashing service up to $1,000 for depositors. Contents of safe deposit boxes were available to holders, and trust operations were transferred to another institution. Depositors seeking a simple payment of their insured deposits were handled at the teller windows of the main bank building or at the motor office in the parking lot. Those with more complicated problems were sent next door to the Energy Building of the bank for personal interviews. Loan customers were reminded that their obligations were still valid and that FDIC would expect the loans to be paid according to terms.

Isaac and I both wanted to be there to see the DINB begin paying out money, hopefully with no hitches. As our meeting in Washington closed down Monday night with Conover's insolvency finding, we went to our homes in the same neighborhood of Great Falls, Virginia, to pack our suitcases. He picked me up on the way to the airport, and we flew down to Oklahoma City with a number of staff personnel in two chartered jets.

After receiving extensive advice on the state of the banking industry from our taxi driver, we arrived at the bank shortly after midnight. On the way he pointed out the new Penn Square tower under construction. All the lights were on at the bank, and it looked like absolute chaos. It was swarming with our people and former bank employees hired to work for the DINB and in our liquidation division. There were batteries of typewriters clacking away furiously and a phalanx of examiners with heads down and fingers flying over their calculators.

Penn Square's demise was featured on local television stations; everyone in Oklahoma City knew we were under a deadline to have the DINB opened the first thing Tuesday.

The depositors took it coolly. We opened on schedule and there were, indeed, long lines, but they were orderly. We had promised to keep the DINB open around the clock if necessary; however, the crowd tapered off toward the end of the first day. We were able to close by about seven o'clock for reopening the next morning. The payoff was going smoothly. Tuesday night Isaac and I flew back to Washington.

When we were over the hump with the payoff, we called Newton back for rest and rehabilitation after a week of twenty-hour working days. We sent another Mike to Oklahoma City to take over the DINB—Mike Hovan, a career FDIC examiner who had been my special assistant when I was chairman. Hovan flew to Oklahoma City on Sunday, July 11. Jim Hudson, a career FDIC liquidator, was there heading up the receivership; his job was to sell off Penn Square's assets.

We asked Hovan to see if there might be a way of selling the remaining insured deposits and realizing some premium on them from an acquiring bank. The action would also speed the payoff, since depositors could simply take over their old accounts at the new bank.

Before Hovan could reply, the books had to be balanced. Our staff had been working so hard on the individual deposit accounts that no one had taken time to inventory the whole. In response to heavy pressure from our board, Hovan pledged to get the accounting done and have a recommendation for us by Thursday, July 15. Hovan got his trial balance Thursday as scheduled; it was $107 million out of balance. The bank's books were a shambles.

He said he and Hudson just looked at each other. The variance was so egregious that there was no way to sell those deposits. We would have no idea what we were selling. Several weeks later the disparity was painstakingly resolved.

The DINB was dying down. It did its work in a burst of energy, flaring off millions of dollars of deposits in the first weeks after the closing. Depositors rushed off to open new accounts at other banks. One little bank just down the road grew by $20 million in less than two months. The DINB settled down to a steady payout of funds, on its way to a peaceful demise.

Ninety-five percent of Penn Square's insured deposits were paid out in three months. By September 30, only $10.5 million in 3,527 accounts remained. When FDIC closed the DINB and sold the last deposits to newly established Charter National Bank in August 1983 only $458,000 was left to disburse.

The receivership's job was to liquidate Penn Square's assets. FDIC held an inventory of more than $500 million in assets, as well as the loan participations tangle to unwind. Hudson, who had opened the receivership, was succeeded by Tom Procopio who was in charge for more than a year, and then by Paul Heafy, who had been Procopio's second in command.

The payoff had gone smoothly as far as the insured depositors were concerned. However, it set off shock waves in financial circles. Cries of pain and disbelief echoed from Wall Street to LaSalle Street in Chicago—Continental's headquarters. The payoff left at risk $202 million in uninsured deposits plus an unknown but certainly large number of other claims including the participations. Their payment would depend on our liquidation of the bank's assets. The large participating banks were frantic to find out how badly they were exposed to loss. Teams of bank employees had begun descending on Penn Square even before it was closed to copy loan documents furiously. Many of the loans involved several banks. They were pushing and shoving—physically fighting—to get into the files. Hovan pulled the plug on the Xerox machine to get the attention of the bank representatives. He then laid out ground rules for their file search. The invading bank teams retreated to motel rooms and employed squads of temporary help—Kelly Girls and the like —to continue copying the loan files. Hovan allowed only one copy to be made of each loan file and left it to the banks to have subsequent copies made elsewhere. Local photocopying businesses enjoyed a small boom.

Crisis followed crisis. The former Penn Square employees we had hired began departing to take new jobs or to look for them. Typically, after a bank failure, FDIC hires most of the working-level employees on the spot—all but the top management—and keeps them so long as we have need for their services. As the work load declines, we let them go. For most bank employees, the FDIC stint provides a cushion of a few weeks or more, instead of abrupt termination on the failure date.

Penn Square had a sizable staff to service the participated loans; they received payments from borrowers, deducted Penn Square's share, and remitted the portion due to the participating bank or banks. Other employees were involved in loan documentation and maintaining credit files. The trouble was that Penn Square officers had been doing the participation agreements so fast that the support staff could not keep up with them.

The files we took over were seriously deficient; most were not current; documentation was poor; records were generally disorganized. Under these circumstances we needed the people who had worked the loans and were familiar with them. But the best were leaving rapidly. Of the 383 Penn Square employees we had hired on the day of closing, 110—or 29 percent—left before the month was out.

Such turnover was disruptive. Morale among the FDIC staff nose-dived. Everybody was dead tired. Isaac asked me to go back to see if I could settle things down. So I flew back to Oklahoma City. The weather was searing hot, oppressive. I found our staff struggling bravely under enormous pressure. The situation was constantly changing. They faced a new dilemma, a hard decision, or another unknown every minute.

I surveyed the situation and decided to meet it head on. Hovan and Hudson were instructed to call all the remaining bank employees together. They guaranteed them all a job for at least a year. They would get the full range of FDIC employee benefits. At the time I thought it would cost FDIC money, possibly a great deal, because I expected our operations to wind down considerably within a few months. It turned out the files were in such a mess that we needed many of the remaining bank people for the full year and more.

After our hiring announcement the rush to leave subsided; but receivership employment declined gradually as the liquidation progressed. By mid-1985 we were down to eighty-seven employees, less than a quarter of the number we had begun with three years before.

Penn Square's holdover executives thought they could take advantage of the personnel crisis. A trio of second-level management headed by Tony Williams, executive vice-president, told us that in return for the titles to their cars they would agree to stay on for at least thirty days. They said that the third-tier executives—some eighteen vice-presidents—would stay on for sixty days in return for their cars.

Penn Square executives had a penchant for company limousines. The bank owned a fleet of forty-seven automobiles, ranging from a brand new $19,000 Lincoln Town Car to a $3,600 three-wheeled police vehicle. Most of the cars were at the upper end of the price range—Buicks, Oldsmobiles, a Cadillac—and none was more than a-year-and-a-half old.

We decided not to be blackmailed. Hovan and Hudson

wanted to fire Williams. They told me he was causing disruption in the work force. I said go ahead. He was given twenty minutes to clean out his desk. Williams threatened to take with him most of the Penn Square work force. He left. No one followed. The other executives settled down.

The automobiles, which had been appraised at $485,000, were later sold at a public auction held in the bank's parking lot. It was a festive occasion, a community event. Fancy cars were not the only indulgence of Penn Square's management; some favored expensive office plants. They and their brass planters fetched $80,000. Auctions of art objects and furniture brought another $76,000.

The Side Effects of Penn Square Surface

An evening or two after I had returned to Washington, I was sitting at home reading the newspaper when I suddenly felt cold and clammy. Then I started to sweat and pain shot through my arms. I was scared. My wife, Margie, drove me to Bethesda Naval Hospital. When I walked in, they immediately put me to bed. Doctors and nurses swarmed about me. The next thing I knew I had needles stuck into both arms and was bristling with IVs and other tubes. The doctors kept me hospitalized for four days. After extensive testing they finally decided that it was nervous exhaustion and let me go home. I had not had a heart attack, as I had thought. It was a big relief. I did not tell anyone about it, I just put it out of my mind for a long time.

About a year later, Isaac and I were reminiscing about that Penn Square Fourth of July and I told him what had happened to me. That was funny, he said, because one evening when the worst of it was dying down, he was on his way home from the office when suddenly he felt cold and clammy and started having pains in his arm. He immediately told Edward Oliver, his driver, to turn around and get him to the nearest hospital. The doctors checked Isaac out and held him for four hours; then they decided it was just nervous exhaustion and sent him home. He had not had a heart attack either.

That ordeal was carrying teamwork and the burdens of office a bit too far. We both had been under severe stress and strain. A seemingly endless parade of difficult problems faced Isaac and me during the seven years we worked together, but none was as stressful as Penn Square.

After setting up the DINB, the next problems were handling the participations and disposing of the other assets. Our receivership's first priority was to get rid of the $2.1 billion in participated loans. We had a staff of 140 doing nothing but servicing loans. It was ridiculous since 85 percent of the loan value —$1.8 billion—belonged to the participating banks.

Three of our attorneys working in Penn Square—Mike Burgee, Albert Tumpson, and Don McKinley—recommended that we swap with the participants: let them take over the loans and files since they had the big interest. They could remit the minor portion due us. For the banks, it meant the added expense of servicing, but it gave them control of the assets. Chase Manhattan Bank worked with our lawyers in drafting a "reverse participation agreement." The other banks approved its form.

Negotiating the transfer agreements, however, was far different from actually persuading the banks to take loans out. Some participants wanted to take only selected loans; one balked at taking any loans whatever; all were slow in actually accepting loans. They had their reasons.

The most reluctant recipient was the largest player: Continental. The bank was not eager to recognize the losses in its $1 billion portfolio of Penn Square energy participations. It wanted to hold off at least until after the start of the year so that it would not have to report the losses for the current year.

We prodded the big participants, including Continental. In December, the first month after the transfer agreements, we passed a handful of loans worth $201 million. It was well into 1983 before the bulk of the participations was out of our hands and into the banks'.

In making and renewing the participations, Penn Square officials had developed a routine of calling on one bank, and if that bank refused, then the next bank, and the next. After the participants bought in, some began doing a little checking. If they did not like what they found, they let the loan go by when it came up for renewal in six months and the participation wound up at another bank farther down the line. The worst credit risks tended to accumulate at certain banks, including Seattle First National Bank. It got into the game late. The bank was not a big energy lender, but perhaps when it saw other big name banks involved, it decided it must be okay. One small participant, the Bank of Healdton in Healdton, Oklahoma, took on more than it could handle for another reason: It was controlled by the family of Bill Jennings, the chief executive officer of Penn Square. The Healdton bank was forced to charge off large loan losses and in 1985 was put up for sale by its owners.

By mid-1985 FDIC retained only $211 million of the participations, all for special reasons: Either we had most of the risk in a loan, or it was involved in litigation, or FBI officials had asked us to hold it while they conducted a criminal investigation.

As the true facts gradually unfolded, we realized that the major banks—greedy as they were in doing the deals—in actuality had been defrauded to some extent by Penn Square. Chase Manhattan and Michigan National sued FDIC, as receiver, alleging Penn Square fraud, negligence, and breach of contract in selling the participations. In December 1985 our board approved a settlement of both lawsuits by issuing receiver's certificates for $10 million to Michigan National and $9.5 million to Chase. This gave them a pro rata share of liquidation recoveries. Both fraud cases were complicated and had been arduously negotiated. These were two of the major lawsuits arising out of the Penn Square collapse. We successfully defended seven other lawsuits by the participating banks who wanted a share of the cash we had realized by offsetting borrowers' deposit accounts.* We faced a greater challenge with far reaching implications, however, on the question of whether letters of credit are insured deposits. Seven lawsuits were filed against us by banks holding letters of credit which we, as Penn Square's receiver, had refused to pay. On May 27, 1986 the Supreme Court ruled in FDIC's favor. Letters of credit are not deposits.[2] Two other lawsuits were filed against us by banks seeking preference among the claimants on grounds that wire transfers on loans were made just before the bank was closed. Five credit unions, in suits against us, also sought preferential status on the grounds that Penn Square had deceived them as to its financial condition. All of these suits were pending at mid-year 1986.

FDIC took the offensive against those responsible for the operations at Penn Square and its ultimate demise. In March 1984 we settled for $2.5 million from fifteen outside directors —persons we held culpable only because they did not exercise their oversight function and not because of any involvement in Penn Square's day-to-day activities. Then in June 1984 we filed suit against six insiders whom we held primarily responsible. We sought $80 million in compensatory damages and another $50 million in punitive damages. In July 1984 one of the six consented to a $20 million judgment that could be satisfied with the payment of $2 million. In November 1984 we settled with another director for $70,000 cash and his repayment of a $61,-500 loan to Penn Square. In 1985 we added an additional defendant, Peat, Marwick, Mitchell, and Company, the accounting firm that had given Penn Square a clean bill of health when, in fact, it was in disastrous financial condition. We made claims

---

*In paying off a bank FDIC will deduct the amount owed on loans as an offset against the borrowers' deposits and then pay the net balance.

in 1983 and 1984 on the blanket bond carrier for separate acts
of dishonesty by bank officials and were paid $6.25 million. In
the summer of 1986 more settlements began to fall into place.
Shortly before trial was to begin in the U.S. District Court in
Tulsa, Peat, Marwick settled our $153.4 million suit and soon
thereafter four Penn Square officers settled our $138 million
claim against them alleging unsafe, unsound, and unlawful
banking practices. The size of the settlements, sealed by the
court, were substantial, but far less than the amount sought. All
of the money will go toward dividends to the uninsured Penn
Square depositors and creditors.

In addition, FDIC remains involved in a welter of legal actions growing out of Penn Square. Counting the lawsuits that
Penn Square itself had begun and that we took over as receiver,
and lawsuits that we initiated or responded to after the closing,
we found ourselves involved with more than two thousand
legal actions at year-end 1985. The largest number were bankruptcy proceedings in which FDIC had a claim. These and many
other suits were to collect on loans and other assets of Penn
Square.

On the criminal front, our examiners discovered 451 matters
needing investigation for possible criminal offenses under federal law. Many were fairly minor; some were quite serious.
Evidence was referred to the Justice Department. In 1984 Bill
Patterson, the energy lender, was brought to trial on criminal
charges arising from Penn Square. He was acquitted by a federal
jury in Oklahoma City. The next day he was indicted in Chicago on other charges relating to Continental, along with John
R. Lytle, the Continental officer in charge of the Penn Square
account, and Jere Sturges, a heavy borrower. In August 1986,
the charges were dismissed because too much time had elapsed
since the indictments. Thomas Orr, a Penn Square official who
specialized in horse loans of dubious value, pleaded guilty to
tax evasion and conspiracy to commit bank fraud. In December
1985 he was sentenced to two-and-a-half years on each count,

to run concurrently. His prison term has started but the case is on appeal. Earlier, Clark Long, who had been assistant vice-president, was convicted on two counts of false book entries, one count of wire fraud, one count of false statements, and one count of obstruction of justice. He was sentenced to three years in prison, later reduced to two years.

There is no such thing as a free lunch, but so-called sophisticated investors from all over the country had sent their money to faraway Oklahoma for an extra point or two of interest without asking the question: "Why is Penn Square willing to pay a premium for its deposits?" The Penn Square experience gave us a rough alert to the damage that can be done by brokered deposits funneled into troubled institutions.

Twenty-nine commercial banks, 44 savings and loan associations, and 221 credit unions from all over the nation were involved, all seeking a little more interest while completely ignoring the accompanying risks. Even the House of Representatives' Wright Patman Federal Credit Union took part. As a former employee of the House, I was still a member of the credit union. Among those who appeared on the scene July 6 was a Patman Credit Union official, Aileen Foley, a long-time friend of mine from the Hill.

As receiver, FDIC estimated in June 1983 that uninsured depositors and other claimants would ultimately receive 65 percent on their claims, far less than our over 90 percent average in ordinary closed-bank situations. Proven claims totaled $438 million; the largest single claimant was the FDIC insurance fund that was owed $217 million for amounts it paid to insured depositors. Dividends were paid in March 1983, August 1984, and November 1985, totaling $240.9 million or 55 percent of proven claims. Collections continue as I write this and it is certain that the receivership will continue many more years with ever dwindling returns. Another $536 million in claims has been rejected by the receivership as without merit, and the receivership was sued for part of that amount. The Michigan National and Chase settlements came from some of these suits.

In March 1986 the FDIC board established a loan loss reserve of $82.1 million for Penn Square, our best estimate at that time after more than three years of liquidation and litigation.

There were congressional hearings about Penn Square and this was proper. It was a sorry story that should have been told. After the formal hearings, we were forced to expend time, money, and energy responding to seemingly endless questions from Oklahoma legislators—particularly Senator David Boren and Congressman Mickey Edwards. Time and time again the lawmakers would demand detailed information on what we were doing and then tell the press what they were doing.

Because of my long affiliation with Congress, I treasure congressional prerogatives. Congress is entitled to any information it seeks, within reason. The congressmen asked for a General Accounting Office (GAO) audit. We should have cooperated, but did not. We stonewalled the GAO, although there was nothing to hide that I was aware of. In 1984, when our resources were stretched thin as bank failures mounted, we felt put upon, so Isaac reacted accordingly. We had nineteen open liquidations in the Oklahoma City office alone at the time. In November 1985 the new FDIC chairman, Bill Seidman, met with Boren and Edwards and agreed to cooperate with GAO auditors, so another of the Penn Square tensions is now behind FDIC.

The Penn Square liquidation will be with FDIC a long time, but the myth that a large bank never would be paid off is gone forever.

Chapter VII

Seafirst

The First Major Casualty
from Penn Square

SEATTLE FIRST NATIONAL BANK was the first big casualty precipitated by Penn Square; it came less than a year later. It could have been a smaller Continental crisis, if BankAmerica Corporation had not moved in, contracting to purchase Seafirst just hours before it would have failed.

Seafirst was the largest bank in the Pacific Northwest; crushing Penn Square loan losses drove it into the fold of its vastly larger neighbor to the south. The biggest bank merger in the nation's history united Seafirst Corporation, a $9.6-billion holding company, with the $119.7-billion BankAmerica Corporation. The $129.3-billion combined entity then exceeded New York's Citicorp by $1 billion to rank first in the nation. That standing was reversed in less than a year as Citicorp grew and BankAmerica marked time.

The merger was a consolidation of economic power on the West Coast that would have been unthinkable under any but the emergency circumstances that gave it birth. The merger required a change in state law to permit the interstate acquisition, and that was obtained. It also required the approval of OCC as the supervisor of both banks and the approval of the Federal Reserve System as supervisor of the holding company. These, too, were obtained—all in spite of anticompetitive implications that under normal conditions would have ruled out even the consideration of such a merger.

In this case the only alternative would have been another multibillion-dollar rescue by FDIC. We were ready to step in; ultimately we did not have to. We did go so far as to send one of our senior attorneys across the country, bearing life-saving documents. Bill Isaac and I had informally agreed we would make a massive infusion of capital, if necessary, to buy time for an orderly solution to the bank's impending failure.

The Seafirst story has two components. The FDIC role is described from my personal experience and files; the Cooley-Seafirst-Bank of America sections come mainly from press accounts at the time.

The drama began shortly after Penn Square. Our postmortem showed us how badly Seattle First was ensnared in energy loan participations with the little Oklahoma City bank. OCC and the Fed continued day-to-day monitoring of Seafirst. If word got out that FDIC was showing any unusual interest, the marketplace would quickly have recognized it as a measure of the bank's ills. So we watched from afar as the bank began its losing struggle for rehabilitation.

In August of 1982, little more than a month after Penn Square failed, Seafirst's Chairman William Jenkins said that he would take early retirement. Seafirst recruited carefully for a new head and announced its choice December 23: Richard Cooley, for sixteen years chairman of Wells Fargo & Company in San Francisco. Bank analysts and others were surprised that Cooley would leave Wells Fargo, the nation's twelfth largest bank holding company, in favor of troubled Seafirst, the twenty-sixth largest. Cooley said he relished the challenge.[1]

He took over in Seattle January 3, 1983. One of Cooley's first and most painful duties was to announce the operating loss for 1982—$91.4 million—together with the news that he had arranged a $1.5-billion emergency line of credit with megabanks around the country. An ominous signal, this was the "reassuring" type of statement that boomeranged in the Continental crisis a year hence. Seafirst was suddenly in a very vulnerable funding position. FDIC feared the huge loss was only the forerunner of worse to come. How much worse no one at that point could tell.

A White Knight Appears

Cooley ordered a sweeping assessment of the bank's condition and brought in the bank's outside auditors, Arthur Andersen & Co., to make a special study of the energy loans. BankAmerica was already making its first overtures at acquisition in private conversations with Seafirst officials.

Preliminary figures showed the bank was going to need a major infusion of capital, so big that it might even constitute selling the bank. Cooley flew to New York in the middle of February to talk with Salomon Brothers, Inc., Seattle First's investment banker. The first-quarter loss was mounting so rapidly that it threatened to equal or exceed the entire 1982 loss. Cooley met frequently with officials of OCC and the Fed in San Francisco, and kept his safety net banks informed. As the first quarter drew to a close in March, BankAmerica sent two key officials to Seattle on a low-profile basis to take a closer look at the books of the ailing bank. The first week in April, BankAmerica retained Goldman, Sachs & Co., the New York investment banking firm, to pursue merger. Seafirst, meanwhile, was distributing financial information packages to other possible investors. The next week, Salomon Brothers reported to Seafirst that it had interest from other quarters; however, no strong challenge to BankAmerica's bid ever appeared.

Worried that when it became known the first-quarter loss might be enough to kill any private deal, Cooley flew to Washington, D.C., to arrange the ultimate backup. After stopping in at the Fed, he and his executive vice-president, William Pettit, came to FDIC on Thursday, April 14.

Our Legal Division had determined early on that should the time come, we could take advantage of the new latitude added to Section 13(c) in 1982. The resolution prepared for our board stated that it was our judgment that the bank was in danger of closing and that assistance could be provided as an interim measure "to permit the FDIC to arrange in an orderly fashion the merger, consolidation or sale of the Bank's assets and assumption of the Bank's liabilities."

We could take action without declaring Seafirst "essential." This time we were worried about the domino theory in a different form—not that financial dealings entangled other banks, but that analysts and the financial marketplace might perceive all Penn Square participants as doomed if the first one went down.

The new law, however, presented a new problem: The revised language specified that the assistance must be used to facilitate a merger. Although the revision had been designed mainly for mutual savings banks, it could apply to commercial banks like Seafirst as well. The problem was that if the private deal fell through, we did not know whether we could find a partner for a federally assisted merger at a reasonable price. Our Legal Division determined that the language in the act, "in order to facilitate the merger," did not mean that the combination had to occur at the moment we granted assistance. We could "facilitate" by sustaining the bank as an operating entity, thus preserving its franchise value, while we sought an appropriate merger partner. They had found the interpretation of the law we needed.

The new authority had already been tested—just two weeks before. We had put $25 million into the failing United Southern Bank of Nashville to keep it operating for a short time while we arranged closed-bank mergers for United Southern and four related banks on the same day in May.*

Peter Kravitz, in our Legal Division, had drafted the Tennessee documents and flown with them to Nashville to handle the United Southern loan transaction for FDIC. Doug Jones, our deputy counsel, told Kravitz to stand by because he might have to do the same thing for Seafirst.

The situation in Seattle rolled toward a climax the next week under deadline pressure from the shareholders' annual meeting scheduled for Thursday, April 21. There the bank's first-quarter loss would have to be disclosed. A hidden run among institutional depositors, foreign depositors, and the like had already started. No one knew how it would develop. In Olympia the state legislature was putting the final touches on a bill that would permit the out-of-state acquisition of Washington's largest bank. On Sunday, April 17, Seafirst informed BankAmerica that it was interested in entering purposeful negotiations. BankAmerica said it was interested only in acquisition, not merely a recapitalization, and that it wanted to negotiate straight through to a consummated deal, not an agreement in principle. They agreed the talks would begin in New York in two days at the offices of Salomon Brothers.

Cooley began the week with a final round of base touching and briefing. Leaving Seattle Monday, he flew to Washington and Tuesday morning met with Paul Volcker at the Fed. By afternoon Cooley was in New York talking with some of the safety net banks. That evening he was back in Seattle, preparing for the annual meeting. He left Seafirst's negotiating in charge of Pettit, who brought with him to New York Stan Carlson

*All five banks were part of the banking empire of Jake Butcher and his brother, C. H. Butcher. Sixteen banks in Tennessee failed either as members of the Butcher chain or because of loans purchased from Butcher banks. Jake Butcher is now serving a prison term after being convicted of bank fraud and tax evasion.

from the bank's Seattle law firm. BankAmerica's negotiators were headed by Stephen McLin, senior vice-president and director of strategic planning. Both sides were also represented by their investment bankers. The talks began at 11 P.M., Tuesday, and went on throughout the night.

A Federal Knight

Cooley had asked what we were prepared to do as a backup. Without waiting for the outcome of the private negotiations, Isaac and I discussed the fast moving situation Tuesday night and agreed we should authorize a loan of $250 million to Seafirst. It was something in the nature of an unofficial two member board meeting. Later that night Comptroller Todd Conover was advised and concurred.

Cooley called and was told that we had advanced the federal backup package to a red alert status. Our action, in effect, passed the decision back to Seafirst. The agreement with Cooley was that we would prepare all the legal documents and be ready to transfer the money as soon as he asked that the loan be funded. We were set to do it instantly, upon Cooley's telephone request.

Our stopgap assistance agreement was a subordinated note, payable on demand, so that our board could pull the money any time and trigger the failure of the bank which would lead to an assisted merger or possibly even a bailout. A closed-bank transaction would leave the shareholders at the mercy of the liquidation results. The principal amount of the note was $250 million that would barely cover the bank's losses; if there were a serious run, we might have to go much higher. We incorporated standard key conditions for FDIC assistance: no payment of dividends without FDIC approval, and authority to remove bank officers and directors and to approve their replacements.

The two-track course continued the next day, Wednesday, April 20, with both the federal and private routes taking significant new steps. In New York the negotiators roughed out a first draft of the merger agreement by late afternoon.

In Seattle the bank's law firm sent a letter to OCC formally requesting the regulator's permission for the bank to borrow $250 million from FDIC the next day, Thursday, April 21.

With assistance documents in hand, Kravitz took a plane from Washington to the West Coast. He arrived in Seattle about 7 P.M. and went directly to the law offices of FDIC's local counsel, Lane, Powell, Moss & Miller. Attorney Raymond Haman of the firm and Kravitz immediately set to work revising and redrafting the documents. They were soon joined by Bill Pusch, a lawyer representing Seafirst. They worked steadily until after midnight and then resumed in the morning. The task was done shortly after noon Thursday. All that was needed was bank board approval and Cooley's signature.

Cooley had spent the morning at the Northgate Theater presiding at the annual stockholders' meeting. He had fielded more than a dozen stockholders' inquiries, but he had not answered the big question: How much was the first-quarter loss? He said Arthur Andersen & Co. was still poring over the energy loan portfolio; it would be "at least two or three days" before first-quarter results would be available.

Cooley told the stockholders that Seafirst had purchased $400 million in oil and gas participations from Penn Square and had originated another $800 million on its own. Cooley said the bank's foreign loan portfolio totaled about $1 billion and although it included more loans in Mexico than he would like, he saw no long-term problems.

The final subject was recapitalization. Seattle First was going to need about $200 million in fresh capital, he said, and sale of the bank was an option. Cooley reported that Seafirst's invest-

ment banker had been talking with potential investors of various kinds all over the United States and elsewhere. About five
groups showed continued interest, he said, including two international banks.[2]

The New York Stock Exchange halted trading in Seafirst
stock less than an hour after the meeting ended. Shares were at
14 and one-half, up by 1 and seven-eighths points on a volume
of 272,000 shares traded. The speculators were betting on a
takeover bid that would substantially exceed the current share
price.

At a press conference at the Seattle First building after the
shareholders' meeting, Cooley told reporters emphatically that
Seafirst was, and would remain, solvent. Then he went into a
closed working luncheon with members of the executive committees and the boards of directors of the bank and the holding
company.

"We had to get him and John Davis out of the meeting and
go over the documents with them," Kravitz recalled. Davis was
both a senior partner in the bank's law firm and a director of
the bank. Apparently, the directors had previously authorized
the application. Kravitz told us that Cooley and Davis took a
cursory look at the documents; there were a few words of polite
conversation; then Cooley signed and returned to his director's
meeting. The papers constituted an agreement to borrow $250
million from FDIC. In effect, they turned control of the bank's
future over to FDIC if the loan was made.

When it was over, Kravitz held a dozen documents constitut-
ing the FDIC temporary assistance package to Seafirst. All bore
Cooley's duly authorized signature, and all were undated. They
needed only signing and dating by FDIC to make them binding
contracts.

In New York, meanwhile, the negotiators were refining their
merger document. They had changed the scene of their meetings to the law offices of Davis Polk & Wardwell and had gone
into a new round of discussions Thursday afternoon. It might

lead to a final agreement, but it might not. The talks dragged on through the evening hours and into the night. We waited at the FDIC offices. Isaac kept in touch with Cooley in Seattle by telephone.

By this time, word of the Seafirst's troubles and the ongoing negotiations was so widespread within the financial community that we believed failure to consummate a private deal in short order would be the end of the bank.

We began to question whether $250 million would be enough to maintain confidence in Seafirst and avert a major run, or stop one once it had got started. Our legal division was told to draft new papers providing for $1 billion in assistance.

Fortunately, it never came to that. When negotiations in New York broke up in the wee hours of Friday morning, participants headed back to San Francisco and Seattle, respectively, amid guarded reports that an agreement had been reached. The full Seafirst board met late Friday afternoon to consider and approve the agreement.

BankAmerica executed two copies in San Francisco the next day, Saturday, April 23, and sent them up to Seattle. Cooley added his signature late in the afternoon and at 5 P.M. announced the merger and the $133 million first-quarter loss.[3]

Two important approvals had yet to be obtained: from the stockholders and the Fed. Additionally, the enabling legislation had to proceed through to enactment. Seafirst said it would submit the deal to stockholders for mail balloting within sixty days to be followed by a special stockholders' meeting at which the results would be formally announced. We decided that the shadow federal deal would stay locked in a filing cabinet at FDIC headquarters until the transaction was actually official. Few doubted that Fed approval, stockholders' consent, and the legislative authority would be forthcoming. But just in case we kept the documents on standby.

The out-of-state acquisition bill came through first. Washington Governor John Spellman signed it into law Monday,

April 25. The Fed gave its approval to the giant merger June 22, and on June 28 Cooley announced that the stockholders, too, had put their stamp on it. The merger became effective July 1, 1983.

Cooley later told me our backup plan was just that. He was determined from the beginning to do a deal with the Bank of America. He commented that in this case the Bank of America really performed the function of the FDIC.

The stockholders and management got a much better deal from BankAmerica than FDIC would have given them. The terms of the private transaction left Seafirst a free-standing subsidiary, unchanged in form but owned by BankAmerica with Cooley still its chairman. Where stockholders under an FDIC deal would have to take severe losses, Seafirst stockholders were able to salvage some cash and a stake in the future of the bank. Stockholders got $7.70 a share and part of a preferred share with a beginning dividend rate of 11.5 percent. The cash and stock cost BankAmerica $125 million each. In addition, the San Francisco giant added $150 million to Seafirst's capital base, bringing the total acquisition price to $400 million for the $9.6-billion bank.

The value of the preferred stock was to vary according to the performance of certain Seafirst loans. BankAmerica said that it would absorb a maximum $50 million additional loss on these loans but that any further losses would be charged against the preferred stock. The final accounting was scheduled for June 30, 1988. Cooley later told the press the selected loans included the energy credits, international loans, and some of the bank's national loans. McLin, head of the BankAmerica negotiators, was credited with devising this strategy which we later found so useful at Continental.

FDIC's only obligation was to undo our deal as quietly as it had been done. This proved to be easier than we thought. It was merely a matter of giving back the signed agreement and the note. There was no need for a board meeting to repeal our decision to grant the $250-million loan. FDIC Executive Secretary Hoyle Robinson informed us that what Isaac and I had done that late night back in April did not count as a board meeting at all. He was not there, Robinson said, nor was any person authorized to act as secretary of the meeting. No secretary, no meeting, the executive secretary told us. We had not really approved a $250-million injection—we only thought we had.

Next came Continental.

Addendum

Seafirst filed suit against five of its top executives and its auditor, Arthur Anderson & Co. Pretrial settlements were made in both suits in July, 1986. Without admitting any wrongdoing, the former officers—Chairman William Jenkins; Joseph Curtis, vice-chairman; Richard Jaehning, president; John Nelson, head of the world banking group; and John Boyd, head of the energy division, agreed to a judgment of $110 million. At the same time, Seafirst agreed to look for payment only to the insurance that had provided coverage. The Arthur Anderson settlement was agreed to in principle, but no details were announced. Still pending in September was a dispute with the insurance carriers over the amount of coverage, and a $50 million suit seeking payment to former shareholders alleging that Seafirst and its officers failed to disclose the true financial condition of the institution.

PART FOUR

Continental

Chapter VIII

Seven Days in May

Continental Is Saved
from Certain Failure

USUALLY a bank failure develops slowly as bad management, greed, insider dealings, or other malpractice wear the institution down. In cases of fraud or runs, the failure can be dramatically fast.

Continental Illinois National Bank and Trust Company succumbed to a run in a matter of days. In fact, Continental was the premier run of all time. It did not consist of depositors lining up at the door; rather, it was the lightning-fast removal of large deposits from around the world by electronic transfer.

In December 1978 Continental had been named by *Dun's Review,* a national financial magazine, as one of the five best-managed companies in the country. At year end 1983, Continental Illinois still looked like a big, strong bank. It reported a $25-million profit and declared a fifty-cent dividend for the fourth quarter. Its history since the mid-1970s had been one of growth and burgeoning operating profits. The bank had reached its goal of becoming the leading commercial lender in the nation.

The holding company's annual reports showed that the loan portfolio averaged $11.6 billion in 1976, grew steadily, and peaked at $34 billion in 1982. Net income rose from $128 million in 1976 to a high of $254 million in 1981. Although these pre-Penn Square figures looked spectacular, the ratio of return on assets was not much different from those of other banks of Continental's size. In fact, on this key measure of performance, Continental did slightly worse than its peer group in 1981, the year it achieved its record net income.

Nevertheless, Continental was a favorite in the markets and the darling of analysts as it entered the 1980s. The bank's common stock sold at a premium over other money center banks for three years through 1981. Among the first to perceive that this stampeding growth had the potential for trouble was Sanford Rose, who pointed out in *American Banker* articles in August of 1981 that the universal bullishness of Continental should be tempered with concern.

In an article headed: "Will Success Spoil Continental Illinois?"[1] Rose observed:

> It can be said that Continental's spectacular loan growth in recent years is less a matter of sharp pricing than it is of finding customers to whom the bank has been willing to lend more than the competition. . . . Recently, the company formed a Houston-based subsidiary that is making rather risky discovery loans to small or start-up operators who would not qualify for ordinary bank credit.

The *Wall Street Journal* followed with articles in September and October graphically detailing the riskiness of Continental's lending operations, but observing on balance that the risks were profitable. One article was headed: "In The High-Flying Field of Energy Finance, Continental Illinois Is Striking It Rich."[2]

Then came Penn Square in July of 1982 and Continental's stock dropped from $25 a share in June to $16 in mid-August.

Its credit ratings were downgraded. Fed funds and certificate of deposit (CD) markets began to dry up. The growth-at-any-cost strategy was abandoned; the bank's top priority became funding at any cost to support the weak loans already afloat. On July 25 the bank, at its own request, was removed from the list of top-graded banks whose CDs are traded interchangeably in the secondary markets. Continental's net income in 1982 plummeted by two-thirds from the previous year.

Losing its clout in the domestic markets, Continental turned to more expensive Eurodollar deposits. The Continental funding squeeze came during a series of events that rocked the financial sector: Penn Square, then the Lombard-Wall bankruptcy, next Mexican and Argentine debt crises, and finally a series of corporate bankruptcies. Continental had loan exposure in all of these.

Even so, Continental appeared to prosper. The regular quarterly dividend was paid in August and the stock price recovered to $25 in November of 1982, matching its pre-Penn Square figure. The apparent comeback continued through the second quarter of 1983 as the stock price reached its post-Penn Square high of $26.

The responsible regulators—the Fed and OCC— and the analysts were becoming increasingly aware of the soft spots in its operations. Although the bank had shrunk its loan portfolio to $31.1 billion by the end of 1983 in an effort to control its problems, its burden of nonperforming loans was climbing alarmingly. Newspapers gave good play to stories that nonperforming loans had reached $2.3 billion by the first quarter of 1984. Later, the annual report of the holding company confirmed that bad loans continued climbing to a peak of $2.7 billion for the 1984 second quarter. It was becoming increasingly obvious that Continental was having difficulty turning a profit on its operations. Even though the 1983 earnings of $108 million had rebounded by 39 percent from the lapse in 1982, analysts noted that much of it came from onetime gains and sales of assets. In the first quarter of 1984 Continental's plight became embarrassingly apparent when it sold its profitable credit card operation to avoid a loss and to maintain the corporation's dividend.

The Continental board had seen to the departure of President John Perkins in December 1983 and Chairman Roger Anderson in February 1984. The board installed a new top management team of David Taylor as chairman and Edward Bottum as president; both were promoted from within the bank and neither was identified with the energy problems.

In early 1984 the bank was anxious about its funding. Throughout the early spring Taylor scoured the world for money sources, but all remained quiet on the surface.

The Electronic Run Begins

Until May. Then the run exploded. We do not know for certain, but we suspect it was triggered when American investment bankers made inquiries in Japan to find if there was any interest in taking over Continental. They were not engaged by the bank; they were trying to drum up business on their own. Another theory, subscribed to by some officers still with the bank, is that the sale of the Continental credit card operation to avoid reporting a first-quarter loss together with an untimely TV commentary, was the real trigger for the run. In March the bank made a gross profit of $176 million from the credit card sale; yet, in April it reported net income of only $29 million for the quarter. On May 4, just four days before the run started, syndicated columnist Robert Novak commented on the McLaughlin Group TV talk show that the Fed would loosen up the money supply "only in the event of a bank failure, maybe something like the Continental Illinois in Chicago."[3]

What we do know is that Reuters, the British news agency,

moved a story on its wire at 11:39 A.M. Tuesday, May 8, saying that Continental had denied as "totally preposterous" rumors that the bank was considering bankruptcy. Reuters had picked up on talk that banks in the Netherlands, West Germany, Switzerland, and Japan had increased their rates on loans to Continental. Some of the foreign banks had begun to pull funds out. It was no secret that Continental was heavily dependent on foreign funding, especially since the failure of Penn Square. Money withdrawn by U.S. money managers and institutional investors had been replaced with deposits from abroad.

Ordinarily, Continental would have refused to comment on the rumor by Reuters. Instead, it reacted with a quick denial, perhaps in the hopes of placating the foreign depositors.

The effect was just the opposite. The denial had scarcely been reported when another wire, the Commodity News Service, carried a new rumor: A Japanese bank was interested in buying Continental. The next morning, Wednesday, May 9, the Commodity News Service story was picked up in Japan by JiJi wire service. Japanese money began leaving Continental. As the sun rose in Europe, the European bankers also began to withdraw their funds.[4] The outflows zoomed; in the ten days preceding FDIC assistance, the loss exceeded $6 billion. Inside the bank, all was calm, the teller lines moved as always, and bank officials recall no visible sign of trouble—except in the wire room. Here the employees knew what was happening as withdrawal order after order moved on the wire, bleeding Continental to death. Some cried.

The run took hold domestically when, a little more than twenty-four hours after Continental had said bankruptcy was "totally preposterous," the Board of Trade Clearing Corporation (BTCC) just down the street from Continental withdrew $50 million. The BTCC, a clearinghouse for trading on the Chicago Commodity Exchange, had been a long-standing customer. Word of its defection moved promptly on the wire services, and the panic was on.[5]

The first calls to FDIC for help came late Thursday afternoon,

May 10. Deputy Comptroller Joe Selby called Bill Isaac; Fed Governor Chuck Partee called me. It was clear that we were going to be involved one way or another.

The same day Comptroller Todd Conover issued a statement designed to be calming, but having the opposite effect. He said:

> A number of recent rumors concerning Continental Illinois National Bank and Trust Company have caused some concern in the financial markets. The Comptroller's Office is not aware of any significant changes in the bank's operations, as reflected in its published financial statement, that would serve as a basis for these rumors.

It was, as a House Committee staff report observed more than a year later, "a highly unusual press release."[6]

Friday morning, May 11, Selby and Conover, meeting with Volcker at the Fed, called Isaac to come right over. The situation was deteriorating. Several major banks in New York were trying to put together a package to bolster public confidence in Continental.

Morgan Guaranty Chairman Lew Preston was taking the lead. That afternoon Preston and the Fed announced a $4.5-billion, thirty-day line of credit sponsored by sixteen banks. In addition to Morgan Guaranty Trust, the participants were Bankers Trust Company, Manufacturers Hanover Trust Company, Chemical Bank, Chase Manhattan Bank, Bank of America, First National Bank of Chicago, Mellon Bank, First Interstate Bank of California, Wells Fargo Bank, Security Pacific National Bank, First National Bank of Boston, Crocker National Bank, Texas Commerce Bank, Citibank, and Irving Trust Company. The major lines were provided by the seven largest institutions, six in New York and Bank of America in California.[7]

Over the weekend we waited. It became apparent by Monday afternoon that the bank sponsored line of credit would not do the job. The run accelerated.

An early morning meeting was scheduled for Tuesday, May

15, at the Fed. Attending were Volcker; Partee; three FDIC board members; and the head of the bank supervision divisions, Jack Ryan of the Fed, Bob Shumway for us, and Paul Homan for OCC. We talked over the alternatives. They were few— none really. Volcker and Ryan ran through the list of potential buyers, including foreigners, but it was increasingly clear there would not be time for a merger even if someone was interested. And so far no interest had been shown.

A straight payoff, it was obvious to all, would be so disruptive it might well lead to a national banking panic. Insured deposits we then overestimated at about $4 billion,* barely 10 percent of the bank's funding base. At first glance, a payoff might have seemed a temptingly cheap and quick solution. The problem was there was no way to project how many other institutions would fail or how weakened the nation's entire banking system might become. Best estimates of our staff, with the sparse numbers we had at hand, were that more than two thousand correspondent banks were depositors in Continental and some number—we talked of fifty to two hundred—might be threatened or brought down by a Continental collapse. (We later computed that 179 banks had more than 50 percent of their capital in Continental; 66 of them over 100 percent.)

These were serious numbers. Of even more concern was the certainty that volatile funding lines of all the other big banks in the nation would be cut back or put on hold if the Continental holding company could not meet its commitments. Two very large troubled institutions with excessive funding exposure came into the discussion immediately; the consensus was that they probably would not survive a Continental collapse.

Various scenarios were laid out and they all signaled doomsday. We were reduced to speculation. The only things that seemed clear were not only that the long-term cost of allowing Continental to fail could not be calculated, but also that it might be so much as to threaten the FDIC fund itself.

---

*Our final calculation showed the insured to total just over $3 billion.

In hearings several months later, the House Banking Committee criticized us for not preparing detailed cost analyses before arriving at a decision. We had only hours to decide, days at the most. The off-the-cuff analysis had to depend on the experience, the instincts, and the integrity of those charged with the responsibility—Volcker, Isaac, Conover, and Sprague. The paper trail would have to follow. I was comfortable then and remain comfortable today with the course we took.

We spent considerable time on all the alternatives, until we had satisfied ourselves that none was viable without immediate massive FDIC assistance. Our staff lawyers under Deputy Counsel Doug Jones were instructed to go full speed ahead in developing an assistance plan. They embarked on a day and night marathon, fleshing out an emergency measure to keep Continental alive until we could work out a permanent solution.

Tuesday Volcker, Isaac, and Conover had lunch with Don Regan at Treasury. Secretary Regan suggested we include the major banks in anything we might devise, just as we had done so successfully in the First Pennsylvania case four years before. It was decided to broach the proposal to the seven largest banks as soon as possible. Volcker called Preston and asked him to set up a meeting for 9:00 A.M. the next day, Wednesday, May 16, in New York.

In the Spirit of J. P. Morgan

Preston scheduled the meeting to be held in the Morgan Guaranty board room. Isaac went up late Tuesday to be ready. As host, Morgan was reenacting its role during the panic of 1907. During that time before federal regulators, J. Pierpont Morgan himself had called a meeting of bankers to forge a joint assistance pact that would save the Knickerbocker Trust Company, then in the throes of a fatal run. Morgan wanted to establish a precedent for mutual aid that would sustain all banks through the panic. J. Pierpont Morgan failed. So did Knickerbocker. I hoped our meeting would fare better.

Shortly before 10 A.M., Wednesday, Isaac left the meeting to call me in Washington and suggest I catch the next shuttle to New York. We had assumed the bankers would want to talk about a rescue package and then get back to their boards and maybe have some answers for us early Thursday. So I had stayed in Washington Tuesday night. Instead, the top decision makers of the banks had assembled at Morgan Wednesday morning. They were ready to act and had full authority to do so. All of the heavy hitters of the banking industry were assembled in one room: Preston from Morgan Guaranty; John McGillicuddy, chairman of Manufacturers Hanover; Walter Shipley, president of Chemical Bank; Thomas Labrecque, president of Chase Manhattan Bank; Charles Sanford, president of Bankers Trust; Thomas Theobald, a vice chairman of Citibank; and Sam Armacost, president of Bank of America. (Armacost happened to be in New York to preside over the opening of Bank of America Plaza in midtown Manhattan the day before, so he stayed over.)

Volcker was there, as were Tony Solomon, president of the New York Fed; Gerry Corrigan, president of the Minneapolis Fed and a Volcker confidant; plus Isaac and Conover. The specter of the six-foot, seven-inch Volcker striding into the front door of Morgan at a time of crisis was a matter of concern, so he was asked to use an obscure entrance.

Isaac called me again a few minutes after his first call and said that the run was escalating. There was no more time. We might have to do a deal in New York, possibly that night. I left immediately. Our key staff was already in New York: Doug Jones, our deputy general counsel and the architect of all our tough legal contracts, and Stan Silverberg, head of research.

Back-up attorneys and staff from our bank supervision division kept arriving as the day progressed; our crisis center moved from Washington to New York.

Isaac told me that at the beginning the discussion was about how to save Continental without government assistance. By the time I arrived, the focus had shifted to the role FDIC should play: The action would have to be government led and financed, but the cooperation of the banks would be essential.

The first question was the amount of assistance. It could not be too low—that would not restore confidence. It could not be too high—that would scare the hell out of everybody. So we finally settled on $2 billion. That was the right number, everyone agreed, enough to inspire confidence without convincing the markets that the bank was so bad it could never be saved.

Volcker left the meeting for a few hours in the early afternoon to get an honorary degree from Columbia University. His appearance had been scheduled for a long time. If he did not show, it would be attributed to the Continental problem and would escalate the crisis. So Volcker had to go get his honorary degree.

After a four o'clock recess, the bankers and regulators reassembled about six o'clock, again at Morgan. The bankers said they wanted to be in on any deal, but they did not want to lose any money. They kept asking for guarantees. They wanted it to look as if they were putting money in but, at the same time, wanted to be absolutely sure they were not risking anything. I said I would not vote for such a sham. Volcker kept pushing for a decision and FDIC action that night. Tomorrow might be too late. We finally adjourned shortly before ten o'clock without any conclusions, agreeing to meet again early the next day.

Volcker stuck to his "el cheapo" cigars during the evening. I enjoyed two really good ones from the Morgan cigar box. The coffeepot was well used; the cognac bottles untouched.

The meeting reassembled Thursday morning, May 17, at the FDIC regional office at 345 Park Avenue. Isaac and I were there about 6:00 A.M. Both of us had sleepless nights. Conover arrived a little later; the bankers began filtering in about seven o'clock. A few of the players from the banks had changed, but the replacements were similarly high-ranking executives authorized to make on-the-spot binding decisions. The bankers were still saying they wanted to join in the rescue package, but they had not lessened their demand for guarantees. Isaac finally told them bluntly that either the banks were at risk or they were not in. One banker sat in a chair in the hallway reading the Franklin and First Pennsylvania precedents. Perhaps he was looking for comfort. It escaped me what he hoped to find.

By 7:30 A.M. we had made little progress. We were certain the situation would be totally out of control in a few hours. Continental would soon be exposing itself to a new business day, and the stock market would open at ten o'clock. Isaac and I held a hallway conversation. We agreed to go ahead without the banks. We told Conover the plan and he concurred.

So we had our board meeting in a small room at the FDIC regional office. Not in the conference room. The bankers were using it. We did not even take seats at a table. The three board members—Isaac, Conover, and myself—simply stood around a desk and held the three-minute meeting. Doug Jones was pressed into service as acting secretary. He scratched out the resolution on a legal pad. It took some time to later reconstruct all of the documents to support our action.

The proposal before us was simple, straightforward, and by far the largest in FDIC history. It was to make a subordinated loan of $2 billion to Continental. The infusion was designed to buy us time to work out a permanent solution. The original draft provided that the note could be called at any time for any reason by the chairman of FDIC. One man able to call a note for $2 billion! Conover objected, I agreed with him and Isaac readily assented, although he has never been averse to power. We amended the resolution to say that the *board* of FDIC could call the note at any time, and the motion then carried on a three to zero vote, with no further discussion.

Meetings were going on all around us. Bankers were in one room; our staff was in another. Attorneys from the banks and FDIC huddled in the hallways. Draft language appeared on scraps of paper.

We told the bankers what we had done and immediately notified the press. Eight minutes later it had not appeared on the business wires, so Preston called Reuters with an urgent plea to move the news. Our press man, Alan Whitney, called from Washington to report that Joe Coyne, the Fed press spokesman, had orders to issue a Federal Reserve press release about the FDIC action. Isaac gave Whitney simple instructions: "Tell Coyne that if the Fed wants to put up the $2 billion, they can announce it any way they want." Whitney made the announcement.

The morning statement was fuzzy on the point of who provided the $2 billion because at the time we did not know if the banks were going to be in or out. The bankers were still talking it over among themselves. Isaac and I left for Washington. Our lawyers stayed in New York working on language with the bank lawyers.

Citicorp was the final holdout for ironclad FDIC guarantees against loss by the banks. Walter Wriston, the Citicorp chairman, was in California. Isaac called Volcker in Washington, who then called Wriston to tell him that Citicorp was the obstacle. Citicorp came around.

About four o'clock we got word from Bernie McKeon, our regional director in New York, that the bankers had agreed to be at risk. Actually, the risk was remote since our announcement had promised 100 percent insurance. The seven banks took $500 million of the note and laid part of it off onto other banks. Eventually fifteen banks joined in the package. The story came out that afternoon that we put $1.5 billion in and the banks, $500 million. But what really happened was that FDIC put in the original $2 billion note on its own, and the banks later bought a quarter of it.

Anatomy of a Press Release

The formal press release that followed was more than just an announcement of the assistance. It was a carefully framed, integral part of the plan itself.[8] The following anatomy of the document is an interesting reflection of the board's state of mind and the uncertainties of the crisis we were seeking to address. The press release was issued jointly in the name of the three agencies: FDIC, the Fed, and OCC to show our united front. Further, the two key paragraphs had been drafted in consultation with the seven major assisting banks as a way of admitting them to full partnership in the rescue. The text gave notice up front that the assistance was temporary, intended to ensure the bank's liquidity, and to allow us the time needed to resolve the bank's problems "in an orderly and permanent way."

Since we did not want "temporary" to be interpreted as "volatile," we made it clear that the money would be there as long as it took "to enhance the bank's permanent capital, by merger or otherwise." The message in the last four words was that all options, except payoff, were open and at that point we had no idea what we would do in the nature of a permanent solution.

We made careful note of the private participation to show that this was not a government alone deal. We said the $2 billion would come from FDIC and "a group of commercial banks," without specifying how many banks and how much they would put in. That was because at the time we issued the press release we still did not have those specifics. We knew by then only that we had a commitment from the lead banks to underwrite $500 million, part of which they hoped to lay off to other institutions. We said that the loans to Continental would bear a market rate of interest, and we noted that the FDIC portion was being granted under Section 13(c)(2) of the act. We had made an essentiality finding, but it was not mentioned in the press release.

The third paragraph caused more hassling among the regulators themselves and with the banks than all the rest of the press release put together. And well it should have. It was the essence of the rescue. This paragraph granted 100 percent insurance to all depositors, including the uninsured, and all general creditors. It read as follows:

> In view of all the circumstances surrounding Continental Illinois Bank, the FDIC provides assurance that, in any arrangements that may be necessary to achieve a permanent solution, all depositors and other general creditors of the bank will be fully protected and service to the bank's customers will not be interrupted.

Its purpose, quite bluntly, was to stop the run and prevent recurrence. We had to have stability. The guarantee was extraordinary but not unprecedented. We had given similar public assurances to buy time for a permanent solution for Greenwich Savings Bank in New York City in 1981 and for the United Southern Bank in Nashville, Tennessee, in 1983. These two were also granted 100 percent insurance by press releases. Only the Continental guarantee, however, touched off a nationwide debate that to this day continues to raise questions and generate controversy.

On May 16 we could not have given such a guarantee—failure and payoff of the bank was still a possibility. On May 17 after infusing $2 billion into the bank, we could make the guarantee because it then would be more cost effective to do an assisted merger or a bailout than a payoff. The bank had $2.2 billion in remaining bank capital, plus our $2 billion. A merger would meet the cost test; it would be cheaper than a payoff where we would lose our $2 billion. Also, our May assistance was based on the "essentiality" law, so presumably a bank that is essential could not be allowed to fail no matter what the cost.

The fourth paragraph of the press release said that the bank-sponsored line of credit, arranged the preceding weekend before FDIC entered the picture, would also remain in place until a permanent solution was developed. The line had been expanded to twenty-four banks to provide $5.5 billion in unsecured loans.

The next paragraph—the Fed paragraph—was the other portion of the Continental press release that was worried to death. It set forth the conditions under which the Fed, as lender of last resort, would make its loans. FDIC and the banks wanted an up front promise from the Fed for unlimited funding. This was not to be. After much reworking, the paragraph evolved into the following awkward and obtuse final version:

> The financial assistance package is designed to enable the Continental Illinois Bank to resume normal patterns of funding in the market to meet its liquidity requirements and to operate normally in other respects. As a part of the overall program, and in accordance with customary arrangements, the Federal Reserve is prepared to meet any extraordinary liquidity requirements of the Continental Illinois Bank during this period.

In translation, the first sentence means that Continental should do its best to obtain funding from every other source before going to the Fed. The second sentence says that the Fed will lend to Continental only on a secured basis (such are the "customary arrangements")—a sore point with FDIC whose loan was wholly at risk. The paragraph also said what it had to say: The Fed would lend to Continental to meet "any extraordinary liquidity requirements." That would include another run.

All agreed that Continental could not be saved without 100 percent insurance by FDIC and unlimited liquidity support by the Federal Reserve. No plan would work without these two elements. The press release told the world that they were, indeed, in place and Continental would not be allowed to fail. Later, in critiquing the rescue, our staff recommended that should the occasion ever again arise the press release should be written in clear, simple, unequivocal English.*

As If Continental Were Not Enough

Although preoccupied, immersed, and almost overcome with the Continental problem, FDIC still had to meet its other obligations during those trying days in May. The Western National Bank of Casper, Wyoming; the State Bank of Mills, Wyoming; the First National Bank of Snyder, Texas; and the First National Bank of Rushford, Minnesota, all failed on May 4. Then came the National Bank of Carmel, California, the Mississippi Bank of Jackson, and the First Continental Bank & Trust Company of Del City, Oklahoma, all closing on May 11.

The Continental Illinois announcement came May 17, followed the next day by the failure of the Planters Trust & Savings Bank of Opelousas, Louisiana; the Bledsoe County Bank in Tennessee; the Washington National Bank of Chicago, and the Bank of Irvine, California. The May onslaught continued one week later with the failure of the First National Bank of Prior Lake, Minnesota.

Continental and twelve other banks all had to be handled within a few days of each other in May. It was a month to long remember; but we had little time for reflection—the tide continued in June with ten more failures. More importantly, we were under pressure to fashion the permanent solution for Continental that our emergency assistance implicitly promised.

No one knew how much time we had—certainly less than we would have liked.

*We didn't even bother to discuss the "community" to be served in our press release. After our lengthy and agonizing deliberations about the community finding at Unity, it was clear that we could do whatever we wanted, so the three following bailouts had only perfunctory discussions by our board about community. At Commonwealth we talked about the State of Michigan; our resolution defined it as the "upper Great Lakes region." At First Pennsylvania we talked about the State of Pennsylvania and adjoining states; our resolution defined it as the "Delaware Valley region." At Continental we talked of the nation and the world; our resolution defined it as "the trade area it serves, plus the regional and national banking community."

Chapter IX

May to July

*Search for Continental
Solution Is Underway*

WITHIN a few days of the Continental collapse, we embarked on a search for a suitor who would take over the problem for us.

It would be costly to FDIC, we knew, but from the beginning we hoped that a government-supported private takeover or merger could be arranged. The search was on in earnest far and wide, banks or individual investors—every lead was explored.

At the start, another dangerous rumor briefly diverted our attention and threatened to compound our problem. The hearsay this time concerned Manufacturers Hanover, the nation's fourth largest banking company with $75 billion in assets. Their scenario was chillingly similar to what had brought on the Continental crisis. The widely circulated story was that Manufacturers Hanover was having trouble finding buyers for its short-term obligations in European money markets.* It sounded like the kind of funding crisis abroad that had tripped up Continental. Also, the bank and the regulators reacted again in the same way as in the Continental situation. Both vehemently

*Manufacturers Hanover stock dived 11 percent in one day.

denied any problem. The press reported that "a top Federal regulator, who asked not to be identified, said the rumors were 'reckless and spurious' and said he was 'livid'."[1] Even the people who were in the business of moving deposits around were telling the press that Manufacturers Hanover was having no trouble taking in the money it needed. But in Continental's case, David Taylor's public debunking of the rumors and Comptroller Conover's statement implying there was nothing wrong with the bank had both backfired and exacerbated the situation.

Yet, there is no right way to react to a rumor affecting confidence in a bank. There is no way of knowing whether a statement or silence is better for defusing life-threatening gossip. What bankers hope may prevent a stampede may just as well accelerate it. So all we could do was hold our breath and hope. Would Manny Hanny fall on top of Continental? The fourth and eighth largest banks—totaling more than $100 billion in assets—failing together? And then what would come next? The whole financial system seemed in jeopardy.

On Thursday, May 24, just one week after our Continental announcement, heavy selling of bank stocks drove down the stock market generally. The Manny Hanny rumors had spooked the markets.[2]

We braced ourselves. Friday came. Nothing happened. The rumors vanished. The story almost disappeared from the press. Just a twenty-four-hour virus? Manny Hanny later reported: "We didn't have any difficulty funding in any instrument, in any currency, in any maturity."[3]

As chairman, I had played the major role in the First Pennsylvania bailout. Now it was Bill Isaac's turn to take the lead. As soon as we had breathed our sigh of relief from the Manny Hanny scare, Isaac asked FDIC Research Director Stan Silverberg to head up the staff group that would be reconnoitering and negotiating a permanent solution for Continental. It was to be a difficult sixty days for the tightly knit group.

One of the lessons we had learned from the previous bailouts was that the FDIC board was better off one step removed from the negotiations. In the first three we were deeply involved, conducting the face-to-face negotiations ourselves. This time it would be the staff on the front lines. By no means had we removed ourselves from the process. Silverberg reported daily to Isaac and was in constant contact with Conover and me so that we had intimate awareness of the negotiations and ample opportunity for input.

At first Silverberg's unit was interrupted by urgent inquiries. Anxious depositors and creditors wanted to know what was meant by the FDIC guarantee in the May 17 press release. Large sums were at stake. Many calls came from overseas. Silverberg told them it meant we were considering direct assistance to Continental, or a live bank merger. If the bank were closed we would arrange a purchase and assumption transaction. In any scenario all uninsured depositors and creditors would be fully protected. We would not do a payoff. This was what they wanted to hear; but Silverberg felt that somehow his assurances did not satisfy them. "It was as if they were thinking, 'Well, can we really trust you?' " he said. He took it philosophically. If we were the creditors, and the bank was over there in some far-away country, and we were dealing with their government, we just might be a little skeptical, too.

In Search of a Permanent Solution

Silverberg flew to Chicago for his first meeting with Continental management during the last week in May. With him were two key members of his team, Jim Marino and David Cooke, both experienced bank analysts. At the meeting were Continental Chairman David Taylor, President Ed Bottum, Treasurer Robert McKnew, the late Joe Anderson then executive vice-president, and General Counsel Robert Brennan, plus outside

advisors: Rodgin Cohn of Sullivan & Cromwell was their outside lawyer; Don Opatrny of Goldman, Sachs & Company,
their investment banker. The eye opener, Silverberg reported to
us, was that the outsiders seemed to know more about the
situation, the condition of the bank, and the courses that had
to be explored than did the Continental people.

At the outset Continental and their advisors had sketched out
a plan to transfer out $4 billion of the bank's bad assets with
FDIC assistance and to downsize the bank principally by selling
foreign branches. FDIC would be receiving about 13 percent of
the holding company stock. In short, the bank management still
did not realize the depth of the problem and certainly at that
point did not realize FDIC was not going to do a wholesale
bailout of the Continental stockholders.

Discussion of various bailout formulations continued in the
ensuing weeks as the quest for a different solution continued.
But after that first meeting the idea of only a token dilution of
the stockholder ownership was no longer discussed.

Meanwhile, our assessment of the patient's condition was
underway. Paul Fritts, our regional director, again had the good
fortune to be in the right place at the wrong time. He had
headed our Philadelphia region when we dealt with the First
Pennsylvania crisis.* Fritts, now at Chicago, embarked on a
crash analysis of Continental, choosing Tom Wilkes to lead the
effort. Wilkes, a seventeen-year veteran bank examiner, was
called off another job in late May and after extensive preparation entered the bank with a forty-person staff on May 25. He
had assembled the cream of our examiner force.

For the next month Wilkes and his crew were on a pressure
cooker assignment as they worked with OCC's examiners and
bank employees to construct a cross section of the bank. Their
information was funneled back to Washington where a crew of
analysts massaged the figures. This group was headed by Roger
Watson, deputy chief of research, assisted principally by David
Cooke, Jim Marino, and George Unthank. Their task was to

*When Bill Seidman became FDIC Chairman, he named Fritts Chief of the
Division of Bank Supervision, the top career job at the corporation.

modify assumptions, make earnings projections, and generally
to assure our board that any solution we finally agreed to would
do the job. We were concerned about making the assistance too
thin or channeling it in the wrong direction. Either way we
would be faced with the problem again in another year.

The legal problems were challenging. Our deputy counsel
Doug Jones called on attorneys Barbara Gersten and Barbara
Monheit to develop documents for any possible solution and to
coordinate with the bank's lawyers; the bank's outside counsel;
and attorneys from the Fed, Treasury, and OCC.

So this exercise started out like all the other tough ones. The
staff was preparing for any eventuality while the board was
deciding what to do. While FDIC and the top management of the
bank searched for a solution, the bank employees had to contend
with demoralizing rumor after rumor: The bank will close tomorrow. Scores of FDIC cars were parked around the corner. The
government would not help. The papers and television stations,
searching for facts, were not reluctant to pass on rumors. It was a
nightmare job for the bank employees, but most stayed on.

Clearly, the first thing the bank needed was room to try to
make a deal on its own. No one thought there was much chance
of that, but it was important the bank should have the opportunity. We had to know that all avenues for a private solution had
been exhausted before we could move in with a government-
directed transaction.

At Continental's behest, Goldman, Sachs had been searching
for a buyer for several weeks. Soon after the May rescue, two
major New York banks sent in teams to review Continental's
loan files. Chemical Bank, the nation's sixth largest with $55
billion in assets, dispatched a hundred employees to Chicago
for a concentrated effort over a long weekend. Citicorp, the
nation's largest bank, sent in a smaller group over another
weekend. First Chicago, Continental's crosstown rival, also
took a look. Since they had many of the same customers, the
reviewing banks were able to compare their own ratings of
specific borrowers with Continental's. In most cases, Chemical,
Citicorp, and First Chicago found that Continental had rated a

debtor much higher as a possibility for repayment than they had. The findings of all the banks agreed that Continental was in worse shape than they had thought, or than we had thought.

There were, of course, differences between the banks' assessments and ours. Wilkes's FDIC crew arrived after the Citicorp, Chemical, and First Chicago teams had gone. Our examiners stayed much longer, doing the detailed analysis we had to have. So Continental in May and June was hit with successive waves of outside examiners, in addition to OCC's staff which continued in the bank throughout. There was a free sharing of information, and we benefited from being able to compare the different federal and private views of Continental's condition.

While Continental sought to pursue its own destiny, the FDIC task group concentrated on the two broad options that would be available to us if it came to that: a financially assisted merger with all depositors and creditors being made whole in the process; or a bailout, which would continue the Continental presence but have essentially the same result on depositors and creditors. A bailout also would allow for some residual stockholder benefit and would guarantee the holding company noteholders against loss.

In the first alternative, we would need discussions with possible merger partners, including the same ones Continental was talking with. In the second, we would have to recruit a top management team.

Merger Candidates

Our shopping list of potential acquirers of Continental was short. Not many institutions would have the size, financial resources, and management necessary to swallow the $41-bil-

lion ailing giant of the Midwest. The logical prospects were
Citicorp and Chemical in New York and the hometown candidate, First Chicago; all of them wanted to talk. Even though we
approached every other megabank in the nation, these were the
only three that showed any signs of interest.

Barry Sullivan, chairman of First Chicago, was definitely interested. He had left Chase Manhattan to take the top job at
First Chicago in 1980, not long after Tom Labrecque had won
the Chase presidency. A combined Continental-First Chicago
would have created about a $75-billion bank, close to the size
of Chase, the nation's third largest bank. He would be in a
prestigious spot.

Although acquisition by the larger New York institutions
seemed promising, there were legal and structural problems.
Illinois law prohibited acquisition by an out-of-state bank; that
would have to be changed before an interstate solution could
become possible. It was the same hurdle Seafirst had to clear in
Washington. In addition, Illinois law prohibited branching so
that Continental and all other banks in the state had only one
office. That made Continental considerably less desirable for an
out-of-stater looking for major market penetration through a
far-flung branch network. The limits that a single-office structure impose on deposit gathering had contributed to Continental's predicament. Seeking to transcend that constraint, its management had gone abroad in its search for funding and had
made the bank heavily dependent on foreign markets.

Rumors of a takeover by a Japanese interest had touched off
Continental's near-fatal run; and foreign purchase was among
the options we were pursuing. The ironic reality was that there
was little interest—really no interest at all—among foreign
banks in acquiring Continental.

We had a few feelers from abroad, but nothing serious ever
developed. One Japanese institution, Sanwa Bank, did indeed
visit Continental and later purchased its leasing operation. A
major Canadian Bank, the Bank of Montreal, communicated

tentatively. In Chicago LaSalle National Bank made some preliminary inquiries. LaSalle was itself a $1.5-billion institution
and was, therefore, far too small to handle Continental, but
LaSalle is owned by a Dutch parent in the $45-billion range.
After LaSalle President Bob Wilmouth touched base with
its Amsterdam parent, Algemene Bank Nederland, LaSalle
dropped out. Two major British institutions, Barclays and
Lloyds, seemed to be logical prospects but were not interested.
Earlier, Lloyds had counted itself out after preliminary merger
discussions. Goldman, Sachs made other unsuccessful contacts
in Canada, Germany, and Switzerland.

We did get an inquiry from Standard Charter, a South Afri-
can-based bank and owner of the $8-billion Union Bank in Los
Angeles. They were seeking a spin-off that would give them a
midwestern bank in the under $10-billion range. The inquiry
occurred just as the Illinois legislature was taking up the out-of-
state acquisition bill. An unrelated amendment appeared to
prohibit any acquiring bank from doing business in South
Africa. Whether Standard Charter took the hint or simply followed its own counsel, it did not pursue its inquiry.

Besides merger, another alternative was a buyout of the bad
loans, leaving Continental to go it alone freed of its debilitating
energy, shipping, and real-estate assets. Continental itself had
explored this approach earlier in the year in talks with the Bass
family of Texas. Later FDIC had discussions with the Basses.
The Bass-Continental negotiations foundered on price. The
talks were prolonged and were finally overtaken by the May
crisis.

The loan takeout idea, however, and our commitment to find
strong new management remained the pillars of any govern-
ment-assisted package FDIC would negotiate. In the end, the
entity that took out the Continental loans was FDIC. The bad
loans were the most serious and most conspicuous problem. In
a smaller bank, such as First Pennsylvania, it would not have
mattered so much. In fact, we took nothing out of First Pennsylvania; we left the bad loans in because with new capital First

Pennsylvania could manage. But Continental was different; its bad loans amounted to about half the size of the entire First Pennsylvania Bank. They had to come out. The balance sheet had to show that.

FDIC and Continental continued their separate searches for a merger partner, but it was fast becoming evident there could be no deal without massive FDIC assistance. Even with that, there was only cautious interest with many ifs.

Perhaps no single bank was big enough to merge with Continental. Citicorp's Vice-Chairman Hans Angermueller in the last week of May had been quoted in the press as saying: "The totality of a $40 billion to $42 billion bank is simply too large an organization. There might be segments of it that might be of interest, but I think it is a very large bite for any institution, domestic or foreign, to take."[4]

If Citicorp could not merge Continental, who could? Angermueller's statement seemed to hint at another alternative: that Continental could be broken up and its segments sold to two or more banks. A catchy name for the concept—the "Continental divide" approach—promptly took hold, but the idea itself never did. We had previously explored and then abandoned such an approach at First Pennsylvania. The one bank we had split up in 1978, Banco Credito y Ahorro Ponceno, in Ponce, Puerto Rico, produced an accounting nightmare that took special FDIC teams years to resolve.

Continental, meanwhile, was doing something about its size. Soon after our temporary infusion of funds, Continental began selling off assets. In a few weeks it had shrunk itself by $5 billion. The action would make merger a little more possible, but the major benefit was to reduce the bank's daily funding requirements.

As May rounded into June, Silverberg with his core duo of Cooke and Marino flew from Chicago, where they had been having conversations with Taylor and his advisers, to New York to meet the suitors, if indeed they were.

Silverberg talked with Angermueller about Citicorp's interest. Citicorp had been helpful to us in promptly sharing its assessment of Continental's loan portfolio. But in its view, the problems were so severe that they dampened even Citicorp's ardor for acquisition. We heard a great deal from Citicorp about how bad Continental was; yet, the big bank did not take itself out of the picture entirely. A format for a permanent assistance package was discussed even if Citicorp itself did not deal with us. The format was based on FDIC removing a chunk of the assets—most of the bad loans—and putting in capital. Citicorp further suggested that the subordinated debt put in by FDIC and the banks participating in the temporary assistance package be made convertible to common stock, so that there would be a kind of collective ownership of Continental. This proposal was discussed very early.

It reflected the attitude that Citicorp, though not interested in buying the Chicago bank outright, might be interested in investing in it. Citicorp would take options on it and manage the bank for us for a price. But Citicorp did not want the general exposure to loss of ownership. Citicorp may also have been worried that two and one might not necessarily make three. In a market where Citicorp could now raise $2 billion and Continental $1 billion, the two banks combined might not be able to raise $3 billion.

Citicorp's proposal remained an option throughout our negotiations and search; it was never high on anyone's list within FDIC, but it was always there. Stan Silverberg reported that Bob Boyd of Citicorp's governmental relations staff had been very active in the effort to get the out-of-state acquisition bill through the Illinois legislature.

From our standpoint, the overwhelming drawback was that the Citicorp proposal gave us no assurance we would have a permanent solution for Continental. Citicorp was offering its reputation, its name, and its people. That was a lot. But in our view it was not enough. We wanted Citicorp to have a solid financial, at-risk investment in the revival of Continental. At some point Citicorp simply removed itself from serious discussions, but left the door open a crack if we really had to have them.

Chemical's approach was somewhat similar to Citicorp's and initially they seemed to be available as a merger partner. By mid-June, however, they removed themselves as an active suitor. The managers of the nation's sixth largest bank holding company told us their early investigation of the Continental loan portfolio had so convinced them of the magnitude of the problem that they would in no way be interested in acquiring Continental. Like Citicorp, Chemical generously shared its findings and evaluations with FDIC and was positioned to stay alive as a long-shot option throughout our search.

Although not interested in an acquisition, Chemical gave us a proposal to work the bad loans for us. In return for its services on collecting or recovering on the loans, Chemical would get expenses and a guaranteed fee plus an incentive based on receipts. However, the incentive was up in the big numbers.

Silverberg told Chemical's people we would keep them in mind. Chemical had bought Continental's credit card business the preceding March for $176 million and we had started out thinking Chemical might be a more eager suitor than it was showing itself. Still, at this stage we were not convinced the interest was not there. As things worked out, Chemical did come back to talk with us later—on the eve of the final transaction.

As the news of our Continental odyssey continued in the press the flow of feelers continued, mainly about acquiring parts of Continental or some of the loan portfolio. Silverberg heard from Merrill Lynch & Company, Inc.; Victor Palmieri and Company; Lehman Brothers; Bear, Stearns & Company Inc.; and a number of banks. None addressed our real problem— reviving and capitalizing Continental.

On the home front, First Chicago's candidacy as a merger partner was an inevitable question. The two big midwestern banks were long-standing competitors for dominance in the largest money center between the coasts. Hardly friendly rivals, their antagonism was well-known throughout the industry. First Chicago had not forgotten the short shrift it got from Continental in the 1970s when First Chicago was experiencing severe earnings problems of its own and Continental was expanding voraciously. Now the situation seemed to be reversed. After four years of new management, First Chicago was on the mend. Continental now needed aid. Could there be a shotgun wedding? Bank analysts shook their heads and said it would never work. They spoke of deep-seated resentments and a "clash of corporate cultures."

FDIC's view was negative from the outset. The numbers were not right. First Chicago was about a $36-billion bank, slightly smaller than Continental. Ideally, we would have wanted a merger partner substantially larger than the takeover target so that it would have the financial and managerial resources to make the merger work. More important than this, the number that really concerned us was the size of the merged bank, $75 billion. Far larger than all other Chicago banks combined, it would have a stranglehold on the banking business in that area and throughout the Midwest. First Chicago was too small to handle a merger, but too big to be merged.

So we met the First Chicago officers with a skeptical eye when they came to see us on June 4. They were led by Chairman Sullivan. Like Citicorp and Chemical, First Chicago wanted to make the point about how bad the Continental loans were. But that seemed to be the major thrust of First Chicago's presentation. The bank's executives laid it on so thick that when they left, Isaac and I just sat there shaking our heads. It made us think that they were not really serious about a deal, that this was just an exercise they had to go through. Whether that was true or not, the session confirmed our opposition to a First Chicago deal.

I said, "Bill, I can't support this because of the concentration

problem." Isaac said he could not support their proposal because he did not think First Chicago could handle it. So for
different reasons both of us were against it from the start.

On June 5 during State Senate hearings to consider the interstate acquisition bill, First Chicago projected uncertainty.
Chairman Sullivan testified that he would want some federal
protection against another run before his bank would go ahead
with an acquisition. He asked how First Chicago could "immunize" itself from possible legal claims against Continental and
its former officers. He estimated such claims could run to hundreds of millions of dollars. He raised such obstacles as tax
considerations and the status of Continental shareholders.

Yet, despite the hurdles they brought up, First Chicago remained interested enough to have its own version of the outof-state takeover bill introduced. That measure contained two
important variations from Continental's bill: It would have reserved for First Chicago the right of first refusal in the event of
an out-of-state bid, and it would have allowed out-of-state
bids only from those states which had reciprocal laws permitting Illinois institutions to enter them. New York has such a
law; if Illinois enacted the First Chicago bill, that institution
would be able to acquire banks there. The contending bills
threatened to tie things up in the legislature.

First Chicago pursued its quest for several days more. Lee
Kimmel, of Salomon Brothers, Inc., the New York investment
banking firm engaged by First Chicago, came in for exploratory
talks with Silverberg's task group. The presentation was equivocal, and Silverberg sensed disagreement within First Chicago
about what to do. The stockholders already gave their opinion
of the proposed takeover: On May 21, when First Chicago made
known its interest, its stock fell to $21.75 a share, down $1.375.
The price continued to drift downward toward the $20 mark.

Silverberg finally told Kimmel outright he did not believe
First Chicago could come up with enough capital to make the
deal acceptable from a regulator's safety and soundness point

of view. First Chicago must have come to the same conclusion on its own. The press reported a four-hour Saturday meeting at the bank involving key officers and directors. Whatever happened, on Monday, June 11, First Chicago formally took itself out of the running. In a public statement, the bank said it had "instructed its investment bankers, Salomon Brothers, to inform Goldman, Sachs, investment bankers for Continental, that First Chicago should not be considered further as a potential merger partner for Continental."[5]

That made things easier all around, certainly for us. We did not want to be in the position of having to rebuff the only in-state bank that would appear to the public to have a chance of taking over Continental.

The next day, Tuesday, June 12, the last takeover candidate, in-state or out, publicly eliminated itself. Chemical announced that it had "decided not to pursue further the possibility of a merger" with Continental.[6]

Two weeks later on June 26, with no merger partner in sight, Illinois Governor James Thompson signed the Continental out-of-state acquisition bill into law. After First Chicago's departure rendered its objections moot, the Continental bill had proceeded unhindered through the legislature.[7]

Continental's Last Resort

The next move obviously was up to FDIC. We started regular interagency sessions in mid-June. While Continental was still trying to find a go-it-alone solution, we were drafting a stand-alone federal assistance package in case it would come to that. Besides Isaac and myself, off and on the meetings were attended by Todd Conover, Joe Selby, and Mike Patriarca from OCC;

Chuck Partee, Jack Ryan, and Mike Bradfield from the Fed; Si
Keehn, president of the Chicago Fed; plus a swarm of supporting FDIC staffers.

We were moving into July and facing another deadline. Continental would soon have to report its second-quarter operating
result. It would, of course, show a huge loss; and we were
concerned that the news would precipitate a new run. The
second quarter loss finally reported was $1.158 billion, more
than four times greater than any quarterly loss ever reported by
an American bank.[8]

We had to get a deal wrapped up. The cure had to be announced simultaneously with or a little ahead of the bad news.
While we had been doing our interviewing, negotiating with
prospective new heads of Continental, and structuring our
stand-alone transaction, we still kept the door open to any
last-minute offers from the private sector.

Despite continual speculation in the press about potential
investors, only two interests actually came to FDIC for last-
minute discussions. The first was Chemical Bank coming back
for a last go at it. This time Walter Shipley, Chemical's president, outlined a deal reminiscent of Citicorp's, except that the
FDIC exposure to loss would be a little greater. There would be
an exchange of preferred stock. We still believed there was not
enough financial commitment on Chemical's part.

A week later we had our final offer. It came from the Bass
family of Fort Worth, Texas. The family's fortune originated in
pioneering oil and gas development. It now extends into major
stock holdings, hotels, ranches, and real estate. No outsider is
quite sure of the family's wealth because it is all privately held.
The family is headed by Perry Bass and his four sons: Sid,
Robert, Edward, and Lee.

The Basses approached us with a deal they had been working
on for several weeks, with the help of the New York securities
firm of Drexel Burnham Lambert Incorporated. It was an outgrowth of the private transaction they had discussed earlier

with Continental. The Bass deal involved the removal of bad loans, but it had the additional twist of packaging the loans as high-yield, high-risk securities. These types of instruments are known as "junk bonds" in the industry, and Drexel specializes in dealing in them.

To our way of thinking, the Basses were late in coming to us, late in making their examination, and late in putting their deal together. Their lateness made us uncertain of the extent of their interest. By this time we had gone through enough negotiations with other parties to know that we were not interested in simply having the bad assets taken out of Continental. That was not really a solution to the problem. Our interest was in recapitalizing the bank. Only after we made this clear did the Basses fashion a proposal based on buying the bank and recapitalizing it.

Silverberg talked at length about the details with Richard Rainwater, the Basses' deal maker, who had formerly been at Goldman, Sachs Inc. and who was a Stanford Business School classmate of Sid Bass. Rainwater was talking about taking out as much as $5 billion in loans and putting $800 million in Bass family capital in. Our analysts concluded the proposal would leave FDIC with too much risk. We would have to put in capital through the purchase of preferred stock, but our stock would be cashable only if the bank did extremely well. The Basses also wanted the Fed to guarantee to keep the discount window open to them an unreasonably long time—a period of years.

Finally, Sid Bass, the eldest brother, came in to see Isaac and me. We talked for a long time. We were tossing around a lot of big numbers. Near the end of the session, I said: "Bill, I wonder if these folks know that we're talking about very large amounts of up-front cash." Sid Bass responded that it would be no problem. They could have all they needed by tomorrow.

We were willing to wait, but there were other concessions in the structuring of the transaction that had to be made. We let Bass know what we needed and then parted. A few days later the Basses dropped out. They let the word be known through

Continental. The bank's president, Ed Bottum, told the press on Tuesday, July 17: "At this stage, the Basses are not an active participant."

This was not unexpected from the nature of our talks with the Bass family. That left FDIC as the last resort for Continental. That was not unexpected either. We were putting the finishing touches on our stand-alone deal. After the Basses' departure, we gave the signal to our staff to go full speed ahead.

We were now down to one option—bailout.

Chapter X

The Treasury Tiger

Treasury Complicates the Rescue

IF DEALING with the major banks was difficult, working with the Treasury Department proved to be nearly impossible. It was a classic case of bureaucratic harassment fueled by a desire to demonstrate who is the boss.

The Treasury troubles surfaced the final ten days before we approved the transaction. At first we were surprised, then concerned, and finally relaxed. In the end we handled the problem by ignoring the Treasury bureaucrats. The administration desperately wanted us to save Continental; but Treasury, at the last minute, proposed FDIC change the plan in a way we feared would doom the undertaking to failure.

After two months of intensive effort in which we saw the alternative solutions evaporate one by one, we concentrated on the one viable option—bailout. The bank would have to be, in effect, nationalized. FDIC would take an immediate 80 percent ownership with the strong possibility of our owning much more within a few years. We planned ultimately to resell Continental to the public.

This was the solution we developed in conjunction with OCC, the Federal Reserve, Continental itself, and a group of the nation's largest banks. The Treasury Department had not been involved, but Todd Conover, who reported directly to Treasury Secretary Don Regan, assured us that Treasury people had been kept informed. Some had attended our meetings.

As our plan neared completion, we scheduled a briefing on Friday afternoon, July 13, for Regan at the Treasury. We met in the secretary's conference room, a small chamber just off Regan's office, furnished with a table barely big enough for the principals. Attending were Paul Volcker and Chuck Partee, our three board members, and a handful of staffers: Doug Jones, Stan Silverberg, and Bill Isaac's deputy, Meg Egginton, from FDIC, and Deputy Secretary Tim McNamar and Assistant Secretary Tom Healey of Treasury.

We went back to the beginning, reviewing the considerations that had influenced us two months before in the meeting at Volcker's office when we determined that Continental had to be saved. Regan and Volcker raised the familiar concern about a national banking collapse, that is, a chain reaction if Continental should fail. Volcker was worried about an international crisis. We all were acutely aware that never before had a bank even remotely approaching Continental's size closed. No one knew what might happen in the nation and in the world. It was no time to find out just for the purpose of intellectual curiosity.

In the Midwest alone, the collapse would have severe repercussions for local banks. By then we had estimates that some 2,100 small banks had $6 billion in deposits and Fed funds in Continental. Dozens might be pulled down or seriously damaged in the Continental undertow. At the minimum, the loss of the correspondent relationships would leave a gaping hole in the nation's banking network and send a host of small banks scurrying to find another big brother.

We talked about the effect on fiduciaries—they might feel duty bound to take uninsured funds out, not only of Continental, but from other large banks as well, including several that we knew were not in the most stable condition. We did not want that snowball to get started. Finally, there remained the unavoidable fact that Continental was the largest commercial lender in the nation. All the borrowers would have to cast around for other lending sources; new credit relationships would have to be established. The thousands upon thousands of checks working their way through the payment system would bounce. It would be chaotic throughout the Midwest, and the chaos would surely spread.

This was the situation, and the gloomy recap only heightened our sense of urgency. Our solution was bailout. We told Regan why and laid out our plan in full detail. The secretary listened closely. He asked penetrating questions and took copious notes on a yellow legal pad.

Then we experienced our first tremor of trouble. McNamar and Healey suggested we again consider closing the bank, then arranging a closed-bank merger or some other solution that would not protect the holding company creditors. Isaac responded that FDIC was prepared to handle a closing by the comptroller from day one. We had readily been persuaded by the Fed that closing the bank would be irresponsible for the reasons we had just discussed. As to a merger on a closed or open-bank basis, there was no hope; and we described our intense, ultimately futile search to find a taker.

We had long since rejected the idea of paying off the bank. After May 17 it was not an option. Technically, FDIC could have done so, but it would be a long, painful process. Although Continental Illinois had over $30 billion in deposits, 90 percent were uninsured foreign deposits or large certificates substantially exceeding the $100,000 insurance limit. Off-book liabilities swelled Continental's real size to $69 billion. In this massive liability structure only some $3 billion was within the insured limits, scattered among 850,000 deposit accounts. So it was in our power and entirely legal simply to pay off the insured depositors, let everything else collapse, and stand back to watch the carnage. The payoff of Penn Square with its 24,500 accounts and Sharpstown with 27,300 had taken several weeks each.

Continental had more than thirty times as many accounts. Further, liquidation of so vast an enterprise as Continental's would take decades. Uninsured depositors and general creditors, including hundreds of correspondent banks and small businesses, would be plunged into uncertainty. They would have to wait on protracted and unpredictable returns on the liquidation to find if they could recoup any part of their losses. Many, we feared, would become ancillary victims of the collapse. We went over it all again and came to the same conclusion—we should not do a payoff, and there were no takers for a merger on reasonably acceptable terms.

Regan told his staff not to raise the closed-bank issue any more. When the meeting ended, we left believing we had now made all the major decisions and that we had Regan's concurrence in our course of action. We were rapidly disabused of that notion. The hint that we faced serious interagency difficulties was not long in exploding into reality.

Treasury Begins to Second Guess

Within the next ten days, in rapid fire order, we were told again by Treasury that we should consider closing the bank; then that our aid should go to the bank and not the holding company. Next we were told that our plan was illegal; then that what we were doing was poor public policy, and finally that we had violated the Federal Financing Bank Act. I will describe these attacks in more detail later.

The real issue, the divisive question, was how to handle the holding company. Should it be saved? Must it be saved? Could it be saved? These were the questions that caught us up in the most bitter debate ever between the bank regulators and the administration. And, as often happens in Washington, what started out as a legitimate difference of opinion on policy, ended as a constantly escalating confrontation. The only issue at the end, it seemed, was: "Who will win?"

The assistance agreement was rounded into final form in the turbulent days after the Treasury meeting. As we fended off the Treasury barrage, our lawyers were simultaneously reducing the agreement to writing; our joint regulators' group was working out strategy; and Isaac, Conover, and I were negotiating with prospective new management for Continental.

Beginning Monday, July 16, our interagency regulators' group worked daily on the ripening agreement in the FDIC conference room. This big room has a large boat-shaped table for principals and seats for staff in the perimeter around them. There are no windows; it is a place for serious uninterrupted work. McDonald's did a brisk business as mounds of hamburgers, french fries, and coke were piled on a corner table for those who felt the need for sustenance during the marathon meetings that often went well into the night. Our target was to make an announcement on Monday, July 23; we missed this date by three days because of a last-minute change in our management team for the bank.

The last issue to decide was how we would treat stockholders. Our working plan was that FDIC would be given a stock package equivalent to two-thirds of Continental Holding Company's shares, a preemptive controlling interest. The third of the shares still held by the private shareholders was to be put at risk to absorb whatever losses FDIC might suffer on the bad loans to be taken out of Continental. Now that we had made the key policy decisions, we hired Morgan Stanley to get Ted Dunn's expertise in structuring the deal so that it would be accepted in the markets. Dunn had impressed us with his practical problem-solving skills when he represented First Pennsylvania in bailout negotiations with us a few years earlier.

A new, potentially serious controversy arose Thursday morning, the 19th, when Isaac unexpectedly broached a new approach on the stockholder matter. It was to take a significantly larger share of the stock up front—85 percent, instead of 67 percent—and simply leave the remaining 15 percent with the stockholders. It was not much, but it would be theirs free and clear and not at risk to absorb further losses.

Conover was immediately and adamantly opposed. There was no way he would vote for such a plan. It was too protective of the stockholders, he said.

I whispered to Isaac, "I hadn't heard anything about this. Where did this come from?" Isaac said he had been up until 1:00 A.M. with Dunn and some of our staff people, and they had convinced him this was a better, more straightforward way. Isaac said that he was now convinced that the 85–15 percent split was cleaner and would save confusion and confrontation in the years ahead.

It was a major shift in position for Isaac. He had voted consistently in failed bank cases to make stockholders pay the penalty, as I did. So I knew it had taken some highly unusual circumstance to make him consider guaranteeing the bank's shareholders a return, even on a fractional basis.

Not wanting to cut the discussion off entirely I suggested that I might consider a 90–10 percent split, but probably not. Conover would not budge. He was dead set against any approach which left the bank shareholders free from risk, no matter how small their ownership share. Under no circumstances would he support such a plan.

So FDIC's three board members took the dispute to the treasury secretary that afternoon. Volcker again participated. Isaac made the presentation. He handled the alternatives fairly, giving the advantages and disadvantages of both approaches. He spoke without notes; he was concise, and he fairly addressed all the nuances and details.

It was Regan, ultimately, who made the decision. He said there was no way we could not have the shareholders at risk. After the meeting, as we were walking back to the Treasury

Department elevator, I asked Isaac, "Well, what do you think?"
He responded: "Well, I guess I lost."

So we went back to the old format, except that instead of a
67–33 percent split of the stock, it ended up 80–20 percent. In
retrospect, even the 80 percent figure was far too little. Goldman, Sachs had proposed a warrant offering to the stockholders
and Dunn and his associate, Harrison Young, also were concerned that we had left the stockholders with no incentive to
vote for our reorganization plan. Since the old stock was com-
promised, they proposed that we offer stockholders a stake in
the new Continental. My view was that the shareholders had
little choice but to vote for the plan since the alternative, a bank
failure, would wipe them out. The stock options they proposed
were a modest sweetener. They required the stockholders to put
up new money, that would translate as an infusion into bank
capital; we planned to sell stock to the public eventually anyway. It was just as well to have the stockholders start now. If
the options also applied some psychological salve to stockholders' wounds, so much the better. So we tossed in the options
and changed the split to 80–20.

The issue that had seemed so important Thursday morning
faded rapidly from our minds. It was settled. But we were
becoming concerned, even alarmed, at the emerging hostility of
Treasury toward our plan. We had been getting ominous signals
during the preceding two days. McNamar was making persistent inquiries. By memo and telephone he raised issues: Did we
believe we had the legal authority to tailor a deal that went
through the holding company? Would we not be exceeding the
law? I thought Treasury was being unreasonable, although
there was room for an honest difference of opinion.

The second meeting with Regan had done little to dispel our
apprehensions. We had disposed of the stockholder question in
a brisk and orderly fashion, and then the focus of the meeting
jumped abruptly to the holding company issue. A Treasury
Department lawyer, Margery Waxman, challenged us on the

legality theme, citing specific points of law as though she were embarking on a court argument.

Doug Jones responded. He was intimately familiar with the assistance provisions of the FDI Act since he had helped draft them two years before. He also knew the case law on the rights of an agency to construe its own act. And he had been working day and night on the Continental case itself. He efficiently parried the Treasury lawyer's thrusts and the meeting soon developed into a legal debate.

At one point—I suppose to stop the discussion—Isaac again offered to handle a closed-bank transaction which would wipe out all the shareholders at a stroke. Again Regan and Volcker rejected this course out of hand.

On the surface the dispute was simple. In fact, it was complex. We would have preferred to place the new capital directly into the bank rather than using the holding company as a conduit. Realistically it would not work because the holding company had indenture agreements which would have been violated, triggering accelerated repayment of debts and forcing the holding company toward bankruptcy.* Some of the covenants had no mechanism for obtaining a waiver of default. In any event, the issue was largely academic at Continental since the holding company had other assets roughly equal to its liabilities even if its investment in the bank was valued at zero. Thus, as a practical matter, the holding company's creditors would not have lost much, irrespective of the structure of the aid program. Further, if we saved the bank we would be saving the holding company at the same time. The issue was one of precedents and appearances.

Treasury objected to placing FDIC junior to the existing creditors of the holding company. In addition Treasury was concerned that the precedent would undermine the validity of

*The Continental covenants said: "will not sell, grant a security interest in, or otherwise dispose of any shares of the capital stock of the Bank or permit the Bank to issue any shares of capital stock except to the Corporation or a subsidiary of the Corporation."

the theory that expanded nonbanking powers could be safely separated from subsidiary banks by lodging them in parent holding company subsidiaries. At that time Treasury was pressing Congress for an expanded bank powers law.

What it came down to at the end was that we could save our honor and massage our prejudices by allowing the holding company to fail. Or we could save the bank.

The FDIC plan ultimately adopted included $1 billion in preferred stock placed in the holding company to be immediately downstreamed into the bank as equity capital. *The result:* a strong bank with a favorable balance sheet, adequately capitalized, with a prospect of market acceptance and a prosperous future.

Treasury's proposal, which was rejected, would have put $1 billion in debt directly into the bank, but it would have done nothing to enhance the bank's equity capital. *The result:* a weak bank with crushing debt, woefully inadequate capital, a balance sheet that would frighten away bank analysts, leaving no prospect for recovery in the foreseeable future.

The second meeting with Treasury left us at loggerheads. In place of consensus, we had conflict. In place of support, we had dissent. We felt that Treasury had done a 180-degree flip-flop.

We were bewildered. Just before the meeting broke up, I asked what Treasury was trying to do. Treasury Secretary Regan said to me: "This is 1984; we might look at it differently another year"—a hint that the administration was seeking to distance itself from the largest bailout in history during a presidential election year. On the other hand, it might have been just the simple issue of who was in charge: Treasury or FDIC. We departed with quite a different feeling from the one we had taken away from that same office less than a week before.

Later the same day, Isaac received a telephone call from Volcker who told him he would be getting a call from Secretary Regan. Volcker said Regan would suggest that FDIC ask for an opinion from the attorney general on the legality of our proposed deal. The call came a few minutes later, but what Regan had to say was that he had already asked for an opinion by the attorney general.

Isaac told Secretary Regan, as I listened, that he did not believe the Justice Department had any jurisdiction in the matter. The case was absolutely within FDIC's discretionary authority under the law, and we would not be bound by the attorney general's opinion. We expected, of course, that the opinion would be stacked.

Treasury would not give up. Isaac and I were in the office all day Saturday and Sunday trying to untangle a last minute hitch with the prospective management team. Late Sunday night Conover called and said Treasury just had to talk to us again. So we said, "Sure, we'll talk to them."

Conover said he would notify McNamar and come down with him. FDIC's three board members, together with Egginton, met about 10:30 Sunday night in Isaac's back conference room. McNamar was alone for Treasury. For more than two hours he went over Treasury's case with us, expounding the department's views on why the holding company should not be rescued. There was little new in his presentation. We maintained our position: There was no point in starting a rescue of the bank that was doomed to failure.

McNamar embarked on a disparaging analysis of our proposal as "bad public policy." He cited all the reasons why it was poor policy to give lenders to the holding company any preference.

Technically, the priority meant that if at some future date Continental should fail and be liquidated, the holding company lenders would get their money before FDIC. However, the whole purpose of our permanent assistance package was to prevent the failure of Continental. Indeed, we had made the determination that the bank would not be closed—it would not fail. We would own it and we would make further investment if necessary. We had said so at a press conference. The press release making this pledge was formally and unanimously approved by our board. If Continental would not be allowed to fail, then the priority issue was moot.

Finally, I responded that we all agreed that nobody wanted to bail out the holding company creditors. But that was not the question. We had to end up with a viable bank. We did agree to jointly seek legislation to solve the holding company indenture problem for the future. In early 1986 a solution still eluded us. Legislation to allow an override of such covenants in the future might be possible, but a retroactive law seemed both unfair and unlikely. And there was not much point in seeking a law that did not address our real problem—the restrictive covenants already in place in every troubled big bank holding company we were watching.

What bothered me most—it concerned all of us—was the fact that if we were to preserve not only Continental, but several other similarly situated large institutions, we would have to make good on the loans that had been made to the Continental Holding Company. This spotlighted the unfairness factor in spades. We were paying ransom to the wealthy foreign depositors so they would not institute a nationwide banking run.

The Attorney General Surprises Us

On Tuesday, July 24, the attorney general's opinion came in. We were surprised and more than a little pleased to see that it favored us. The opinion said our proposed package appeared to be within the broad grant of discretionary authority that Congress had given us. It said: "A credible and factually justified basis, consistent with the Act, for choosing one method of assistance over another, would probably satisfy a reviewing court."

On the priority point, the attorney general's opinion found that nothing in the law requires FDIC to hold a privileged lender position after assisting an insured bank. "Indeed," the opinion noted, "the Act expressly permits the FDIC to occupy a position subordinate to the rights of depositors and other creditors." The opinion also said that the law does not require that FDIC assistance to troubled banks may not have incidental effects which benefit shareholders, management, or creditors.

The lack of a prohibition, of course, does not mean that the purpose of FDIC assistance was to subsidize creditors or investors. FDIC's policy was just the contrary. Our primary objective was to protect the small depositor and preserve confidence in the banking system. We believed that those who put money at risk—the lenders and investors—should continue to bear that risk, including paying the penalty when the bank failed.

We had established a long track record on this point. The attorney general's opinion quoted at length from testimony that I had given before a House subcommittee in 1981, when I was chairman of FDIC, working for the passage of more flexible and modernized live-bank assistance authority under Section 13(c). It was in the wake of the First Pennsylvania crisis. I testified and the attorney general quoted me:

> Structuring of a 13(c) assistance transaction requires careful balancing. Sufficient assistance must be provided, yet care must be exercised to assure that shareholders and management do not unduly benefit. Our purpose is to protect depositors and assure the maintenance of adequate banking services in the community. The stockholders and management are expected to bear the consequences of the bank's financial difficulties. As was the case with First Pennsylvania, severe restrictions are placed on management and on the rights of shareholders as a part of any 13(c) transaction until such time as the FDIC's financial commitment has been repaid and the bank's viability restored. While these restrictions are not punitive in nature, they usually are onerous. Because of the Corporation's limited use of its 13(c) powers as well as the strict limitations placed on management and ownership in connection with its use, the industry does not regard 13(c) assistance as a "bailout" which would justify the assumption of excessive risk in other institutions. We have been very selective and careful in our use of this power in order that such a perception would not arise.

The attorney general's opinion said: "We are unable to conclude on these facts that the FDIC's proposed transaction is inconsistent with its legitimate objectives." Further, "we conclude that the transaction probably would not be held to exceed the FDIC's statutory authority."

The opinion recommended that FDIC "articulate carefully and thoroughly its reasons for selecting a particular course at the time the transaction is finally approved."[1] This was done on July 25 as our staff provided the board with a detailed memorandum analyzing the options we had considered along the way to our final solution.[2]

Among these options were: (1) to close the bank and immediately merge it into a newly chartered institution capitalized by FDIC; (2) to have FDIC buy subordinated debt in the bank and upstream it into equity at the holding company; (3) to have FDIC make a capital contribution to the bank in return for preferred stock in the holding company. We had discarded each option as being more costly to FDIC and less likely to achieve the desired result. The staff paper concluded for the record that adopting any of the alternatives would make the future viability of the bank less certain and ultimately could require further outlay and losses by FDIC.

We were elated at the attorney general's response. We thought that was finally the end of it. We underestimated the extremes to which Treasury would go; it remained persistent to the point of antagonism.

Treasury Continues Second Guessing

Before the day was out, FDIC faced two more thrusts: The first was a call to Isaac from the *New York Times* asking for comment on the Treasury secretary's memo on the proposed Continental transaction. Isaac's response was: "What memo?" It turned out that after seeing the attorney general's opinion, Treasury had taken its case elsewhere. A memo over the secretary's signature labeled the Continental assistance package "bad public policy."

I presume that since the package was not illegal, "bad public policy" was the next worst thing that Treasury could call it.

The memo was nominally addressed to Comptroller Conover, Chairman Isaac, and Chairman Volcker. I am not sure the addressees were intended as the primary audience, especially since it contained nothing that we had not discussed again and again. The fact is the newspapers had the memo before we did.

The next day the *New York Times* had a lead article on the business page describing the memo as "extraordinary criticism in a four-and-one-half page memorandum." The first paragraph of the news story said:

> Treasury Secretary Donald T. Regan told the three Federal banking agencies today that their draft plan to keep Continental Illinois National Bank and Trust Company from failing was "bad public policy" that "represents an unauthorized and unlegislated expansion of Federal guarantees."[3]

The Regan memorandum referred to our late Sunday night meeting with McNamar and said that all three FDIC board members agreed that the best public policy was for the creditors of the holding company to be in a subordinated position to FDIC.

This was true. But the memo made no mention of our reasons for sticking with our course despite the fact or that what Regan was proposing would sink the bailout. There was no way to structure a deal his way and still have a viable bank.

The first page of the Regan memorandum will give you a feel for the atmosphere at the time.

> As you know from our meetings and your discussions and phone conversations with Deputy Secretary McNamar since Wednesday of last week, Treasury has serious reservations about the FDIC's current proposed assistance package for Continental Illinois Corporation.
>
> First, while the Office of Legal Counsel has concluded that "the transaction contemplated probably would not be held to exceed the FDIC's statutory authority," it recognized that the issue is not clear and that choosing this transaction increases the

legal risks. The OLC also emphasizes the need for the FDIC to offer a compelling rationale for providing aid to the holding company rather than the more straightforward, direct bank assistance provided in the First Pennsylvania situation. A rationale which is consistent with the FDIC's statutory authority has not yet been provided.

Second, we believe that it is inappropriate public policy to place the FDIC in a position which is junior to the existing creditors of the holding company.

We believe it would be preferable, for both legal strategy and policy reasons, to provide assistance directly to the insured bank and obtain whatever is appropriate from the bank holding company in return for that federal assistance, similar to what was done by the FDIC with First Pennsylvania.

Against this background, we oppose proceeding with the Continental Illinois assistance package as outlined in the draft "Memorandum of Agreement in Principle for the Recapitalization of Continental Illinois National Bank and Trust Company of Chicago" . . . dated July 21, 1984. We believe it is bad public policy, would be seen to be unfair vis-a-vis past FDIC/Federal Reserve bank supervisory policies, and represents an unauthorized and unlegislated expansion of federal guarantees in contravention of Executive Branch policy which lacks explicit Congressional authorization.[4]

Publicly, Isaac had no comment. Privately, he hit the ceiling. We talked about it. This disruption occurred at a very sensitive time—just two days before we were to wrap up the assistance package and name the bank's new top management.

Isaac asked, "Are you still with me?"

I said, "Yes, of course."

He said, "Even if Conover votes against it, either because he's been instructed to or otherwise?"

I said again, "Yes, Bill. This doesn't change anything."

Isaac said, "Good." He was going to fire off a letter answering the memo from Treasury. I told him not to answer it. A response would just escalate the dispute. Forget it, and let the Treasury memo have its play. Isaac did not answer the memo. There was no follow-up story.

Ultimately, Conover voted with us. He qualified his vote with a strong statement about the unwanted side effects of benefiting the holding company noteholders, but he voted for the permanent assistance package we had crafted. "At no time," he said later, "did anyone hint, or even breathe, anything to me about how I should vote."

Volcker was clearly in our corner. That was reassuring. On July 25 Michael Bradfield, general counsel of the Fed, supplied us with a detailed sixteen-page opinion which concluded:

> Accordingly, based on the language of the statute, its remedial purposes, its legislative history, and principles of statutory construction, it is my view that the proposed assistance package is consistent with the FDIC's authority under Section 13(c) of the FDI Act and is authorized by law.[5]

The second thrust from Treasury that Tuesday was another memo: this one from Waxman to Egginton. It accused us of violating the Federal Financing Bank Act. The act was a housekeeping measure intended to give Treasury control of the timing for the marketing of government obligations by any federal agency. That was so the Treasury could choose the most advantageous time to sell federal debt instruments and could prevent competition among new government issues in the marketplace.

Treasury leveraged that into a claim for jurisdiction by stretching the term "obligation" to include the participations we sold to the seven megabanks in the $2-billion infusion in May. The first two paragraphs of the memo give the tone:

> Under the Federal Financing Bank Act ("FFB Act"), the prior approval of the Secretary of the Treasury is required for any obligation issued or sold by a Federal agency. For purposes of the FFB Act, the FDIC is a Federal agency. Accordingly, the assistance package proposed for the Continental Illinois Bank and/or Continental Illinois Corporation should be submitted to the Secretary of the Treasury for his approval prior to the issuance or sale of any obligation by the FDIC. In this regard, I note that the

FDIC has already sold obligations, i.e., participations in the (May 17) note that it purchased from Continental Illinois Bank.

Every effort should be made to correct this situation as soon as possible. Please inform me of what steps the FDIC is taking to comply with the terms of the statute before any final decision is made on the Continental Bank assistance package.[6]

At this point we had been working around the clock for weeks; we had the assistance package in final form and were in the last delicate stages of negotiating with a new management team. In less than thirty-six hours we were to announce the final Continental package to the world.

What the memo did not say was that the Secretary of the Treasury had urged us to solicit the banks in the first place. That was in May. Now in July he was turning around and telling us that these participations were in violation of the law.

We regulators had considered asking major bank participation in the May loan before the secretary got involved. We discarded the idea because we feared the consequences should the banks refuse. At the time the run was at a gallop. If the story got out that a half-dozen of the biggest banks in the country had refused to put money into Continental, it could have spurred a stretch drive that would have meant the bank's ruin.

So we thought it better to infuse the $2 billion ourselves initially and then, as Continental steadied, to approach the banks and ask them to buy in. At Regan's urging, we reversed ourselves and asked the big banks to go in with us at the outset. He proved right; they did come in. But we went through a lot of anxious hours while the banks temporized and equivocated before they finally took the plunge. Fortunately, no story leaked.

I am not a lawyer, but I can only conclude that whether participations are "obligations" or not, we must have had the secretary's permission to sell them since he asked us to. In fact, he insisted on it.

There were humor and irony in this turn of events, but at the time I was in no mood to appreciate them. In its grasping at straws I thought the Treasury Department had come up with the last straw. But I was wrong. The final straw was yet to come.

Before the day was out, that same hectic Tuesday, Conover came over to FDIC and said that we had to go back over to the Treasury Department.

"Why?" Isaac asked.

"Because they want to talk to us again," Conover said.

"After the *New York Times* and the Federal Financing Bank Act, they want to talk to us again?" I said.

Conover said, "Yes."

I said, "I'm not going. Enough is enough."

Isaac said he was not going either.

The next morning Conover told us they had the meeting at Treasury anyway, without us, and had gone over the Treasury option again. To what purpose I did not know. We were through analyzing. We had made our decisions. We had the assistance agreement in final form. And, we were on the verge of signing the management team, the final hurdle we had to pass.

A Reflection

All in all, the Treasury Tiger excercise was an absurd one, conducted in the highest traditions of the nation's capitol. Treasury started out by confusing oranges and apples and it was all downhill from there: First Pennsylvania had a cancerous interest rate mismatch; Continental was drowning in bad loans. Different problems required different solutions. In First Pennsylvania we put money into the bank and saved the holding company. In Continental we put money into the holding company and saved the bank. Either way, the stockholders and noteholders received an outright gift from FDIC. All we could do was hold down the donation to the bare minimum.

Chapter XI

Choosing the Management

*The Swearingen-Ogden Team
Is Selected*

WHO would run Continental for us? Ironically, the management question that was the last to be decided had been the first addressed. At our very first strategy session following the May 17 rescue, as we sought a permanent solution, Bill Isaac had insisted that we talk about management first. I wanted to start talking about how to structure a viable plan, but Isaac was adamant. In retrospect, he was right.

All the careful, well-thought-out transactions in the world would do no good if we did not have the right people to carry them out. What we were talking about was capability and confidence—able executives. Just as importantly, executives brought in from the outside showed that the shop was under new management and that the market had a reason to give it a chance.

As Stan Silverberg set out on his fieldwork and Continental went prospecting for a private deal on its own, our board embarked on a talent search for new management in case we should have to do the bailout and take Continental over. On our own and in the strategy sessions with the Federal Reserve and OCC, we pursued our search. Anyone with an idea as to who could run Continental for us found ready listeners. Suggestions came from Citicorp, Bank of America, and many other sources. We wanted the most capable banker we could get.

One name that came up right away was Tom Theobald, vice-chairman of Citicorp.* He had been one of three contenders for the chairmanship to be vacated by the retirement of Walter Wriston in August, and it had just been announced that the top job would go to John Reed, another Citicorp vice-chairman. To us Theobald seemed a logical choice for the Continental job, except for one thing: Theobald told us, "No," right away; he was not interested under any circumstances. Hans Anger-mueller, the other Citicorp vice-chairman who had been in the running for Wriston's job, also declined to be considered.

Bill Ogden's name also was mentioned very early—another logical candidate. He had left Chase Manhattan as a vice-chair-man and chief financial officer in March 1983. Ogden had ex-tensive experience in bank operations and international lend-ing. He had wide contacts abroad and seemed to be the ideal person to try to get back all those foreign deposits that had fled Continental.

Another early starter was Dick Cooley, chairman of Seattle First. We had been impressed with him—his coolness during the Seafirst crisis early in 1983. Our deliberations focused on bankers. These were all we considered. After all, banks should be run by bankers.

Then, amid our ruminations one day, Si Keehn, president of the Chicago Fed, observed it was a shame that none of these fellows came from Chicago. What we really need, he said, is someone with strong hometown ties—a member of lots of

---

*Ironically, Theobald later was to become Continental chairman, succeeding our initial selection.

boards of directors, a well-known figure within the Chicago business community, a capable executive himself, an acknowledged leader, someone who needed no introduction.

"Well," said Isaac, "whom do you have in mind?"

"John Swearingen," Keehn said. "But you can't get him."

It was as if Keehn had pushed a button in everyone's mind. We all looked up together and nodded mutual assent. The room began to buzz. Swearingen. He would be absolutely right. The former chairman of Standard Oil of Indiana had in his twenty-five years built the company from a noncontender into the eighth largest industrial concern in the nation. Swearingen was prominent in Chicago business circles and respected throughout the world. Most importantly, he was a proven, tough, successful manager. He was a long-time member of the Chase board, but he was not a banker. We brushed that aside. It was unanimous. We wanted Swearingen. Keehn thought we could not lure him out of retirement, but it was easy. Isaac called him. After trying retirement for nine months, Swearingen was ready for a new challenge.*

Elated though we were, we still had to consider the very practical question of banking experience. Managing a $40-billion institution was no small undertaking, especially for someone who has never run a bank. So we decided Swearingen should have a capable, experienced banker to operate the institution. We would recruit a management team and Swearingen would be the father figure. We continued our search for a bank executive.

Ogden wanted the job, and we thought for a while that Cooley did, too. Conover was pushing for Cooley, his fellow Californian, because he knew him and was impressed with the job Cooley had done at Wells Fargo & Co. before going to Seafirst. Isaac and I would have taken either one, although I felt much more comfortable with Cooley. We had them in for interviews. Part of the time the entire board would talk with one of them; sometimes each of us would spend time alone with the

*I later wondered whether Keehn came up with the idea on his own, or did it initiate with Swearingen.

candidate. We discussed each other's concept of the job and the perception of what our expectations would be. We told them that FDIC policy would be strictly hands-off daily operations. We looked for style of leadership and tried to envision how each would address the Continental challenge. Both held up well under scrutiny. We settled on Cooley, but we were reluctant to let Ogden go. Ogden had other interests and said he needed an answer promptly. We asked him how long he could stay available. He said a week or two at the most.

Over the next two weeks, both Swearingen and Cooley were in and out of Washington. We began a running exchange on everything from the scope of the job to tactics on specific problems, all of which helped us to get to know each other better. We brought in OCC's examiners to give a full-scale presentation on Continental, warts and all, especially the warts. Swearingen and Cooley took the most recent Continental examination reports to study. Their questions were penetrating and seemingly endless. Swearingen was the expert on energy business; Cooley on energy loans. The exposure to energy loan losses is what brought Continental down.

Our understanding was that they would run Continental with no FDIC interference. Our role would be limited to that of stockholder, with the stockholder's perogatives of approving the tenure of management, including the board of directors, and changes in stock structure. Compensation would be worked out later, but it would be fair and commensurate with their responsibilities. At no point did we shake hands on a deal. However, our board believed we had an understanding with Swearingen and Cooley if all the pieces fell into place as we expected they would.

Swearingen was retired and relaxed. Cooley, with his career ahead of him, was more concerned. He hired a lawyer. Dan Persinger, in our legal division, suggested we do the same. We retained Jack Murphy, of the Washington office of Cleary, Gottlieb, Steen & Hamilton, and got a future FDIC general counsel in the bargain. Since we had settled on the Seafirst chairman for the job, we thought Murphy's work would be just to iron out a few wrinkles in the contract. So we asked David Taylor, Continental's new chairman, to schedule a meeting of his board for four o'clock Monday, July 23, to approve the transaction, including the new management. We gave Taylor no names.

Late in the week before our planned announcement Murphy brought us a disquieting report. He said that Cooley's attorney was insisting on a number of provisions, including a clause guaranteeing three years' pay for Cooley if he left at any time for any reason. That probably would have killed the deal, but at about the same time Cooley called Isaac and bowed out for personal reasons.

Three years later I asked Conover if he knew the real reason for Cooley dropping out. He had talked to Cooley before, during, and after the negotiations. Conover said he was not certain, but his impression was that the contract was not the problem. Cooley had just recently moved to Seattle to take over Seafirst and did not relish another move; his stature was growing with Bank of America. Probably he perceived that no matter what partnership arrangement was made, Swearingen would emerge as the dominant figure.

Some time after the fact, I talked about it with Cooley over breakfast at the Rainier Club in Seattle. Cooley said he bowed out due to a combination of factors: His job at Seafirst was still unfinished; the Bank of America officials were urging him to stay; the attorneys apparently had not been able to work out adequate indemnification clauses; and we already had Swearingen on board. "You don't need two bosses," he said.

Less than a week to go, and half of our management team had disappeared. Our press releases had been drawn up with the management paragraphs blank; biographies and pictures of Cooley and Swearingen were ready to be inserted at the last minute. That was to avoid leaks. It had turned out to be good planning for this unexpected reason.

Isaac and Conover both called Ogden. He flew in that night and quickly agreed to come on board. We still hoped to reach a final agreement that weekend. We had no trouble deciding that Ogden would receive a compensation package identical to Swearingen's, whatever that turned out to be. But the big question was whether they could work together as a team. They had known each other for twenty-three years as Ogden worked his way up the Chase ladder and Swearingen served on the Chase board. There was no need for getting-acquainted pleasantries.

Swearingen and Ogden talked with us Saturday and Sunday, but the important discussions were between the two of them closeted together most of the weekend. They had a problem. Each wanted to be the boss.

The discussions continued into Monday. We waited. There was nothing we could do. Dave Taylor called from Chicago, asking, "What shall I do about our board meeting today?" Isaac told him it would have to wait.

The Management Team Is Chosen

As the talks went on Tuesday without any sign of progress, we agreed that Swearingen was the key but we wanted Ogden, too. At one point Ogden told me, "You have to make a decision." After four futile days, he was ready to leave. Isaac stepped in with a last-ditch effort. "Wait. Don't go home," he told Ogden, "we'll get you a room at the Madison Hotel." Swearingen already had a room there. Isaac told the two men to have dinner together and to keep on talking—to work it out.

The solution was Solomon-like. Isaac told me he came up with the idea in the middle of the night. Swearingen would be chairman and chief executive officer of the holding company and Ogden, chairman and chief executive officer of the bank. We figured that in the end Swearingen would wind up as the real boss, but it looked fuzzy, since they both had a chairman title. Ogden would have the major responsibility in day-to-day bank operation. We hoped the fragile agreement would hold together. We were not sure.

That left the compensation package as the last hurdle. In addition to salaries of $600,000 each, both would receive 400,-000 stock options. We had offered 200,000; Swearingen asked for 400,000. Finally, at my urging, Isaac took Swearingen aside and said, "You win—400,000 it is." The options to buy stock at $4.50 a share can be exercised until August 13, 1994.

When we were discussing the compensation, Swearingen said he needed another two weeks to look at the books before he could give us a final answer. He knew, of course, that we were under time pressure.

Our position was that the bank was in bad shape and every-body knew it; two weeks or two months was not going to change that fact. He did not have to worry about stepping in and having the bank collapse under him because we were not going to let it fail. We told him if he took it over and got it straightened out, he would be a hero. A rich hero. They both stood to make millions if they turned the bank around. It could mean billions to FDIC if they did.

About noon Wednesday we reached an agreement with Swearingen and Ogden in Isaac's back conference room, and we all shook hands on it. Our new managers should be in Chicago when we made the announcement here in Washington, we said. "Oh, I've already got a ticket on that two o'clock plane," Swearingen responded. He had it in his pocket all along. Such self-confidence. A plane was chartered to take Ogden to Chicago with a stop at his home in Connecticut for a clean shirt. The plane had mechanical problems, so Ogden did not get to Chicago until late that night. Swearingen and Ogden arrived at the bank together the next morning; bank employees delight in telling the story that neither had enough change to pay the taxi driver.

As soon as Swearingen and Ogden left our offices, Isaac telephoned Taylor and asked him to call the Continental board together at 4:00 P.M. that afternoon. Ever fond of the dramatic moment, Isaac waited until the board was assembled to telephone again and tell Taylor he could inform his board it would be Swearingen and Ogden. Taylor later told me the board was stunned, surprised, and delighted. Also chagrined that they had not thought of the obvious choice—Swearingen. The Continental board readily gave its assent to the FDIC permanent assistance plan and the management agreements. We had kept our negotiations with Swearingen, Cooley, and Ogden absolutely confidential. All press speculation was off the mark. I had never heard of some of the names mentioned.

That evening the Congress was informed and that episode may have contributed to some of the later congressional criticism. We gathered around a speaker phone as Isaac outlined the transaction to Senators Jake Garn and Bill Proxmire and Congressmen Fernand St Germain and Chalmers Wylie. These four constituted the chairmen and ranking minority members of the House and Senate banking committees. The phone connection was poor, the transaction complicated, and a five-way dialogue is hardly conducive to mutual understanding. Copies of our press release were dispatched to the Hill to flesh out the story for them.

Our own board met the next day at 8 A.M., Thursday, July 26, an unusual hour to approve an extraordinary transaction. A press conference was set for 9 A.M., one floor up in our employees' cafeteria; press and television crews were already assembling. The board met in closed meeting with the usual roomful of key staffers who were unusually quiet. Some had been intimately involved in the negotiation and preparation; others had known only that a landmark assistance transaction was being shaped in the conference rooms and executive offices of FDIC. Our familiar board room had an air of suppressed tension, of expectancy.

The meeting went off a bit like a stage set. There was no discussion. There was nothing left to discuss. Instead, each member made short remarks for the record, some of us working from notes. When my turn came, I let show some of my frustration and indignation over the Treasury harassment with its political overtones. I said:

> This is clearly the most difficult and important decision an FDIC Board has had to face in our 50-year existence. I am confident and very comfortable that we are taking the course that public policy dictates. . . . The resulting institution will be smaller, immeasurably stronger, and well-positioned to profitably serve the banking needs of its customers. A banking panic will have been averted. While the FDIC will be the major stockholder, the bank will be run by the new management without interference.
>
> This is the fourth time in 13 years that the FDIC has approved long-term assistance transactions to rescue a failing bank deemed essential to be saved. I have participated in developing and approving the transaction in all four instances. Never before have I been so confident of success. . . . We have studied, analyzed, and rejected all conceivable alternatives. We have carefully considered all the public policy questions. We have an unequivocal legal opinion upon which to base our action. While the responsibility is totally ours, we have consulted at length, in depth, in detail, and in person with the Secretary of the Treasury and the Chairman of the Federal Reserve, and the solution we have before us incorporates the basic principles they both very forcefully advocated when we first discussed options. Specifically, they both argued that we must not close the bank, nor devise a package that would harm holding company markets. The fear was that other bank failures, large and small, would be triggered, probably on a massive scale.
>
> After the deal was put together, the Fed held its position, but Treasury took a 180-degree detour. I do not know why. What I do know is that we have a bipartisan board or a nonpartisan

board and the fact that we are united in the decision that this is the proper course to follow shows that we cannot, we will not, and we do not and we did not allow any political considerations to color the decision we are about to make.[1]

All the labors, deliberations, and anxiety of the past ten weeks culminated in a board meeting that had taken less than a quarter of an hour. We voted to approve the plan, three to nothing, and the three of us went upstairs to face the press and the television cameras.

The Deal

The permanent assistance package Isaac described to the press looked complicated. Actually, it was just a two-bank maneuver: (1) take out the problem loans and create what amounted to a bad bank for them; and (2) leave the performing loans in the surviving good bank, Continental.

Here is how the transaction fit together:

1. We agreed to take over $4.5 billion in bad loans and gave Continental $3.5 billion for them. We paid by assuming $3.5 billion in debt that Continental owed the Federal Reserve. That meant Continental had to immediately write off a $1-billion loss.
2. We replaced the loss that was written off by injecting $1 billion in new capital into Continental Illinois at consummation. We did this through a stock purchase in the holding company that was required to downstream the proceeds immediately into the bank in the form of equity capital.
3. The $1.5 billion in FDIC temporary assistance and the $500 million put up by the major banks was repaid upon consummation. The effect was to reduce FDIC's immediate cash outlay from a $1.5-billion loan to a $1-billion stock ownership.

4. Our stock purchase included 32 million junior preferred shares valued at $720 million. Although it is not voting stock, it is convertible into 160 million shares of common or voting stock upon sale to a third party. This gives us effective control over 80 percent of the common stock. The remainder of our purchase was $280 million worth of adjustable rate preferred stock.

5. All of the outstanding common stock—40.3 million shares—was transferred to a new holding company, Continental Illinois Holding, where it will remain for up to five years, until 1989. The bad loans are being worked and all the collections, minus expenses, are used to pay interest and principal on the Fed debt we assumed. At the end of five years, if $800 million or more of the debt remains unpaid, FDIC has an option to acquire all of the common stock at a nominal price. If the loss is less than $800 million, then FDIC can acquire a pro-rata share.

6. Current shareholders were given the option to buy one share of new common stock for each share of old, up to 40 million shares. The price was $4.50 a share for the first sixty days and $6 for the succeeding twenty-two months, until September, 1986, when the options lapsed. This could have produced a maximum of $240 in new equity capital for Continental but the results were disappointing as the stock price never rose much above the conversion trigger. A total of 14.7 million warrants were exercised, producing about $25 million from the $4.50 options and about $36 million from the $6 options.

7. FDIC left operation of the bank entirely to the new management team.

8. The Federal Reserve will continue its lending assurance throughout the term of FDIC assistance.

9. FDIC took over all claims against former management, bonding companies, accounting firms and the like, and agreed to apply recoveries from these claims against the Fed's debt we assumed.

The bank was required to trim its size and lending reach to facilitate the cure. That was handled by the Fed as supervisor of the holding company. Chairman Volcker in a July 24, 1984, letter to FDIC set forth the understanding:

> As we have discussed on a number of occasions, we share the mutual objective of restoring Continental Illinois Bank to a position where it can be funded on a self-sustaining basis with-

out FDIC capital or a special Federal Reserve commitment of liquidity assistance. That objective requires that the Bank, for some period, will need to reduce its assets while concentrating primarily on its prime market area in the Mid West.

The assistance plan being prepared is a major step toward accomplishing a return to health on this basis. To reflect these understandings with Continental management, the Board is entering into an agreement with Continental Illinois Corporation providing for the establishment by that company of a plan to reduce its consolidated assets in an orderly way.

The target was for a bank in the $25-billion to $30-billion range. That was a big comedown from the bank's $41-billion peak, but it was still a pretty good sized bank.

The assistance package was also being aired at a Continental press conference in Chicago. There, the old management, Taylor and Bottum, shared the platform with the new, Swearingen and Ogden. It was announced that Taylor and Bottum would be made vice-chairmen and would stay with the bank in which they had made their careers.*

Ironically, after all the administration pressure, President Ronald Reagan congratulated us on our action. Larry Speakes, the White House press secretary, quoted the president from Air Force One, en route to California at the time of our announcement: "It was a thing that we should do and we did it. It was in the best interest of all concerned."[2]

Addendum

By November of 1985 Continental had sufficiently recovered so that FDIC authorized the bank to upstream $60 million in earnings to the Continental Holding Company to finance preferred stock dividends which were five quarters in arrears. The dividends paid December 31 included $14.6 million to the publicly held preferred and $40.9 million to the FDIC-owned pre-

*In June 1986, Taylor moved to Irving Trust Co., a unit of the New York-based Irving Bank Corp., as vice-chairman.

ferred. The private holders received cash; FDIC received additional preferred shares in lieu of cash. Additional dividends totaling $10 million were approved in February 1986, all cash.

Continental's special borrowing arrangement with the Fed was terminated in August 1985 and by mid-December it had also ended use of the special funding safety net provided by the other big banks. In March 1986 Moody's Investors Service, Inc., upgraded the debt ratings of Continental.

The bank was on the way to recovery and a return of Continental to public ownership loomed as a possibility. In May 1986 the FDIC board engaged Morgan Stanley & Co. Inc. to advise if a public stock sale or a private placement is feasible, and if so, when and under what conditions.[3] On October 16, Bill Seidman told a National Press Club audience that FDIC intends to sell 50 million shares of Continental Illinois Corporation common stock before year-end, thus reducing government ownership by about 30 percent.

Chapter XII

Liquidation

The Fed, the Board,
and the Bad Loans

FINALLY, we now had a deal. It had been approved by FDIC and the Continental board and announced to the world. All we had to do was wait sixty days until the stockholders' vote. Nothing else could happen to derail the transaction. Right? Wrong.

On Tuesday afternoon, September 25, Si Keehn, president of the Chicago Fed, called Bill Isaac and said he was going to file a public lien against Continental's assets the next morning—the day of the stockholders' meeting. Keehn said he felt there was not sufficient collateral to secure possible future borrowings.

Keehn had given us a warning several weeks before at one of our final interagency meetings. He cited the law stipulating that Fed loans must be "secured to the satisfaction of such Federal Reserve bank." We did not believe he was serious. In September Continental borrowings from the Chicago Fed were running at $6.6 billion, fully secured, and there remained a huge backlog of eligible collateral. Why raise the issue?

Keehn was concerned because FDIC's 100 percent guarantee against loss would lapse when the permanent solution went into effect upon stockholders' approval. Clearly FDIC was not going to let Continental fail. After all, we owned it. We were faced with a nonissue that could blow the deal. If the Fed was worried about getting its money back, how could we expect investors around the world to have faith in Continental?

Our attitude was that the Continental package was built on interagency trust and cooperation. It turned out we were wrong. The Fed, apparently, is the lender of last resort if it wants to be, and it does not want to be unless it is fully collateralized. The megabanks had been reluctant to take on any risk. The Chicago Fed said it would refuse to do so.

Isaac told me he was on the phone until 1:30 A.M. the morning of the stockholders' meeting, talking to Volcker and Keehn. Volcker finally persuaded Keehn to hold off temporarily.

The Fed did not file its lien the day of the stockholders' meeting, or the next day, or the next. We continued to negotiate. In the ensuing months Mike Bradfield, the Fed general counsel, and Jack Murphy, our chief counsel, exchanged repeated drafts of a specific FDIC guarantee to the Fed against any losses in Continental. Nothing was ever executed. As the borrowings from the Fed subsided so did the argument. But at year-end 1985, the basic issue had not been resolved.

Unaware of our last-minute interagency difficulties, the stockholders had their meeting and announced their vote overwhelmingly approving the assistance package. The agreement was signed and went into effect the same day, September 26, 1984.

The Continental Board

We had put off a decision on Continental board membership until last. In the ensuing weeks we took up the question of how to treat the board responsible for policy direction and supervision of management when the bank was being led down the road to ruin. The assistance agreement stated explicitly that no one could serve on the board over our objection.

Too well we remembered our agonizing experience at First Pennsylvania where we interviewed and researched each board member and made godlike decisions on who could stay and who would go. We decided we would do just as well to handle the Continental board on a formula basis.

Those who were on the board during the years Continental adopted its disastrous expansion policy would be asked to leave. Newcomers could stay. It was as simple as that. We set an arbitrary cutoff date of 1980. All the policies and investment practices that led to the bank's downfall were in place by that time; the directors who were then on the board had condoned them.

We left it to Continental to do the announcing, and in a statement on December 3, the bank said that ten of the board's sixteen directors would not be standing for reelection at the annual stockholders' meeting the next spring.[1]

This left only Swearingen, Ogden, and the four directors who had joined Continental after 1980 still on the board: Weston R. Christopherson, former chairman and chief executive of Jewel Companies, Inc.; Frank W. Luerssen, chairman and chief executive of Inland Steel Co.; John M. Richman, chairman and chief executive of Dart & Kraft, Inc.; and William L. Weiss, chairman and chief executive of Ameritech.

A week later Christopherson announced that he, too, was departing. A nonbanker, like Swearingen, Christopherson had left Jewel Companies, Inc., after its takeover by American Stores Company in mid-1984. He stepped into the banking world at the top by becoming chairman and chief executive officer of the Northern Trust Company, Chicago's fourth largest bank with assets at the time of $6.7 billion.

Some of those dismissed went public with their reactions.

"Incredible," said Robert Malott, chairman of FMC Corporation. He accused us of "imposing our judgment on the directors' qualifications."[2]

"Cheap shot," said James F. Beré, chairman of Borg–Warner Corp. He was referring to a story circulating in Washington the day before the departures were announced in Chicago by the bank.[3] Earlier, Beré had given a more restrained comment: "It's difficult for me to see how a mass exodus of board members is in the best interests of the bank."[4]

Vernon Loucks, president of Baxter Travenol Laboratories, Inc., told the press that William Johnson, chairman of IC Industries, Inc., Beré, and Malott, in particular, had "worked their butts off to save the bank. When things start going bad, everybody wants to find scapegoats," Loucks said. He cited figures showing he had devoted far more time to Continental board and committee meetings in 1983 and 1984 than any of the other boards he sat on. He told the *New York Times:* "This is going to require a whole new definition of what's going to be expected from board members. People will be far more discriminating before they commit themselves to spending that type of time. We all have jobs that are more demanding than a directorship."[5]

Despite their views, at least one prestigious local publication —*Crain's Chicago Business*—supported the FDIC action. Parrying Malott's reaction that the dismissal was "incredible," *Crain's* said editorially: "The 'incredible' element in the Continental Bank disaster was the negligent performance of the board of directors over the past two years. The ouster of ten board members—most high-ranking Chicago chief executives—seems, if anything, too lenient." *Crain's* called it "an abdication of responsibility by a board of directors stocked with Chicago's business elite."[6]

Time magazine, in a long reach of imagination, likened the dismissal to the execution of Rear Admiral John Byng by the British in 1756 after Byng had failed to repel a French siege of the English position on Minorca. *Time* summoned up Voltaire's comment that "it is good to kill an admiral from time to time to encourage the others."[7] We did not see it quite so bloodthirsty as an execution, but as Loucks and Voltaire divined, we did indeed intend to send a message—and a strong one—to those who take their bank director resonsibilities too lightly.

The new, truncated Continental board recruited aggressively to fill the vacancies, and in January and February of 1985 appointed five new directors: Archie R. Boe, formerly president and director, Sears, Roebuck and Co.; Francis E. Ferguson, formerly chairman of the board and currently member of board of trustees, Northwestern Mutual Life Insurance Company; John H. Johnson, president and director, Johnson Publishing Company, Inc.; Leonard H. Lavin, chairman, president, chief executive officer, and director of Alberto-Culver Company; and Richard B. Ogilvie, partner in the Chicago law firm of Isham, Lincoln & Beale and formerly governor of Illinois.

These new members, along with Swearingen, Ogden, and the three remaining holdovers, made a ten-member board. All were elected at the annual meeting April 22 at the Art Institute of Chicago. In July 1985 the board was expanded to thirteen with the election of James W. Cozad, vice-chairman of Amoco Corp.; O. C. Davis, chairman and chief executive officer of Mid-Con Corp.; and Whitney MacMillan, chairman and chief executive officer of Cargill, Incorporated. Continental again had a full board.

At year-end 1985 a series of legal actions were pending; they were aimed at the pocketbooks of some of Continental's former officers and directors, its auditing firm, its insurers, and the bank itself. Two of these suits originated prior to FDIC's involvement with Continental. These are: (1) a securities fraud class-action suit brought by stockholders against the bank, certain individuals, and Ernst & Whinney, the auditor; and (2) a derivative action brought on behalf of Continental against certain individuals and Ernst & Whinney. The second suit was taken over by FDIC as part of the assistance package. The two suits were consolidated by the courts, and a trial was scheduled to start in the spring of 1986. However, settlement negotiations begun in late 1985 continued into 1986. The litigation involves large sums and is exceedingly complex; there was no way to predict its course or outcome.* A third suit, initiated by FDIC, was aimed at voiding, at least partially, the golden parachute severance agreements that former Continental Chairman Roger Anderson and former President John Perkins made with the bank prior to their departure. The suit is still pending at this writing.

The new management team, as we had expected, had its tense moments. Differences between Swearingen and Ogden erupted and surfaced in the Chicago press. Individually and together, the two came to Washington to talk with Isaac. Once, Isaac flew to Chicago for an airport meeting with Swearingen, Ogden, and the holdover board members to negotiate the primacy issue. A protocol was worked out: Swearingen would be the executive to whom the board would look as being primarily responsible, but Ogden would also have access to the board.

This seemed to work. It was the logical solution. Swearingen, after twenty-five years as top man, could accept no other role. Ogden would have a three-year audition to see if he could earn the top job when Swearingen stepped aside.

---

*In August 1986, the U.S. District Court gave final approval to a settlement whereby Continental and its former top officers agreed to settle the class action suit for $45 million. Still undecided are the amount of the derivative suit damages, the extent of auditing firm culpability, and how much the insurers will pay FDIC on the directors' and officers' liability policies on which the insurance carriers are vigorously denying liability.

By the fall of 1985, when Swearingen and Ogden came to Washington to discuss the bank's progress and plans with us, the two gave every appearance of being a smooth-working, congenial team. They clearly were enjoying the challenge and the satisfactions of their assignment.

The Liquidation Challenge

The new managers ran the "good bank" for us; that is, the Continental that was left after FDIC took out billions of dollars of bad loans. The "bad bank" into which those loans were transferred was in actuality FDIC; we devised a dramatically new approach for handling it. We had to.

The Continental transaction presented FDIC with its most difficult liquidation challenge ever. The $4.5 billion in book value of troubled loans we were to assume represented a doubling of the stockpile of bad assets already being liquidated by FDIC. New employees could not be hired and trained in sufficient numbers in time to be of much use to us at Continental.

What we arrived at was a separate agreement within the assistance package by which Continental would attempt to collect on the bad loans for us. We had done something similar in the United American Bank (UAB) failure in 1983 when we contracted with First Tennessee, buyer of the failed bank, to work UAB's bad loans. That arrangement proved unsatisfactory and was terminated. The difference in the Continental case was that the bad loans had been Continental's and bank employees were familiar with them. We hope for better results.

The agreement required Continental to set up a separate department and to provide space and equipment; FDIC would compensate the bank for overhead. The bank appointed Garry

J. Scheuring, an executive vice-president, to head up the unit; by year-end 1985, it had eighty employees. In late 1985, Scheuring moved over to Continental and was succeeded by David O. Nordby.

The agreement required the bank to "seek diligently to collect all amounts due" with the goal of "maximization of return." Besides outright collections, the bank had authority to sell loans or to achieve realizations on collateral. The bank was also responsible for litigation on loans. Operating budgets and advances on loans required FDIC approval; I headed the Committee on Liquidations, Loans, and Purchases of Assets that considered such proposals each week.

FDIC had full rights of oversight, including the right to place its own observers in the collection unit. FDIC could terminate the agreement or the handling of any loan or all the loans at any time for any reason; the bank could terminate on 180 days' notice.

Incentive compensation was negotiated separately in the spring of 1985. The bank would get $1 million for the first $500 million in gross collections plus a scaled percentage on net collections, beginning at 0.6 percent on the net between $250 million to $1 billion and rising to 2.25 percent for the net above $3 billion. The sharply rising incentive reflected the greater difficulty of collecting on the poorest quality loans. As a stick-with-it bonus, the bank would get a payment equal to one-third of all previous incentive payments if it fulfills the five-year term of the collection agreement. Probably, the maximum the bank will realize will not exceed 2 percent of the net.

Continental transferred $3 billion in loans at the time of the transaction and has the right to transfer an additional $1.5 billion over a three-year period. The plan was structured in this manner to provide Continental ample opportunity to select the really bad assets for transfer to FDIC. By year-end 1985, Continental had transferred $581 million and thus has leeway to select $919 million more in bad loans by September 26, 1987.

The ultimate recovery of any value by the original Continental stockholders turns on the results of the liquidation of the $4.5 billion in transferred assets. Every $20 in losses gives FDIC the option to buy a common share at a pittance—$0.0001 per share. This translates to $800 million in losses as the trigger figure where the stockholders are wiped out. In May 1985 Continental issued an estimate that the losses could range between $600 million and $800 million.[8] Early in 1986, after eighteen months of experience with the liquidation, both the bank and the FDIC estimated that the losses on the transferred assets will exceed the trigger point by a considerable margin. FDIC financial reports were then restated to show a $700 million reserve for losses for 1984 and an additional reserve of $600 million for 1985, or a total estimated loss for FDIC of $1.3 billion.* These figures assumed that FDIC will assume ownership of all 40.3 million shares remaining with the stockholders, giving FDIC control of all 200 million common shares.

There remains a long-shot possibility that the original stockholders would receive some value. The contract provides the option of paying $20 a share to the FDIC in lieu of surrendering the stock. Such an eventuality, triggered by a spectacular rise in Continental's stock price, is not anticipated. However, the Continental statement said: "It cannot and does not express any view as to the likely occurrence of such factors."[9]

The final calculation of overall cost of the rescue of Continental must await the public sale of the stock by the FDIC. No one now can predict what it will bring in the marketplace, or when it will be sold.

Meanwhile, the work of collection goes on. Not surprisingly, many debtors did not like the idea of paying up. Very surprisingly, some of them went so far as to sue to prevent us from collecting. One real estate partnership that owed $42 million,

*The FDIC board in the spring of 1986 doubled the corporation reserve for losses, skyrocketing it from $2.2 billion to $4.5 billion. The increases included: $1.3 billion for Continental; $500 million for bank failures prior to 1985; $500 million for the 120 bank failures and assistance transactions in 1985.

another that owed $34 million, and two other borrowers that owed $140 million between them went to court in a futile attempt to prevent Continental from transferring their loans to FDIC. They would prefer Continental over FDIC as their creditor—nervy, coming from people whose debts were a part of the Continental problem.

The FDIC Liquidation System

What Continental does for FDIC under contract in Chicago is just one station of a far-flung liquidation empire. It gets bigger every time another bank fails. With the single exception of Continental, this empire is staffed and operated by our own employees. As in Chicago, their job is to collect money owed to banks that failed, those debts turned over to FDIC. That activity, rarely pleasant, has produced rude awakenings for increasing numbers of delinquents who find their loans in the hands of FDIC. These borrowers—including energy speculators, near-bankrupt farmers, and others—view FDIC far differently from its traditional image as the good guy protector of deposits. To them FDIC is the debt collector in the black hat. Yet it is a necessary function and a fascinating one as well.

FDIC's liquidation operation is best described as something akin to the duties of a mortician. When a bank dies, FDIC tidies up the remains and disposes of them.

The deposit insurance cycle begins when a bank is closed and FDIC is appointed receiver. The first task to is take custody of the bank. A team of liquidation personnel, gathered from throughout the nation, assembles in the vicinity of the bank the night before the closing. This is done in great secrecy since a hint that FDIC is mustering could start a run. Those who got the word and took their money out would have an unfair advantage over other depositors.

Once the bank is closed, the FDIC team works around the clock, usually over a weekend, to prepare for either a payoff of depositors or sale of the bank, depending on what the board decided. In either instance, the insured depositors have access to their money in short order, usually the next banking day.

In many instances, the initial task is formidable. New York City's Franklin National Bank, which failed in 1974, operated 108 branch offices; its closing required a force of 778 FDIC personnel, most of whom were examiners from around the nation on temporary assignment. For the unexpected closing of the First National Bank of Humboldt, Iowa, in 1982, FDIC people battled tornadoes and then a snowstorm to get to the bank. Trips that should have taken a few hours turned into two-day ordeals with some employees finally arriving after hitchhiking on tractor trailers or being transported in state police cars.

The weekend of the Humboldt travails, we also arranged mergers for a failing $2 billion savings bank in Philadelphia and a small Virginia bank for which no buyer could be found until nearly midnight Sunday. It is not unusual for FDIC's board to meet late at night on Fridays, Saturdays, or Sundays to handle a failed bank.

In the early days—the 1930s—failed banks were very small. In 1940 even after seven years of averaging fifty failures a year, the assets acquired by FDIC for liquidation stood at just $136 million. Then FDIC's liquidation function was easily handled.

For the next thirty years, as the failures dwindled, so did FDIC's liquidation workload. The asset inventory did not again reach the 1940 level until 1971. In the 1970s and 1980s, both the number and the size of failed banks increased dramatically. The Penn Square failure in 1982 alone left FDIC with a tangle of loans that will take years to resolve. In 1983 the $1.4-billion

First National Bank of Midland, Texas, and the series of
Butcher bank failures in Tennessee brought the book value of
FDIC's bad assets to the then unheard of total of $5 billion.
Then came Continental, driving the inventory beyond the $10-
billion mark, reflecting more than 142,000 different assets. Be-
sides Continental, there were 338 other active liquidations of
failed banks at year-end 1985. In its over fifty-year history
FDIC handled and concluded 537 other liquidations.

The accelerating pace of bank failures spurred the corporation to find new, more efficient ways to handle the job before
the task got out of hand. One tack was to be more restrictive
about the assets retained. In a payoff where there is no purchaser of the bank, FDIC must receive and liquidate all assets.
In a closed-bank sale, FDIC can be more choosy and take only
the lousiest assets. FDIC's job is to absorb the loss after wring-
ing whatever recovery it can out of assets that made a bank go
broke. There is no point in dumping somebody else's bad loans
into a good bank and creating a new problem. The same old
assets would wind up in FDIC's lap again, anyway. So FDIC is
being more aggressive in passing the best of a failed bank's
assets to an acquiring bank. That leaves the corporation free to
concentrate on the worst assets. For many years, the purchasing
bank acquired only the bank premises and the good installment
loans; it had a sixty-day option to purchase any of the remaining assets. In 1985 FDIC began passing good-quality commercial and mortgage loans to the acquiring bank and allowing that
bank a period in which to send the lemons back.

Part of FDIC's new effort was simply to hire more staff. By
year-end 1985, our liquidation force of 3,300 represented nearly
half of the total FDIC employment of 7,125. The liquidation
staff has increased tenfold since 1981 when we had fewer than
one hundred active liquidations, most of them small. During
the 1940s when FDIC was handling some 400 open liquidations,
the staff numbered about 1,600. By 1950 after FDIC had liquidated much of that backlog, the entire Division of Liquidation

had only thirty-two full-time positions, including secretarial and support workers.

Another major innovation has been the consolidation of work sites into larger production-type operations. During the sleepy years each liquidation was handled individually. A liquidator was named, moved to the site, and stayed until the assets were disposed of or until he or she was called to a new closed bank. In the 1980s FDIC opened regional offices in Atlanta, Dallas, Kansas City, Chicago, New York, and San Francisco, with subregional offices in 23 areas of the heaviest bank failure activity.

Under this new procedure, the liquidation still begins at the site of the closed bank, but the assets are quickly pulled into a subregional or regional office where they are segregated by category and worked by specialists. This approach makes possible economies of scale and the mustering of legal and marketing expertise.

FDIC's liquidation activities are not a fire sale or forced liquidation in any sense of the word. The law requires FDIC to get the maximum possible recovery out of an asset, no matter how poor it may be. So the staff is prepared to negotiate a sale, solicit bids, hold an auction or do whatever else it may take to dispose of an asset, or to wait to get a better price if that is in FDIC's best interests. Further, FDIC works loans—that is, prods borrowers into making their payments according to terms of the loan and may renegotiate loans to give the borrower some time in return for a higher interest rate or a better ultimate return to FDIC. If an asset is an ongoing business—a motel or restaurant, for example—FDIC is prepared to keep it operating to preserve its value until the corporation can market it advantageously. What FDIC cannot do is throw good money after bad, advancing more funds to a borrower with no prospect for repayment.

Besides maximizing the agency's return as its statutory fiduciary responsibility requires, this businesslike approach also minimizes the impact on a community. FDIC does not depress a local market by dumping assets indiscriminately within a short time after the bank's closing. In fact, the FDI Act requires liquidations to be conducted "having due regard to the condition of credit in the locality."

The immense volume of bad loans FDIC acquired from Continental and scores of other failed banks and the collapse of the Midwest farm economy in 1984 and 1985 put this policy to the test. Suits by and against borrowers mushroomed. In their desperation and distress, farmers asked FDIC to forgive their loans, make new loans, extend old loans, or allow some other indulgence. FDIC's policy has been forbearance to the extent the law allows.

As collections accumulate in a liquidation, FDIC periodically declares dividends which are paid pro rata to all uninsured depositors and creditors, including itself in lieu of insured depositors. In a few rare cases, creditors may ultimately be paid in full, including interest. More likely, however, creditors will receive 80 to 85 percent of their claims. If anything should be left after all claims and liquidation expenses are paid, it goes to shareholders. Receiverships of failed banks, like any receivership, are conducted under the jurisdiction of the courts, and sales of assets by the receiver are subject to approval by the courts.

Liquidations may take years; recent large failures may require ten years or more to complete. The Public Bank in Detroit and San Francisco National Bank liquidations have endured almost two decades and they were still on the books when we established reserve for losses in early 1986. Liquidation of Franklin National Bank in New York and U.S. National Bank in San Diego continues after more than a dozen years apiece. The speed of liquidation depends largely on the number and size of acquired assets and their salability.

Among the unusual assets bequeathed FDIC by failed banks was *And They're Off,* a partially completed motion picture about the horse racing industry starring Tab Hunter and Jose Ferrer. The exotic assets the corporation has acquired over the year are legion. One I was particularly fascinated with as a history buff was General Custer's knife and a shirt from one of Sitting Bull's warriors adorned with scores of scalps.

After FDIC acquired a large almond orchard near Bakersfield, California, in the U.S. National Bank failure in 1973, squirrels ate 25 percent of the crop. Then almond prices fell by half, so operations were abandoned and FDIC sold the property at fire sale prices. Even this did not work. The buyer returned the land and it had to be sold again. The process was repeated in 1985 as we reacquired the property through foreclosure. Some assets seem to be destined to stay in our inventory in perpetuity.

In 1978 the corporation took over a loan collateralized by a Chicago warehouse filled with a million pounds of meat. After the refrigeration broke, the rats took over. The liquidators drew the line at becoming exterminators. Actually, FDIC had little say since it was not the proprietor of the warehouse, merely a creditor. Needless to say, our chances of collecting on a mortgage of several hundred thousand dollars went as bad as the meat.

FDIC also has had interests in oil tankers, shrimp boats, and tuna boats and has experienced many of the pitfalls facing the maritime industry. An oil tanker ran aground; a shrimp boat was blown by a hurricane onto the main street of Aransas Pass, Texas; and tuna boats were idled when the price of tuna dropped sharply. Other liquidation assets have included several taxicab fleets, countless idled oil drilling rigs, distribution rights to an X-rated movie, a coal mine that was on fire the day the bank was closed, a horse training facility with two inept race horses and quarter horses greatly overvalued at several million dollars, thousands of art objects including an antique copy of the Koran, a collection of stuffed wild animals, and all types of real estate including churches and synagogues. FDIC has taken over as many as 400 single-family mortgages and as much as $500 million in international loans from single bank failures.

Legal Fees Explode

Legal work inevitably accompanies liquidation, and legal fees eat up an inordinate percentage of the recoveries. We live in a litigious society; that is never more apparent than in the liquidation business where stakes are so high.

In 1985 FDIC spent a staggering $36.2 million in outside legal fees, up from $22.2 million in 1984.* Much of the increase is attributable to Continental. The *National Law Journal,* which did its own survey of outside legal fees in 1983–84, found that FDIC spent far more than all other federal agencies combined, although information from some agencies was incomplete.[10] The message, however, is very clear: The explosive growth in legal fees is a problem that needs to be dealt with. As I left FDIC the new General Counsel, Jack Murphy, who had been very careful and defensive at first, was replacing more expensive outside counsel with FDIC attorneys, and expanding on a computerized file system initiated by Frank Skillern to better monitor our legal efforts.[11] To date FDIC has withstood extraordinary White House pressure over the years to make FDIC's general counsel a political appointee. He hires the outside law firms.

The assets in their wonderful variety make FDIC probably the most diverse conglomerate in the country. Certainly no private concern would wish to pursue so many different lines of business. Nor does FDIC. Our sole purpose is going out of business. That we have not been more successful at it—in fact FDIC has acquired far more inventory in recent years than it has disposed of—is a striking testament to the continuing shakeout of the banking industry in the mid-1980s.

What does this tell us about the future, which must be viewed in the context of the past? What's past is prologue.

*The outside legal fees stood at just 7.5 million in 1981, my last year as chairman. Legal confrontations escalated from 6,000 lawsuits in 1980, to 16,500 in 1984, over 20,000 in 1985, and was headed past the 25,000 mark in 1986.

PART FIVE

Where Do We Go From Here?

Chapter XIII

Lessons Learned

History Does Tell Us Something

THE REGULATORS learned two lessons of import while passing through the bailout episodes and, at the same time, handling multiple and increasingly difficult bank failures throughout the nation.

First, the policies and practices of bank management that lead to failures can be curtailed to some extent but they are going to be repeated. Unburdened with the experience of the past, each generation of bankers believes it knows best, and each new generation produces some who have to learn the hard way.

Second, the incredible tangle of jurisdictional overlap will make the strong regulatory presence needed to restrain the excesses an impossibility, unless there is a major restructuring of the agencies—consolidation.

The Repeat Factor

The first lesson is the inevitability of repetition. Continental is an example of a big bank that forgot its history and was condemned to repeat its past. In 1937 the bank paid its insurance assessment under protest. It sent FDIC a check for $831.96, with a note arguing that the deposit insurance law was invalid and unconstitutional. Continental gave notice that it waived none of its constitutional rights, including the right to a refund.

It was a macho move—Continental was just then coming off a federal bailout. Four years earlier, it was the first major bank in the nation to be rescued by the same federal government whose intervention it so vehemently protested. That time the Reconstruction Finance Corporation (RFC) was the white knight. Continental was brought to its knees in the Great Depression by the same kind of bad loan syndrome that nearly ruined it fifty years later. The investment was different—utilities in the 1930s, oil and gas in the 1980s—but the fallacies were the same: concentration of assets, out-of-territory lending, and pursuit of growth at any cost. And the motivation in both instances was absolutely the same: Go for the fast buck; a bigger bank means more compensation for its management.

Reflecting years later on the rescue he had crafted, RFC chairman Jesse Jones wrote:

> Continental was a great correspondent bank—a bankers' bank —in which a large proportion of the country banks of the Middle West and many in the South and Southwest kept accounts. Had it collapsed, the effect would have been frighteningly felt in fields and towns and cities over a large area of the country.[1]

This is still true today, except that Continental's reach extends overseas now, and the repercussions of the bank's failure in 1984 would have been felt worldwide.

Continental was not alone in its desire for gain at any cost. Earlier, Commonwealth and First Pennsylvania had "bet the bank" on interest rates. They lost. Both purchased vast quantities of long-term securities with the expectation that interest rates would fall and give them a windfall profit. Both got their windfall when interest rates went up; it blew them right out of the water.

Like Continental, Penn Square and Seafirst emphasized unhealthy growth and disregarded loan quality. Their pattern was to book egregious concentrations of credit in the vulnerable energy sectors of the economy without adequate investigation and documentation.

Seafirst, already dominant in the Northwest, seems to have embarked on its fatal involvement in the energy loan morass from a desire to grow anywhere. Penn Square was an unbelievable mix of sharp and shady practices. In all instances, management let temptation overpower judgment.

This record of repeat behavior points to the greed factor that remains the major—often the only—reason for a bank's failure. Banks fail in the vast majority of cases because their managements seek growth at all cost, reach for profits without due regard to risk, give privileged treatment to insiders, or gamble on the future course of interest rates. Some simply have dishonest management that loots the bank. A 1986 FDIC survey concluded that criminal misconduct by insiders was a major contributing factor in 45 percent of recent failures.

For many years I believed and often stated that these were the only causes for bank failure. Today, after witnessing the effect of the recession on banks in the farm and energy belts, my thinking has been adjusted. Severe economic conditions can and do create an environment that causes failures of banks that would have survived in better economic climates. Even so, in these depressed areas we see most banks survive. Management —either its excesses or its abilities—remains the determining factor of whether a bank lives or dies.

This tells us that the regulator's supervisory approach must be strengthened and improved to meet the challenge of the years ahead. We have long known that that unseemly growth and concentration of risk are danger signs; yet, too often the regulators have allowed such unsafe practices to continue. Individual banks should not grow faster than the economies they serve, and the regulators should no longer allow them to do so. New methods for dealing with erring banks have been proposed; these include the levying of deposit insurance premiums based on risk or requiring bank capital levels based on risk. These proposals are intriguing and, perhaps, should be adopted. In my opinion, however, they can never be a sufficient deterrent to those who roll the dice with their institutions. In this computer age as never before regulators can ferret out banks that exhibit the symptoms of greed or abuse, including runaway growth rates. Regulators must greatly expand the use of this capacity to track down offenders in the early stages and to police them with a more rigorous application of old-fashioned cease and desist orders, including removal of offending bank officers if necessary. All this can be done with existing authority; it merely requires more diligent practice.

In the fall of 1985 all three bank regulatory agencies, the Fed, FDIC and OCC, announced plans to step up their examination and enforcement procedures and to begin looking closely at such previously ignored risks as off-book activities. Let us hope these encouraging plans are followed up aggressively and relentlessly. One example, the OCC has placed full-time examiners at each of the twelve largest national banks. Another, the FDIC planned to participate in the examination of seventeen large national banks in 1986 under a newly negotiated examination protocol.

The Struggle for Turf

The second lesson learned addresses the phenomenon I call a "running turf fight." It has had deleterious effects on the supervision and handling of problem banks for too many years.

You have seen how the background and personalities of the individuals involved play a continuing role in the decision-making process. Solutions are not developed by formula, but rather through an intense give and take where confrontation is often the major ingredient. The regulators, comprised of a mix of dedicated career officials protective of the agencies they serve and an ever changing group of political appointees, find themselves unable—not to mention unwilling—to surrender prerogatives to the common good. The turf fight has a long history. One flagrant example is the San Francisco National Bank.

Shortly after nine o'clock the night of Friday, January 22, 1965, Deputy Comptroller Bill Camp notified Ed DeHority, our chief of the Division of Bank Examination, that he had just closed the San Francisco National Bank. Camp had appointed FDIC receiver, as required by law in the case of national banks. FDIC could take care of the depositors and start its liquidation at will.

It was a bolt out of the blue. Previously OCC had not given FDIC the slightest hint that the $54-million San Francisco National Bank was in trouble. Now FDIC was faced with what would be the largest payoff and liquidation the corporation had undertaken up to that time. Without notice, the staff had done no advance preparation.

To add insult, it was the second time that day the comptroller had done it to FDIC. Earlier, he had closed the Brighton National Bank of Brighton, Colorado, also without prior word. Fortunately, Brighton was a much smaller bank—$2.3 million in deposits—and FDIC knew something of it from state sources.

Admittedly, San Francisco and Brighton come from the era when Comptroller Jim Saxon wielded noncooperation like a blunt instrument. He made no bones about it; he regarded national bank regulation and supervision as a private preserve of his office. Saxon was grudging about sharing information or working together with anyone, including his colleagues on the FDIC board. Saxon went so far as to boycott some FDIC board meetings and occasionally sending a deputy in his place. It was then that the president ordered the establishment of an Inter-agency Coordinating Committee to force the regulators to talk with each other. This committee later was succeeded by the congressionally mandated Federal Financial Institutions Examination Council. Saxon refused to give bank examination reports to either FDIC or the Fed unless those agencies paid for them. He was the consummate turf protector.

Saxon was extreme, but the theme of jealousy over jurisdiction continued under his successors. The running turf fight continued through the failures of the $1.3-billion United States National Bank in San Diego in 1973 and the $3.7-billion Franklin National Bank in New York City a year later.

The turf fight was repeated in the Penn Square failure, complicating our payoff and liquidation problems that would have been immense even under the best of circumstances. The ferocity of the Continental run caught everyone by surprise, even though we had known for some time of the bank's volatile situation. FDIC should have been participating in the bank's examination after it was placed in a problem status in June 1983. Instead, we stuck with protocol leaving oversight to the primary supervisors, OCC and the Fed. Sanford Rose, writing in the *American Banker* fifteen months after the crisis, reported he was quoting a 1981 OCC examination report proclaiming that "Continental is adequately staffed with both sound lending officers and scientific personnel to handle current relationships and meet continued strong growth anticipations." Calling it "one of the least prescient evaluations ever made," Rose wryly suggested FDIC should consider suing OCC.[2]

Periods of cooperation and confrontation ebb and flow, depending on the players; this certainly will continue so long as we have so many separate competing agencies with strong-willed leaders. For example, confrontation escalated again during Bill Isaac's term at the FDIC. Time and again Isaac enjoyed fights with Todd Conover at OCC, Tim McNamar at Treasury, Paul Volcker at the Fed, and such disparate groups as Merrill Lynch & Company, Inc., money brokers; the Federal Home Loan Bank Board; the General Accounting Office; Kansas bankers; Oklahoma congressmen; the Bureau of Indian Affairs; and others on an endless list. The end product: many press clippings. I supported Isaac on the substance on most of these issues; he was right, but my approach would have been to work out compromises that by definition mean there are no winners and no losers, and something gets accomplished.

The problem among the agencies stems in part from tangled jurisdiction. A 1977 report by the United States Senate Committee on Governmental Affairs opens with the following paragraph:

> Regulation of American commercial banking is intricate, labyrinthine, baffling, and remarkable. It is divided not only between the States and the Federal Government but also, within the Federal Government, among three autonomous regulatory agencies. Its roots go back as far as 1864, which makes it older than railroad regulation, frequently cited as the oldest form of economic regulation in this country. Its statutory authority, on the Federal level alone, is divided among seven major enactments. Undeniably, it contains seeds of a significant amount of overlap, duplication, and inconsistency.[3]

The situation led Arthur Burns to conclude that the "most serious obstacle to improving the regulation and supervision of banking is the structure of the regulatory apparatus." In short, it is a jungle. It affords banks some latitude to shop for the most lenient regulator; a practice that Burns said nurtured a "competition in laxity" among the agencies.[4]

In their relentless pushing against the constraints of the law, the banks are represented by multifarious lobby groups. Each group represents a more narrowly defined segment of the industry and each clamors for some tiny advantage for its members' special interest. As in many areas of Washington life, there are far more bank lobbyists than regulators.

The state scene presents its own set of problems affecting bank regulation; not the least of these is the revolving door used by state banking commissioners. In the ten years preceding 1986, the 50 states have had 187 different bank supervisors. California and Kentucky head the list with eight each. Most are political appointees; their constant turnover seriously weakens any contribution the states could make to more effective supervision.

As long ago as 1937, the Brookings Institution advanced the idea of a single banking agency. In 1962 Robbie Robertson, vice-chairman of the Fed—a man who served twenty-one years, longer than any other as a Fed governor—called for putting some reason into the regulatory structure. In the 1970s Senator William Proxmire, then chairman of the Senate Banking Committee, added his support. The Hoover Commission in 1949, the Hunt Commission in 1972, and the FINE study in 1975 all called for some type of agency consolidation.

After the Senate Committee on Governmental Affairs endorsed the proposed consolidation in the 1977 study, momentum seemed to be growing, but the idea was derailed in a typical congressional ploy. Instead of consolidation, in 1978 Congress created still another regulator—the Federal Financial Institutions Examination Council—made up of the heads of the Fed, FDIC, OCC, the Federal Home Loan Bank Board, and the National Credit Union Administration. The council was supposed to facilitate interagency cooperation.

I was chosen vice-chairman at the council's organizational meeting in 1979, soon after I returned to FDIC as chairman. The tone was set on day one. FHLBB representatives generally were silent or they abstained on any issue of consequence. They did not appear at all interested in supervisory standards, honest accounting rules, or adequate capital standards.* The Fed, FDIC, and OCC representatives eyed each other warily. NCUA people knew they were different. Nothing had really changed.

Some good has come from the council in terms of administrative matters, but the essential problems were not addressed. Today the council remains a stepchild and is generally considered additional debris cluttering up the bank regulatory scene.

In private discussions with President Jimmy Carter, and later with his domestic policy advisor Stu Eisenstat, I endorsed consolidation of the regulators. The proposal was placed on the Carter legislative agenda, but the project was put aside in the crush of other business.

Left to our own devices and increasingly outraged as the lack of prior notice of failing banks was repeated, Isaac and I determined to do something about it. First, we attempted to work out with the Fed and OCC a system of early warnings and joint examinations of problem banks. There was much talk of cooperation, but no agreement.

So Isaac and I brought the issue to a head by overriding our colleague on the FDIC board, Comptroller Conover, and ordered FDIC to examine a series of OCC's troubled national banks. We acted under Section 10(b) of the FDI Act, which had never been used before. The provision gives us, as insurer, authority to examine any insured bank. Previously, we had deferred to OCC in the examination of national banks and to the Fed for its state member banks. We had limited our examinations to the state-chartered banks that were not members of the Federal Reserve System and hoped OCC and the Fed would keep us informed about the others. By voting over the objection of the comptroller, we were violating long-standing protocol and serving notice that we would no longer remain passively

---

*These chickens came back to roost in the late 1980s as Savings and Loans failed in disgraceful numbers.

dependent on OCC's indulgence if we thought there was a problem we should know more about.

After a series of decisions to examine national banks, Conover succumbed to the pressure and entered into serious discussions. In February of 1983 Isaac, Conover, and I cut the framework for a deal during a long afternoon around the pool at Tucson's El Conquistador Hotel where we were attending a joint OCC-FDIC examiner conference. Tension was in the air. While the three of us talked for two hours, examiners from both agencies, fearing loss of jobs, eyed us warily from a distance. No one was in the pool.

The talks set the stage for a formal agreement signed on December 2, 1983, too late to be of any help at Continental. Nobody lost a job, and FDIC now gets the early information it needs. We created a cooperative program in which FDIC joins OCC in examinations of certain national banks, including all problem national banks. No agreement was reached with the Fed. Countless drafts were exchanged, but it became increasingly clear that the Fed was waiting us out. Both of our terms had run their course during the negotiations and Isaac and I were soon to be replaced.

Despite our agreement with OCC, it is the Fed's "wear 'em down" attitude that will prevail in the interagency contention if Congress does not address the issue. Agreements can be changed with the players, and all three of us who signed off on the only agreement in place have left our agencies. The standoff in interagency relations will continue until the long overdue consolidation that is every day becoming more urgent. As interstate banking develops, so does the job facing the supervisory agencies and the threat to the insurance fund. Groups of states have already passed reciprocal laws that permit interstate mergers within their respective groups. Major banks, particularly in the South, responded immediately with announcements of significant interstate mergers. By October of 1986, some type of interstate merger authority was in place in thirty-seven states. The next logical step will be to expand the reciprocal boundaries until full nationwide interstate banking is realized—perhaps by the end of the decade. In a variety of other ways—loan production offices, credit card operations, takeovers of failed savings and loan associations— the large banks are already buying their ways into other states. The result will be an increasing concentration of economic resources and a multiplication of banks that may be too big to let fail.

Although the bid to achieve a unified regulatory structure was thwarted, the issue will not die; it only becomes more pertinent. The most recent proposal for comprehensive reform was produced in July 1984, after more than a year of study by the task group of thirteen senior federal officials headed by Vice-President George Bush.[5] Its key provision is to create a unified federal banking agency, headed by a single director who would report to the Secretary of the Treasury. In short, it would politicize bank regulation and supervision.

As we learned in the Continental chapters, the intrusion of political judgments can cloud evenhanded regulation, particularly in time of crisis. Politics, like greed, threatens to become a lesson that goes unlearned. What this second recurring lesson tells us is that the bank supervisory structure must be rationalized to deal with the challenge we face. It must be done in a way that keeps the regulators insulated from political influence.

In my judgment, a consolidated independent banking agency should be created with the responsibility of regulating and supervising all banks and their holding companies, regardless of their chartering authority or Fed membership. The agency should be headed by an expanded seven-person board whose chairman would be named by the president, and whose membership would be balanced to insure that all of the competing interests have a voice. Public members who are not beholden to any of the regulated institutions are a must.

Next, the public policy debate. Should megabanks be allowed to fail?

Chapter XIV

The Public Policy Debate

*Serious Questions Are Raised
About Bailouts*

THE MOST significant theme of this book I call "The Debate," capitalizing it because of the overriding importance of the issue. Should megabanks continue to receive favored treatment?

There is no question they do now. Of the fifty largest bank failures in history, forty-six—including the top twenty—were handled either through a pure bailout or an FDIC assisted transaction where no depositor or creditor, insured or uninsured, lost a penny. In effect, the forty-six enjoyed 100 percent insurance protection. The four lonely exceptions that will be described later were the result of unusual circumstances.

These favored forty-six major banks ranged from Continental, which had in excess of $41 billion in assets shortly before bailout day in 1984, to the $115 million United Southern Bank in Knoxville which failed in 1983. The pattern continues through the second fifty largest failures, down to the $30-million range. Four out of five in this group also were afforded 100 percent protection. The one hundred largest failures and how they were handled shows the favoritism in stark reality.*

Smaller banks simply do not fare so well. Sixteen failures in 1984 and another twenty-nine in 1985 were handled through some variation of a payoff. The uninsured, thus, were afforded something less than 100 percent protection. Twenty-five of the 1985 payoffs were for institutions with under $30 million in assets; twelve had under $10 million. Twenty-two of these banks were in communities with a population of less than 5,000.

Over the past twenty years, forty-three of the one hundred smallest bank failures were handled by payoffs, including thirty of the smallest fifty. Although most of the failed small banks that were paid off had relatively few uninsured deposits, that is no answer to the fairness issue. A customer with a portion of his deposit uninsured in a $6-million farm community bank that cannot be sold is not treated the same as a customer with a similar deposit in a larger bank that can be sold or bailed out.

Furthermore, as managers of the smaller banks can and do argue vociferously, one reason they have few uninsured deposits is because customers are afraid to leave more than the $100,000 insured amount with them.

Since most depositors in the smaller banks have full insurance protection because account balances are below the insurance limit, on the surface it appears not to really matter how the failure is handled. But it does. The real hardships in a bank failure fall on the loan customers who suddenly find themselves shifted from a continuing banking relationship to a "pay your debts now" mode. Many cannot. And the hardship cases abound.

There is no dark plot to be unfair to small banks. The dispar-

*See the list of the one hundred largest failures in the appendix.

ity in treatment arises from a combination of the law that pre-
scribes how bank failures must be handled, an attitude of the
regulators that megabanks must be saved under any circumstance, and the fact that many banks in small depressed rural
communities cannot be sold at any reasonable price.

No consensus exists that the present system is appropriate.
The feeling among many academicians, congressmen, observers, critics, and the general public is that large banks should be
allowed to fail the same as small ones. There was no real need
for the Continental bailout or the three stepping stones that
preceded it, the argument goes; after all, our free enterprise
system is designed so there will be both winners and losers.

This issue was raised, in successively higher decibel levels,
each time we did a bailout. Ironically, the question does not
occur when a failed bank is sold with precisely the same effect
on depositors and creditors as a bailout. The difference: The
bailouts have afforded some stockholder protection and debt
securities were honored.

I agree with the critics in the abstract. Now that I no longer
have to make the decisions, it is therapeutic to join in the
chorus: All failing banks should be treated the same. But no one
who holds the responsibility could possibly agree.

Over the years, I have been in the forefront advocating measures to cut down on the enormous advantages the large money
center institutions have over their more than 14,500 smaller
counterparts that make the American economy work in every
town and hamlet in the nation.

Yet, with this admitted bias toward the community banks,
three times I blinked when faced with what would have been
the largest bank failure in history—Commonwealth, First
Pennsylvania, and finally Continental. Why? Simply because
the information before us—the facts at hand—convinced me in
each instance that the nation just could not tolerate a failure of
that magnitude at that time.

The big bank-small bank issue has preoccupied me since I

first joined FDIC in 1968. That is because it represents the essence of bank regulation—how to give fair and evenhanded treatment to all institutions while at the same time protecting the public interest.

Some fifteen years ago, not long after I joined the FDIC board, I asked Paul Horvitz, then our research director, to assemble six of the leading academic experts to assist me in understanding the big bank–small bank argument which raged even then.

The following 1971 memo from my files is instructive:

> Last month we had a group of economics and banking professors at the Corporation for lunch and during the discussion they were adamant in their position that "big banks never close." By their definition, anything over $10 million in deposits would be beyond the small category.

The memo said that most of the 490 failed banks handled by FDIC up to that time were in the $1 million or less category; only seventeen exceeded $10 million in deposits.

> The largest was the $93 million deposit Public Bank in Detroit which failed in 1966 and was merged into the Bank of the Commonwealth with Corporation assistance.
>
> The largest bank in which a salvage operation was impossible and insured deposits had to be paid off was the $78.9 million Sharpstown State Bank which failed 60 days ago in Texas and depositors are still being paid.

Nothing much has changed, except now we all are a little older and the numbers are quite a bit larger.

The Continental bailout triggered a public policy debate as soon as we made our $2-billion cash infusion in May 1984. My initiation was immediate. The day after we had acted, I headed for Monterey to attend the California Bankers Association annual conference. It was a long-standing commitment and, I felt, a well-earned respite in my home state. Bankers' conventions always allow ample time for relaxation. After rising leisurely, I strolled over to the opening luncheon. Gus Bonta, the association vice-president, grabbed me. He had a problem. Willie Brown, speaker of the California Assembly, had just called to cancel his luncheon address. Could I fill in?

I agreed. Brimming with our Continental solution, I was proud and eager to share with my homestate friends the dramatic story of how we had saved a linchpin institution of their industry. After recounting the details of our action, I asked for questions. They came in a deluge, along with speeches and arguments. It turned out to be a long luncheon.

It was unfair, my banker friends chorused—inequitable. We had saved Continental just because it was a huge institution, while just two weeks earlier we had let a little bank in Carmel —less than five miles down the road from where we sat—go down the drain. Uninsured depositors and creditors had lost money in the $76-million National Bank of Carmel, unlike those at Continental who were fully protected. Reese Davis, whose County Bank of Santa Cruz took over the Carmel bank, told me that he was serving coffee and doughnuts in the bank lobby, but it fell far short of satisfying the uninsured depositors and the loan customers who were uncertain about their future.

The California bankers were not alone in their wrath and indignation. Over the next few months we received hundreds of letters and calls from individuals and members of Congress. Newspapers, especially those in towns that had recently lost banks, editorialized about the disparity in treatment.

From Oklahoma City, where two years before we had paid off the insured customers of Penn Square leaving uninsured depositors and creditors high and dry, there was uproar, with Senator David Boren and Congressman Mickey Edwards leading the outcry. The two legislators embarked on an unrelenting campaign, including introduction of legislation, but mostly a whirlwind of letters and press releases criticizing FDIC.

After suffering a spate of bank failures, the Banking Committee of the Nebraska Legislature drafted a resolution to sue FDIC on grounds that we had abused our discretionary authority by paying off two failed Nebraska banks.

Father Ronald Battiato, a Catholic priest in Verdigre, Nebraska, helped bring national attention to the epidemic of farmbelt bank failures with a public relations campaign aimed at FDIC. In Minnesota Michael Hatch, the state bank commissioner, threatened to refuse to name FDIC as receiver of a failed bank unless we would agree to make loan advances to farmers and report to him monthly on our activities.

In Washington, D.C., Senator John Melcher of Montana introduced legislation calling upon the Federal Reserve System and FDIC to make available $3.5 billion—the amount of our bad loan purchase in Continental—in direct credit to distressed agricultural lenders. In Oregon former Congressman Charles Porter sued FDIC asking that our assistance authority be declared unconstitutional on the grounds that unbridled use of it could deplete the insurance fund and render us unable to protect depositors up to the $100,000 statutory limit.

Of course, nothing ever came of any of these extraordinary activities, but they do tell you something of the temper of the times. The issue would not subside.

Carter Golembe, the banking guru from Washington, D.C., in a quote to *Bank Letter,* an industry newsletter, crystallized the policy implications that could logically be expected to flow from the Continental precedent:

> If government decides the "national interest" is served by saving big banks, automakers or defense contractors, it should set up a special government agency for the task. Golembe suggested a re-creation of the Depression-era *Reconstruction Finance Corp.* The FDIC's role in the Continental affair, in which it acquired preferred stock, changed management and removed directors, is more akin to the activities of the old RFC than of an insurance agency.[1]

In March of 1985 at the annual convention of the Independent Bankers Association in San Antonio, I found that Continental still dominated the corridor and dinner table conversation nearly a year after the rescue. The question came at me again later in the year at a Chicago conference of the Mid-America Institute for Public Policy Research. My interrogators were banking professors from the leading universities of the nation: Alan Meltzer of Carnegie-Mellon, George Kaufman of Loyola, George Benston of Rochester, Ed Kane of Ohio State, and many others. No bank is too large to fail, these heavy hitters of banking academia told me.

Martin Mayer, a prolific and respected author on banking matters, argued in a *Financier* article in late 1985 that the FDI Act "almost certainly does not permit what the FDIC did" at Continental. He simply did not accept the attorney general's opinion that the transaction was legally structured. Mayer observed correctly that the real difficulty was that foreign holders of debt securities and commercial paper in the holding company would have yanked their $17 billion in Eurodeposits out of the bank if the securities holdings were not fully protected in the bailout. If the holding company was not saved, the bank could not be rescued. The Mayer article points up the fact that the only consensus is that there is a difference of opinion.[2]

Megabanks Play by Different Rules

On June 7, 1985, I addressed the argument head on in a speech before a Boston University School of Law conference. I had been waiting for a scholarly setting to outline my thesis.

I said that, yes, I was comfortable with the "easy" decision to save Continental. It was one of the few megabanks that had to be saved. But I said the nation's banking giants are getting a free ride on their insurance premiums and flaunting capital standards by moving liabilities off their balance sheets. I proposed that Congress accept the fact that a few multinational giants will never be allowed to fail and adjust policies accordingly, specifically to amend the insurance assessment formula to cover both domestic and foreign deposits. The regulators, I said, should address the question of off-book liabilities.* These include future loan commitments, standby letters of credit, and loan sales with recourse. Their use accelerated in 1985 following issuance of new, higher capital standards by the three bank regulators. Shortly before I left the FDIC board early in 1986 we issued proposed rules to address the off-balance sheet problem.

The theme of my remarks was that the major banks of the nation today range virtually unchecked throughout the world, gathering deposits, lending money with abandon, and piling up off-book liabilities—some risky and few capitalized. Further, they have economies of scale and the ability to plaster the nation with credit cards and loan production offices. The list is endless. Small banks that tend to their own very important business of providing the financial life blood to their communities are simply in a different league. Large bank operations today invite some change in procedure and law to address safety, soundness, and fairness considerations that did not exist two generations ago when most of our substantive banking law was enacted.

The problem we had to recognize in dealing with Continental was that the megabank had $30 billion of off-book liabilities in addition to $36 billion in uninsured borrowings, much of it foreign originated. Their total of $66 billion made the additional $3 billion in insured deposits look almost insignificant. Certainly, we could have simply paid off the insured as we had

---

*Items not carried on the bank's balance sheet are unique in that they put the bank to immediate risk although there is no outlay of funds at the time. Since a loss may or may not materialize, the amount of reserves or capital to back up the liability is discretionary with bank management. Most opt not to set aside any substantial amount.

done in sixteen small bank failures in 1984, but scores of large and small institutions—perhaps hundreds—would have been in serious jeopardy if Continental could not have met its commitments. We believed the very fabric of our banking system was at stake.

Our bailout which protected Continental's entire $69 billion structure cost the bank the bargain basement sum of $6.5 million in insurance premiums in 1983. Small banks pay proportionately far more for their insurance and have far less chance of a Continental-style bailout. The disparity in premiums is an outgrowth of the development of international banking. The premium, or assessment, that banks pay to FDIC for insurance is based on domestic deposits only. That seemed reasonable a half century ago when the law was passed; foreign deposits then were an insignificant part of our banking operations. Today that is no longer true. Although the vast majority of banks still have no foreign deposits, the major banks are deeply involved.

Table 14.1 shows the ten banking institutions that led in foreign deposits in 1984. They held as many foreign deposits as domestic.

These holdings are neither assessed nor insured but would be protected in a bailout. The disparity, however, is not limited to the small bank versus large bank issue alone; inequities exist among the big banks themselves. Bank of America, the nation's second largest, paid FDIC nearly $40 million in insurance premiums in 1984 while Citibank, which is significantly larger, paid only $18.5 million. The reason: Citibank had a larger proportion of foreign deposits. An outdated law has been overtaken by time and events.*

It was a landmark speech to a receptive audience. Later, our press office received record numbers of requests for copies of my speech from both here and abroad. I did not flatter myself, however, that it would put the large bank-small bank argument

---

*On September 19, 1986 the Senate voted 63 to 32 to assess foreign deposits at an estimated cost of $310 million to the megabanks. However, the reform died in conference on the budget bill.

TABLE 14.1

The Ten Leaders in Foreign Deposits
(In Billions of Dollars)

	December 31, 1984	
	Domestic Deposits	Foreign Deposits
Citibank	$30	$49
Chase Manhattan	25	34
Bank of America	59	30
Morgan Guaranty	14	26
Manufacturers Hanover	23	22
Bankers Trust Company	9	19
First Chicago	12	14
Chemical Bank	22	13
Continental Illinois	8	8
Security Pacific	24	7
TOTAL	$226	$222

Source: Foreign Deposit Leaders (from Call Report data).

to rest. If anything, it escalated the debate.

On August 5, 1985, the chairman of the House Banking Committee, Congressman Fernand St Germain, who conducted thorough hearings on Continental, issued his own statement on the matter:

> A year has passed and I am still not convinced that a $4.5 billion bailout was all that stood between the safety and soundness of the financial system and the doomsday scenarios of our federal regulators. Indeed, the banking system would have survived, Continental's 2,000 or so correspondent banks—the FDIC could never produce the exact number—would have survived, and the American taxpayer would have survived without another government handout.[3]

The chairman's views accompanied the release of a 202-page committee staff report that was sharply critical of bank management, the Fed, and OCC as supervisors, outside auditors Ernst & Whinney, and the federal insurer—FDIC.[4] The report raised fundamental questions about the bailout provision in the law and the sweeping discretion granted to FDIC to say which banks shall be saved and which shall be let to die.

The FDI law, after all, speaks of insuring depositors, not saving the nation. The law states that all insured depositors up to the $100,000 limit are to be protected, and this is done in every bank failure. However, the law further recognizes the need for an escape valve in the event the impossible would occur—failure of a megabank—and incorporates a provision under which the uninsured can also be protected in spectacularly difficult situations. Clearly, something more than simple insurance is expected of FDIC in these instances. But what? And to what extent?

Seeking a Uniform Policy

Disruptive as it may be to the local community and individuals, the truth is the failure of most of the banks in the United States would have no discernible impact on the FDIC fund or on the economy. Nor in the overwhelming majority of cases can they qualify under the very exclusive test of being "essential" to their communities. Acutely conscious of the inequity long before Continental made it embarrassingly clear to the nation at large, Bill Isaac and I set out to achieve a long-sought goal. As our terms waned in the spring of 1984, we created a uniform policy for handling failed banks, one that would be used for all banks regardless of size. It would be the crowning achievement of our common tenure on the board.

Our motivations differed somewhat. Isaac believed that marketplace discipline was being eroded; increasingly FDIC was selling failed institutions in transactions that protected all depositors and creditors. He believed that large depositors, creditors, and investors generally should not have the safe haven accorded to insured depositors. Rather, they should be left at risk so they would have motivation to look for well-managed banks. The scrutiny of such investors would in turn exert discipline on banks to run prudent operations that would attract investors' funds.

While I agreed with this, my major interest was in protecting the unsophisticated depositor or creditor who would suffer when we had to pay off a bank, rather than selling it. Not all investors with more than $100,000 in a bank are opportunists; they often included a widow who had just sold the family farm or a church that was accruing a building fund. These people suffer along with any fast buck investor types if their banks are paid off. They have to wait months, even years, for any recovery on their claims; then they are paid in depreciated dollars.

Our two separate concerns, coupled with the knowledge that we would face an increase and possibly an avalanche of bank failures in the middle 1980s and beyond, led us to develop and test a new, and hopefully, universal system. It was called a "modified payoff" by some, a "deposit transfer with an advance dividend" by others and worse things by many later on. It was a variation of the direct payoff, but it cut down materially on the delay before the uninsured could receive any portion of the money due them. The universal plan was simple in concept, easy to implement. It was fair. It provided some market discipline and, importantly, a minimum of disruption in banking services in the community. The advance, in particular, meant that more money would be circulating in a community than in a straight payoff that stops access to uninsured funds entirely. We believed we had come up with a bell ringer. No change in the law would be required.

Under the plan, when a bank closed, FDIC would sell the bank premises and its good loans to an existing bank in the vicinity, or to a newly created one, which would act as FDIC agent in paying off the insured deposits. FDIC would take over all the problem loans for liquidation as is done in every bank failure. The stockholders would lose their investment and the management would be on the street. So far, this replicated what FDIC had always done in a payoff. The new aspect was the advance dividend. FDIC's Division of Liquidation would be asked to make a hurry up guesstimate of what it ultimately could expect to collect in the liquidation. This estimate of future recovery would be converted to present-value dollars and be paid as an immediate dividend to the uninsured. FDIC would be conservative, rounding the staff estimate down, and then knocking off 5 points for good measure. An estimate of 52 percent ultimate recovery, for example, would be rounded down to 50 and an advance dividend then declared and paid at 45 percent. If the corporation was too generous with this initial dividend, FDIC would eat the loss. If collections produced enough money for additional dividends, they would be paid as soon as possible.

In the spring of 1984, we instructed the staff to try the experiment in various sections of the country, with failed banks of varying size and with different regulators. Banks that previously would have been a candidate for sale were to be included.

Eight were done. In early May we said, "Stop. Let's analyze what happened in detail." It looked like a winner, but we wanted to study the results in depth. Then, if we decided to adopt the plan permanently, we would give advance notice to all, perhaps a year—Paul Volcker thought it should be two years—that this system would be used in every bank failure.

Our Legal Division could find no possible grounds for challenge. Not only were we performing our insurance function of protecting deposits up to $100,000, we were also giving a bonus, the advance dividend. But all the uninsured in every bank failure would be exposed to some risk and probably some loss.

In the early spring, we worked on possible refinements to the new system and developed plans to achieve the widest possible notice of our intentions. We had tested the advance dividend concept in payoffs as well as sales and found it worked well in either situation. Complaints had been minimal. The plan was looking better every day. We were approaching equality in treatment.

Then came May 17 and Continental. Our planning had covered every contingency, except the failure of one of the small handful of multinational giants. The unthinkable had happened.

Our universal plan initiative aggravated the outcry that ensued in the wake of the Continental rescue. It was responsible for part of the fallout that landed on me during my speech to the California bankers in Monterey; the bank failure in Carmel was one of the eight "universal plan modified payoff" banks.

Before Continental there had been no real complaints about FDIC's handling of bank failures. Some grumbling here and there, a little surprise expressed sometimes, arguments from those who had borrowed money from the bank and objected to paying their debts, but no great outcry. The problem and the crescendo of complaints arose, in my opinion, not because of what we did at Continental, but because of a mixture of timing, emotion, perception, and semantics. Not reality. A closer look at these four factors would be useful to understand the outpouring of unhappiness that often escalated to outrage.

First, the timing. With its attendant confusion and unhappiness, Continental occurred on the heels of our universal plan experiment. So much for timing. It could not have been worse.

Second, emotion. The Continental affair exacerbated a series of open wounds in the large bank-small bank face-off. The smaller banks throughout the nation feel put upon in many ways. They believe the New York giants are out to get them and many believe the American Bankers Association (ABA) does not represent their interest. They feel exposed and vulnerable. Battered by deregulation, threatened by the tentacles of interstate banking, bashed first by the OPEC oil price escalation that led to record high interest rates and then by a full-scale recession, depended on by failing farm and business customers they served for generations—all these factors made the small banks feel cornered. Continental provided an emotional outlet and I understood. And I sympathize. The small banks have constituted the backbone of the nation throughout its history. I join them in fighting what threatens them, that is, excessive deregulation in pursuit of profit and an interstate banking system that ultimately could force thousands of them to the wall.

Third, the perception. With the coverage of Continental on television and in the newspapers to an extent afforded no other economic disaster in memory, the perception was that the government had changed the rules at Continental—at no cost, really, except to FDIC and to the standard of fairness. The perception was and is there.

Finally and most importantly, semantics. We can talk of a purchase and assumption, a sale, without negative connotations. We talk of a bailout and there is an explosion. In practice, the effect of a sale or a bailout is virtually the same. The bank stockholders lose, possibly everything, although in a bailout, the stockholders have a better chance at salvaging something. In either instance the management is out. But all the uninsured, both depositors and creditors, are completely protected. The problem loans are taken over by FDIC for liquidation.

The bottom line effect of what is done in a sale every week of the year paralleled what happened in the Continental bailout. What was bailed out was the name, "Continental," the corporate entity. The one real difference: Continental Illinois Corporation debtholders were protected.

Then what is the problem? It simply is as I said in sentence one of the book: Bailout is a bad word.

The reality is that nearly all large bank failures are handled by bailout, either in name or its functional equivalent. Whether they have been pure bailouts as in Unity, Commonwealth, First Pennsylvania, and Continental; or open-bank assistance like that which prevented the failure of seventeen giant mutual savings banks in the 1980s; or the hundreds of routine closed bank sales with FDIC assistance over the years, the results have been virtually the same: Millions of depositors and creditors have benefited from de facto 100 percent protection.

There are, however, always exceptions. The four exceptions in the top fifty failures were: Golden Pacific National Bank in New York City in 1985, with so many unknown liabilities that we had to pay it off; West Coast Bank in Los Angeles and Heritage Bank in Anaheim, both in 1984 and both part of our universal plan experiment; and, of course, Penn Square in 1982. Of the remainder of the less-than-100-percent protection cases, most are very small banks.

The smaller institutions have a greater chance than larger banks of being paid off because of inherent disadvantages. These three factors significantly complicate the attempt to avoid payoffs.

1. Many of these failures are in tiny, depressed rural communities that are already overbanked, with banking alternatives either in the town or within easy driving distance. Taking over such a failed bank simply is not an attractive investment for anyone. In twenty instances in 1985 we received not a single bid for a small failed bank and in five additional instances the only bid received was too small to meet the cost test under the law.

2. Oftentimes the failures occur in the states which do not allow, or severely restrict, branching. In these situations the purchaser must capitalize a new bank in addition to paying a premium for the deposits in the old one, unless the purchaser lies within the county or wherever the branching restrictions allow. This one factor materially increases the investment that must be made and thus reduces the chances for a sale. In branching states, the purchasing bank can simply open the failed institution as a branch with little and oftentimes no requirement for more capital.

3. All national banks and many state banks are not subject to depositor preference statutes that establish a priority for claims against the failed banks' receivership. FDIC can do a sale with a lesser bid required in a depositor preference situation because

all of the depositors, insured and uninsured, can be made whole without exposing FDIC to other claims.

What can be done to relieve these conditions and perhaps arrest the existing tilt toward payoffs of smaller banks? Very little in the case of the tiny community which may be reduced to only one bank, a cafe, a grocery store, and a gas station. There is hope to do some good in the other two instances, but only if state and federal officials are willing to deal with the political considerations.

For years bankers in some states have successfully fought off efforts to open up the competition by loosening restrictive branch banking rules. The bankers' political clout has not lessened, but their attitude is changing in some states. The most notable example is Kansas, which lost thirteen banks in 1985, including three in small communities which lost their only banks.* In early 1986 the state legislature enacted legislation to moderately loosen branching restrictions. Oklahoma took similar action. Nebraska pretended to act by approving a bill allowing branching, but only in the rare case of a community that had lost its only bank within the past three years. Missouri, Wisconsin, and Minnesota approved regional interstate compacts. Iowa was considering action. The Colorado House narrowly defeated a branching bill, thirty-one to twenty-nine.

All of these efforts are being made grudgingly and are severely limited in scope. After all, life is much easier and more rewarding for a small-town banker who can keep all competition away.

---

*The states that led in 1985 bank failures were: Kansas, thirteen; Nebraska, thirteen; Oklahoma, thirteen; Texas, twelve; Iowa, eleven; Missouri, nine; California, seven; Colorado, six; Minnesota, six; Tennessee, five; Wyoming, five.

The Too Big to Fail Factor

Thus, as we have seen, one of those disquieting facts of life is that at some point a bank is absolutely safe—too big to let fail. In congressional testimony following Continental's bailout, Comptroller Todd Conover hinted that the eleven largest banks in the nation were immune from failure. In my Boston speech, I identified the top two as being absolutely safe. The right number is elusive. But it is there, somewhere. Probably any failing multinational institution that cannot be sold through a purchase and assumption transaction or assisted merger to either a foreign or a domestic suitor would be a bailout candidate. The list of super banks is sure to grow as interstate banking, an inevitable fact of the future, will just as inevitably produce combinations that will dwarf the present giants of the industry.

I predict that no matter what the stated policy, the next time a megabank is on the brink of failure, whoever holds the responsibility will make the same decision that we did in the Continental case. Major banks will continue to be treated differently than small ones. I cannot believe that any future FDIC board would allow the collapse of one of the giants of American banking.

It is time to face up to the reality: Despite our best efforts to find other alternatives, certain banks are too big to let fail and some of the smaller ones cannot be saved. It is a bittersweet conclusion; not a palatable pill, coming as it does at a time when we can expect ever mounting numbers of bank failures—probably well over a hundred a year through the remainder of the decade. But it is a fact of life. Our problem bank list that stood at just over 200 in 1980 soared to over 1,000 by year end 1985, and was still climbing. Table 14.2 includes many banks in the impossible-to-save category. To be absolutely fair, all banks would have 100 percent insurance—or none would. Since we

TABLE 14.2

FDIC Problem Banks

Year End	Number	Percent of Total Banks	Percent of Total Banking Assets
1980	217	1.47	1.39
1981	223	1.51	2.28
1982	369	2.50	2.91
1983	642	4.35	6.40
1984	848	5.75	8.63
1985	1052	7.71	8.23
1986 (July 1)	1306	8.98	12.53

SOURCE: FDIC Division of Bank Supervision.

cannot make the system genuinely fair, the job now is to make it fairer. We need to do what we appropriately can to mitigate the megabank advantage and to extend the benefit of big bank treatment to smaller institutions.

How to achieve this uneasy equation? One hundred percent insurance for all banks has been a common suggestion, particularly with the farm bank failure epidemic that seems destined to continue. But it will not work. If all banks were risk-free they would constitute an open invitation to investors who, having nothing to lose, could dump money into them for use in free-wheeling lending and other speculative endeavors. The slight degree of uncertainty we now have preserves at least a modest amount of market discipline.

The use of negative bids would save many banks, but once started down this road FDIC will find there is no end as others line up to get in on the bonanza.* The announcement of the first negative bid payment in July of 1986 prompted a barrage of requests for similar treatment.

Another approach would be to revive the universal plan or some variation of it. But I know from hard experience that no

---

*In a negative bidding situation proposed acquirers would bid on how much FDIC would pay them to take over the failed banks.

matter what version is adopted and no matter how determined FDIC may be to treat all failed banks the same way, when another megabank crunch comes, the policy will be set aside. However, the modified payoff option is certain to be seriously considered. Its growing list of supporters now includes ABA and the major banks that oppose other solutions, such as paying their fair share for insurance on foreign deposits.

For a time in 1985 it was fashionable to speak of risk-related premiums as a possible equalizer. This theory has its appeal— charge all banks in proportion to the risk each presents to the insurance fund—but the concept has too many flaws. For one thing, the methods of judging risk in a bank are simply not good enough; even if they were, the degree of risk can change from day to day. Secondly, the proposals being considered call for only a token additional charge for risky endeavors. Finally, paying a premium for unacceptable risk would cloak the activity in respectability. Nevertheless, FDIC continues to support this concept.

Rolling back the $100,000 insurance limit to a lesser figure has been proposed in many quarters. I agree this would be desirable, but my futile attempts to stop Congress from approving the $100,000 limit suggest to me that there is no political possibility of a rollback.

Another suggestion requiring legislation would be to permit FDIC to create a conservatorship, or alternatively, a full service Deposit Insurance National Bank, or a "bridge bank" to slowly wind down a failing large bank to manageable proportions or to preserve the franchise value until the bank can be sold. Of all the proposals being discussed, to me this shows the most promise.

New ideas about reaching fairness will surface: On his first day on the job Bill Seidman, the new FDIC chairman, talked to me about the big bank-small bank fairness problem. Addressing the issue will be his first priority, Seidman told me. By year-end 1985 he had a task force at work on the issue, and by the spring of 1986 he had a series of proposals for Congress. At his confirmation hearings Bob Clarke, the new comptroller of the currency, also declared the fairness issue to be his top priority.

In March of 1986 Seidman told the Senate Banking Committee: "The time has come to treat all banks alike until we have a mechanism in place to permit any bank to fail, irrespective of size. But at this point that is just not possible."[5]

Seidman, the first businessman to head FDIC, is aggressively testing a variety of new concepts to determine what will work, not only in handling bank closings but also in the liquidation area. If anyone can come up with new solutions, he will.[6] Seidman and I, both of the same generation, survivors of the Depression, proud of our war records, with similar political backgrounds, worked extremely well together. We both were more interested in results than in posturing or publicity. I was sorely tempted when he asked me to postpone my resignation.*

Conclusions

I have traced the history of four major bailouts in this book, and in the process I have not attempted to sugarcoat the facts or suggest theoretical solutions that I know are not attainable. I do have ideas for improving the system.

My answer to the public policy debate is, "yes," megabanks must and will continue to be bailed out if they are failing, but they should pay a price for this protection, and they should be handled so that management and stockholders suffer, as nearly as possible, the same fate as in an outright failure. In order to

---

*Shortly after my resignation I was succeeded by an old friend, C. C. Hope, a retired banker and former president of the ABA.

equalize the cost of insurance protection, the FDIC assessment should be levied on all deposits, foreign and domestic. It is not necessary that the premium raise more money, only that it be made more equitable. Therefore, the general rate should be lowered. The result would be that small banks with only domestic deposits would pay less and large banks with foreign deposits more. FDIC revenue would remain the same.

Making the interstate sale authority permanent is an essential tool that must be retained. It would be improved by lowering the $500 million trigger figure, and also by authorizing the acquisition of bank holding companies where a bank representing a significant share of the holding company assets has failed.* Proposals to include failing as well as failed banks on the eligible list would open up the bailout process to intolerable political pressures.

If adjustments are then made in state and federal laws to provide depositor preference for all banks, and in state laws to permit branching for failed institutions, we would further narrow the disparity of treatment between large banks and small.

Every bank would contribute: The big banks would pay a fairer share for their insurance protection; smaller institutions would give up some of their cherished protection against competition.

Thus, the overwhelming majority—nearly all—depositors and creditors would be protected in a failing bank situation. True, there would still be a few exceptions, but they would be down to the irreducible minimum. We would have de facto 100 percent insurance protection for nearly all banks, the concept that the Congress has objected to so strenuously in the past. My preference is different; in fact I think $100,000 insurance is too

---

*The permanent interstate bill, held hostage for months as it was given a series of short-term extensions, was finally killed in the closing hours of the 99th Congress, the victim of disputes over unrelated banking legislation. It will most certainly be revived in 1987: it is an essential bill that some want to use as a vehicle to close the nonbank loophole; some want to use as a piggyback for expanded bank powers.

high. However, as long as the megabanks receive 100 percent protection we cannot in good conscience deny it to the smaller ones.

A final word: FDIC must retain the "essential" bailout authority. It is a vital tool, and despite the outcry it has been used sparingly, fairly, and successfully. I would not want to be faced with a megabank failure without this ultimate fallback at hand. This book demonstrates the bailouts came only as a last resort and when the national interest clearly is served by its use. Changing the law to bring the administration or Congress into the process would destroy its utility.

If implemented with compassion and care, and if understood by the public, this program will do much to alleviate the present discontent. Every bank failure is a tragedy; nothing will change that.

Although the improvements I recommend are major, I do not want to leave the impression that the deposit insurance system is seriously flawed. Far from it. The system is still strong, still the bedrock of our nation's banking network. The FDIC sticker on a bank's door still means what it says. Insured depositors can still sleep easily and because of that a lot of bankers can sleep easily, too. I leave office with gratitude—to the presidents, congressmen, and governors who have made it possible for me to fulfill this role in life—to my colleagues on the FDIC board and those with the other financial regulators—and to the dedicated cadre of men and women who carry out the government's role. I acknowledge particularly the fine career staff at FDIC whose ability and selflessness I have witnessed personally countless times during the years I have had the pleasure to serve with them.

These are interesting, challenging, and exciting times in the financial services industry, and in a measure I am sorry I will no longer be a part of it. But there is a time to depart, and I do so with pride in FDIC's past achievements and with confidence in this agency's ability to meet the challenge of the future. Good luck to those who follow.

APPENDIX

One Hundred Largest Banks Requiring FDIC Assistance, January 1, 1934,
through December 31, 1985
(in $000,000)

		Assets	Year	Type of Assistance*
1.	Continental Illinois National, Bank, Chicago, Illinois	$41,000	1984	1
2.	First Pennsylvania Bank, Philadelphia, Pennsylvania	8,400	1980	1
3.	Bowery Savings Bank,† New York, New York	5,279	1985	2
4.	Franklin National Bank, New York, New York	3,656	1974	3
5.	New York Bank for Savings,† New York, New York	3,403	1982	2
6.	Dry Dock Savings Bank,† New York, New York	2,500	1983	2
7.	Greenwich Savings Bank,† New York, New York	2,500	1981	2
8.	Western Saving Fund Society† of Philadelphia, Haverford, Pennsylvania	2,113	1982	2
9.	First National Bank of Midland, Texas	1,404	1983	3
10.	Union Dime Saving Bank,† New York, New York	1,400	1981	2
11.	United States National Bank, San Diego, California	1,265	1973	3
12.	Bank of the Commonwealth, Detroit, Michigan	1,260	1972	1
13.	Western New York Savings Bank,† Buffalo, New York	1,022	1982	2

*See key at end of the appendix.
†Mutual Savings Banks which would have failed without an FDIC assisted merger.

(Continued)

		Assets	Year	Type of Assistance
14.	Farmers & Mechanics Savings† Bank, Minneapolis, Minnesota	$980	1982	2
15.	Central Savings Bank,† New York, New York	900	1981	2
16.	United Mutual Savings Bank,† New York, New York	833	1982	2
17.	United American Bank, Knoxville, Tennessee	778	1983	3
18.	Banco Credito y Ahorro Ponceno, Ponce, Puerto Rico	712	1978	3
19.	Fidelity Mutual Savings Bank,† Spokane, Washington	689	1982	2
20.	United States Savings Bank† of Newark, New Jersey	675	1982	2
21.	Penn Square Bank, Oklahoma City, Oklahoma	517	1982	4a
22.	Orange Savings Bank,† Livingston, New Jersey	515	1984	2
23.	Abilene National Bank, Abilene, Texas	446	1982	2
24.	Home Savings Bank,† White Plains, New York	422	1985	2
25.	Hamilton National Bank, Chattanooga, Tennessee	412	1976	3
26.	Girod Trust Company, San Juan, Puerto Rico	399	1984	3
27.	Farmers Bank of the State of Delaware, Dover, Delaware	360	1976	1
28.	American City Bank, Los Angeles, California	272	1983	3
29.	Metropolitan Bank and Trust, Tampa, Florida	261	1982	3
30.	Oregon Mutual Savings Bank,† Portland, Oregon	260	1983	2
31.	City & County Bank of Knox County, Knoxville, Tennessee	244	1983	3

(Continued)

		Assets	Year	Type of Assistance
32.	Mississippi Bank, Jackson, Mississippi	$227	1984	3
33.	The Drovers' National Bank of Chicago, Illinois	227	1978	3
34.	American City Bank and Trust, New York, New York	224	1976	3
35.	Moncor Bank, N.A., Hobbs, New Mexico	205	1985	3
36.	Banco Economias, San German, Puerto Rico	190	1977	3
37.	West Coast Bank, Los Angeles, California	190	1984	4b
38.	International City Bank & Trust Co., New Orleans, Louisiana	176	1976	3
39.	First National Bank of St. Joseph, Missouri	174	1985	3
40.	Golden Pacific National Bank, New York, New York	166	1985	4c
41.	Heritage Bank, Anaheim, California	158	1984	4b
42.	First Peoples Bank of Washington County, Johnson City, Tennessee	153	1983	3
43.	Oklahoma National Bank & Trust Co., Oklahoma City, Oklahoma	150	1982	2
44.	American City Bank & Trust Co., N.A., Milwaukee, Wisconsin	148	1975	3
45.	American Bank & Trust, Orangeburg, South Carolina	147	1974	3
46.	City & County Bank of Anderson County, Lake City, Tennessee	142	1983	3
47.	United American Bank in Hamilton County, Chattanooga, Tennessee	135	1983	3
48.	Auburn Savings Bank,† Auburn, New York	130	1983	2
49.	First National Bank of Oak Lawn, Illinois	120	1983	3

(Continued)

		Assets	Year	Type of Assistance
50.	United Southern Bank of Nashville, Tennessee	$115	1983	3
51.	Public Bank, Detroit, Michigan	110	1966	3
52.	Birmingham-Bloomfield Bank, Birmingham, Michigan	110	1971	3
53.	Bank of Oregon, Woodburn, Oregon	106	1985	2
54.	Northern Ohio Bank, Cleveland, Ohio	104	1975	3
55.	First Continental Bank & Trust Co. of Del City, Oklahoma	103	1984	4d
56.	The Citizens Bank, Ogden, Utah	91	1985	3
57.	East Texas Bank & Trust Co., Longview, Texas	90	1984	3
58.	Commercial Bank, Andalusia, Alabama	89	1985	2
59.	First City Bank, N.A., Oklahoma City, Oklahoma	87	1985	3
60.	Mission State Bank & Trust Co., Mission, Kansas	83	1980	3
61.	Sharpstown State Bank, Houston, Texas	79	1971	4e
62.	National Bank of Odessa, Texas	78	1983	3
63.	National Bank of Carmel, California	76	1984	4d
64.	State Bank of Clearing, Chicago, Illinois	74	1975	3
65.	National Bank & Trust Co. of Traverse City, Michigan	74	1984	3
66.	Golden Valley Bank, Turlock, California	72	1985	3
67.	Shelby National Bank of Shelbyville, Indiana	67	1984	3
68.	The Bank of Commerce, Chanute, Kansas	65	1985	3
69.	Planters Trust & Savings Bank of Opelousas, Louisiana	64	1984	3

(Continued)

		Assets	Year	Type of Assistance
70.	First State Bank of Northern California, San Leandro, California	$56	1976	3
71.	Mechanics Savings Bank,† Elmira, New York	55	1982	2
72.	First National Bank in Humboldt, Iowa	54	1982	3
73.	San Francisco National Bank, San Francisco, California	54	1965	4e
74.	Security State Bank, Weatherford, Oklahoma	52	1984	3
75.	Northwest Bank, White Settlement, Texas	50	1985	3
76.	Dayton Bank & Trust Co., Dayton, Tennessee	49	1984	4d
77.	Newport Harbor National Bank, Newport Beach, California	48	1983	3
78.	Seminole State National Bank, Seminole, Texas	47	1984	4d
79.	Capistrano National Bank, San Juan Capistrano, California	47	1985	3
80.	Farmers State Bank, St. Joseph, Missouri	47	1985	3
81.	First Commerce Bank of Hawkins County, Rogersville, Tennessee	47	1983	3
82.	Farmers Bank and Trust Co., Winchester, Tennessee	46	1984	3
83.	The Des Plaines Bank, Des Plaines, Illinois	46	1981	4e
84.	East Gadsden Bank, Gadsden, Alabama	46	1980	3
85.	Security National Bank of Lubbock, Texas	46	1984	4d
86.	Northshore Bank, Houston, Texas	44	1985	3
87.	Fidelity Bank of Denver, Denver, Colorado	44	1985	3

(Continued)

		Assets	Year	Type of Assistance
88.	Community Bank, Hartford, South Dakota	$42	1983	3
89.	First National Bank of Jacksonville, Alabama	42	1985	3
90.	Republic Bank of Kansas City, Missouri	41	1984	4c
91.	City & County Bank of Roane County, Kingston, Tennessee	40	1983	3
92.	Hamilton Bank & Trust Co., Atlanta, Georgia	40	1976	3
93.	City & County Bank of Campbell County, Jellico, Tennessee	40	1980	3
94.	Swift County Bank, Benson, Minnesota	39	1985	3
95.	Garden Grove Community Bank, Garden Grove, California	39	1984	3
96.	Cherokee County Bank Centre, Alabama	38	1984	3
97.	First Enterprise Bank, Oakland, California	37	1985	4e
98.	West Valley Bank, Woodland Hills, California	37	1985	3
99.	Citizens State Bank of Fulda, Minnesota	37	1985	4c
100.	Halifax National Bank of Port Orange, Florida	36	1985	3

1:   Bailout
2:   Open-bank assisted merger
3:   Closed-bank assisted merger
4a: Payoff—Deposit Insurance National Bank
4b: Payoff—Partial cash advance to the uninsured
4c: Payoff—Deposit transfer
4d: Payoff—Deposit transfer with partial cash advance to the uninsured
4e: Payoff—Straight payoff

NOTES

(Except for newspapers, books, congressional documents,
FDIC Board minutes, and FDIC news releases,
all materials cited in the following notes are
from author's personal files.)

Chapter I / Bailout

1. *Congressional Record,* 26 July 1984, H7957.
2. FDIC personnel changed as we went from bailout to bailout, but some key figures reappear in different positions.

The FDIC Boards

Bailout	Chairman	Director	Comptroller
Unity	Wille	Sprague	N/A*
Commonwealth	Wille	Sprague	DeShazo
First Pennsylvania	Sprague	Isaac	Heimann
Continental	Isaac	Sprague	Conover

*Comptroller Camp did not vote.

The FDIC Division Directors

John L. Flannery	Thomas Brooks
Edward J. Roddy	Margaret L. Egginton
Robert V. Shumway	John J. Slocum
William E. Murane	James A. Davis
Frank L. Skillern, Jr.	Edward F. Phelps, Jr.
David Stickerod	Stanley J. Poling

Bailout	Bank Supervision	General Counsel	Liquidation	Administration
Unity	Flannery	Murane	Slocum	Phelps
Commonwealth	Roddy	Murane	Slocum	Phelps
First Pennsylvania	Shumway	Skillern	Stickerod†	Davis
Continental	Shumway	Brooks*	Davis	Poling

*Brooks was general counsel for the May assistance; Egginton was acting counsel in July 1984.
†Stickerod was acting head of this division.

3. To complete the record we note here two additional 13(c) essentiality cases that are not relevant to the story of the four commercial bank long-term bailouts.

In 1974 the $150-million American Bank and Trust Company of Orangeburg, South Carolina, was declared "essential" and was provided a four-day, $10-million FDIC liquidity loan that later was extended for a few additional days. Less than three weeks after the bank was declared essential, the loan was called and the bank was closed and sold. How essential could it be? Obviously, the bank was not considered essential; the finding was simply a device to buy time to find a purchaser.

In 1976 the $426-million Farmers Bank of the State of Delaware was declared essential and FDIC purchased $40 million of classified and charged off assets —essentially bad loans. The State of Delaware owned 49 percent of the bank stock and by state law the bank was the sole depositor for state funds. Clearly, the essentiality finding went to the state, not the bank, and no one would argue that Delaware is not an essential state.

These two cases, plus four described in the book, constitute the totality of the essentiality findings in FDIC history.

Chapter II / The Legal Framework

1. *Blueprint for Reform: The Report of the Task Group on Regulation of Financial Services* (Washington, D.C.: U.S. Government Printing Office, 1984).

2. The false starts were frustrating, particularly with the $778 million United American Bank of Knoxville, Tennessee, which failed February 14, 1983, just three years to the day before Park Bank. We sold UAB out-of-state and then had to rescind our action. Negotiating with three Tennessee groups, we had tried to craft a sale without closing the bank. These efforts failed and at 5 o'clock Sunday, February 13, bids were accepted in our Atlanta office from eight groups. The high bid, at $65 million, was from Citizens and Southern of Georgia, an out-of-state institution. Under the ground rules of the law, rebidding was called for with the eligibles to include anyone whose bid was within 15 percent of the estimated cost to the FDIC. Three were eligible.

We told our Regional Director Pete Burr to call for rebids at 7:15 P.M. Citizens and Southern upped its offer to $70 million; First Tennessee Corporation, with a first bid estimated to be about $57 million but which did not conform to our bidding specifications, offered to add $10.5 million to the pot, but would not change to a conforming bid. First Union Bank of Charlotte, North Carolina, stood pat with its $51.1 million offer.

Our board reconvened at 7:50 P.M. At this point Bill Isaac said it was a close call but he wanted to sell the bank to First Tennessee. He figured its bid was high because of some of its provisions and our senior staff thought so also, but they were divided on which way to go. Isaac had been negotiating with the chairman, Ron Terry, throughout the preceding day and night, and the bid tracked the negotiations. Acting Comptroller Joe Selby and I believed First Tennessee's bid was impossible to price and, in any event, we should follow the procedures and make the award to the high bidder who followed the ground rules. We were concerned with the precedent we were setting.

Finally, at 8:30 we voted unanimously to go with Citizens and Southern. The sale did not take. Within minutes, the Comptroller advised us that the Citizens and Southern plans for capitalization were inadequate. We reconvened at 8:50 and again at 9:40, and finally made the sale to First Tennessee. It was the longest, most contentious board meeting in all my service at FDIC.

The purchase proved very costly to First Tennessee, which acquired a lot of bad loans in the transaction, and FDIC sweetened the contract on several occasions to the tune of $35 million to reduce the pressure. In February of 1986 we set a reserve for our own loss on the United American deal of $492.9 million.

This sorry experience led us to adopt stern ground rules that were followed successfully in the Park Bank sale. Hopefully, the rules will not be tampered with in the future.

Three other Garn-St Germain sales were attempted but not implemented. In the spring of 1983, we planned to merge five smaller Tennessee institutions and offer the surviving bank for out-of-state sale, but Tennessee Governor Lamar Alexander aborted the plan at the last minute so the five were sold separately in a mass bidding contest on May 27. The local banks got bargains at FDIC expense. On October 14, 1983, the First National Bank of Midland, Texas, a $1.4 billion institution, was offered for out-of-state sale. The winning bidder by a wide margin at $51.1 million was Republic Bank Corp. of Dallas. Still not an out-of-state sale. During the spring and summer of 1984, the Garn-St Germain provisions were used to shop Continental Illinois nationwide, but ultimately we resorted to a bailout.

3.   The leading case on agency discretion is *Dalehite* v. *United States,* a 1953 Supreme Court ruling which stated:
The discretion protected . . . is . . . the discretion of the executive or the administrator to act according to one's judgment of the best course. . . . Where there is room for a policy judgment in decision, there is discretion.
In another Supreme Court case, *U.S.* v. *Shaughnessy,* in 1954 the court provided the following judicial view of agency discretion:
    and if the word "discretion" means anything in a statutory or administrative grant of power, it means that the recipient must exercise his authority according to his own understanding and conscience.

Chapter III / Unity Bank

1.   William E. Murane, memorandum to Frank Wille and Irvine H. Sprague, 27 April 1971.

2.   William E. Murane, memorandum to the Board of Directors re Unity Bank and Trust Company, Roxbury, Massachusetts—Proposed Assistance under Section 13(c) of the Federal Deposit Insurance Act, 28 June 1971; William E. Murane, memorandum to Frank Wille, Irvine Sprague, et al., 30 June 1971.

3.   Board of Directors of the Federal Deposit Insurance Corporation, minutes, 22 July 1970.

4.   "FDIC, Mass. Bank Group to Lend $2 Million in Capital to Bolster Black-Owned Unity B&T," *American Banker,* 28 July 1971.

5. H. Erich Heinemann, "Black Banking, Participation of F.D.I.C. in Assisting Boston Institution Raises Questions," *New York Times,* 4 August 1971.

6. FDIC News Release PR-106, 27 December 1976. (At that time Bob Barnett was FDIC chairman, George LeMaistre director, and Bob Bloom acting controller.)

Chapter IV / Bank of the Commonwealth

1. Committee on Banking and Currency, House of Representatives, Hearings on H.R. 6778, Bank Holding Company Act Amendments, 1 May 1969, 91st Congress, First Session, 1969, p. 758.

2. COMAC Presentation, undated, pp. 3 and 5.

3. Jack E. Edgington and Burton L. Raimi, memorandum to Frank Wille and Irvine H. Sprague, Subject: Bank of the Commonwealth, 24 March 1972, pp. 14–15.

4. Norman Pearlstine, "Chase Takes Over Bank of Commonwealth From Parsons After Default on Loans," *Wall Street Journal,* 15 January 1971.

5. John L. Flannery, Memorandum to the files, 29 March 1971.

6. Presentation Concerning the Bank of the Commonwealth to the Federal Regulatory Authorities, John A. Hooper, 30 June 1971.

7. Alan Miller, memorandum to Director Sprague, Subject: Bank of the Commonwealth, 27 September 1971.

8. Bank of the Commonwealth, Proxy Statement for Annual Meeting of Shareholders, 19 January 1972, pp. 7–14.

9. FDIC News Release PR–6, 18 January 1972.

10. Proxy Statement, pp. 11 and 14.

Chapter V / First Pennsylvania Bank

1. McCarthy, Ried, Crisanti & Maffei, Inc., Credit Critique-Banking: Report on First Pennsylvania Corporation and First Pennsylvania Bank, N.A., 21 March 1980.

2. "First Pennsylvania Is Finding It Harder to Fight Rumors, Erosion of Confidence," *Wall Street Journal,* 24 March 1980.

3. Document entitled First Pennsylvania Corporation, First Pennsylvania Bank, N.A., 2 April 1980.

4. Frank L. Skillern, Jr., draft memorandum to Irvine H. Sprague, Subject: Analysis of the FDIC's Authority Under Section 13(c) of the Act, 11 April 1980; Frank L. Skillern, Jr., memorandum to The Board of Directors, Subject: First Pennsylvania Bank, N.A., Bala-Cynwyd, Pennsylvania, Application for Assistance under Section 13(c), 28 April 1980.

5. Comptroller of the Currency, Federal Deposit Insurance Corporation, and Federal Reserve Board, joint news release: PR-42-80, 28 April 1980.

6. "The Bankers Magazine Interview: John G. Heimann," *Bankers Magazine,* January-February 1986, p. 11.

7. Shirley Hobbs Scheibla, "Untold Philadelphia Story, First Pennsylvania: No Bottom Line," *Barron's,* 13 October 1980, p. 27.

8. *Philip Zinman, Individually and on behalf of all Others Similarly Situated* v. *Federal Deposit Insurance Corporation,* Civil Action No. 80-3281, U.S. District Court for the Eastern District of Pennsylvania (Memorandum and Order Entered 1 July 1983).

Chapter VI / Penn Square

1. Philip L. Zweig, "Oklahoma Bank Strips Oil/Gas Unit Head of Lending Power," *American Banker,* 1 July 1982.
2. The Supreme Court six to three ruling that letters of credit are not deposits overturned a 10th U.S. Circuit Court of Appeals finding in *FDIC v. Philadelphia Gear Corp.* The case involved a standby letter of credit issued by Penn Square on behalf of Orion Manufacturing Corp. to Philadelphia Gear Corp., which tried to collect. FDIC refused to pay. If the landmark case had gone the other way FDIC for the first time would have had to insure about $120 billion worth of outstanding credit, and banks would have been liable for about $100 million in additional annual insurance assessments.

Chapter VII / Seafirst

1. John P. Forde, "Cooley Named to Top Posts at Seafirst," *American Banker,* 23 December 1982.
2. "Seafirst Willing to Consider an Outright Purchase Offer," *American Banker,* 22 April 1983.
3. Teresa Carson and Michael J. Parks, "Bank-America to Buy Seafirst Corp. in Largest US Bank Merger; Washington Governor Signs Measure Allowing Interstate Deal," *American Banker,* 26 April 1983. (The "Chronology of Events Leading up to the Big Deal" accompanying this article was used to coordinate the private negotiations with the alternative FDIC-assisted solution being developed simultaneously within the agency.)

Chapter VIII / Seven Days in May

1. Sanford Rose, "Will Success Spoil Continental Illinois?" *American Banker,* 25 August 1981.
2. Laurel Sorenson, "In the Highflying Field of Energy Finance, Continental Illinois Bank Is Striking It Rich," *Wall Street Journal,* 18 September 1981; Paul A. Gigot, "On the Offensive, Behind Homely Image Of Continental Illinois Is an Aggressive Bank; Its Risks Sometimes Backfire, But Its Cut-Rate Lending Has Yielded Major Gains; Orders for 'Harper's Army,'" *Wall Street Journal,* 15 October 1981.
3. R. C. Longworth and Bill Barnhart, "How panic followed the sun in debacle at Chicago bank," *Chicago Tribune,* 27 May 1984.

4. "U.S. Throws Full Support Behind Continental Illinois in Unprecedented Bailout to Prevent Banking Crisis," *Wall Street Journal*, 18 May 1984; Peter T. Kilborn, Winston Williams, and Robert A. Bennett, "Harrowing Week-Long Race to Rescue Continental Bank," *New York Times*, 21 May 1984.

5. Jeff Bailey and Jeffrey Zaslow, "Continental Illinois Securities Plummet Amid Rumors Firm's Plight Is Worsening," *Wall Street Journal*, 11 May 1984; Winston Williams, "LaSalle St. Supporting Continental," *New York Times*, 17 May 1984.

6. Staff Report to the Subcommittee on Financial Institutions and Supervision, Regulation and Insurance, 99th Congress, First Session, 1985, Committee Print 99–4.

7. "Continental Illinois Gets Rescue Package Of $4.5 Billion Record Bailout Attempt," *Wall Street Journal*, 15 May 1984.

8. Office of the Comptroller of the Currency, Federal Deposit Insurance Corporation, Federal Reserve Board, joint news release, 17 May 1984:

The Federal Deposit Insurance Corporation, the Federal Reserve Board and the Office of the Comptroller of the Currency, together with a group of leading banks, have assembled a comprehensive financial assistance program for the Continental Illinois National Bank and Trust Company. The program will provide assurance of the capital resources, the liquidity, and the time needed to resolve in an orderly and permanent way the bank's problems.

Under the program, the FDIC, together with a group of commercial banks, will provide a total of $2.0 billion in capital to the bank in the form of subordinated notes. This capital will be available for the period necessary to enhance the bank's permanent capital, by merger or otherwise. The subordinated notes bear interest at a rate equal to the one-year Treasury bill rate plus 100 basis points. The FDIC Board of Directors voted to grant assistance pursuant to Section 13(c)(2) of the FDI Act.

In view of all the circumstances surrounding Continental Illinois Bank, the FDIC provides assurance that, in any arrangements that may be necessary to achieve a permanent solution, all depositors and other general creditors of the bank will be fully protected and service to the bank's customers will not be interrupted.

To further augment the financial resources available to Continental Illinois Bank, a group of 24 major U.S. banks has agreed to provide over $5.3 billion in funding on an unsecured basis throughout the period during which a permanent solution is developed. This agreement was arranged between the Continental Illinois Bank and the group of commercial banks, for which the Morgan Guaranty Trust Company of New York is agent.

The financial assistance program is designed to enable the Continental Illinois Bank to resume normal patterns of funding in the market to meet its liquidity requirements and to operate normally in other respects. As a part of the overall program, and in accordance with customary arrangements, the Federal Reserve is prepared to meet any extraordinary liquidity requirements of the Continental Illinois Bank during this period.

The Office of the Comptroller of the Currency—the primary supervisor for the Continental Illinois Bank—has worked closely with the FDIC and the Federal Reserve in connection with the structuring of this program. In the Comptroller's opinion the bank's difficulties will be resolved in an orderly way with the capital and liquidity support provided in this program.

Chapter IX / May to July

1. Merrill Brown and James L. Rowe, Jr., "N.Y. Bank, Markets Hit by Rumors," *Washington Post,* 25 May 1984.

2. "Confidence Game: Large Banks Are Hit by New Set of Rumors, and Stock Prices Fall; Latin-Loan Worries Affect Manufacturers Hanover; Bonds and Dollar Decline," *Wall Street Journal,* 25 May 1984; Gary Klott, "Worries on Banks Jar Markets; Rumors About Hanover Trust Called Untrue," *New York Times,* 25 May 1984.

3. "Manufacturers Hanover," *Wall Street Journal,* 31 May 1984.

4. Richard Ringer, " 'Continental Divide' Approach Gains Favor, Illinois Officials Say," *American Banker,* 4 June 1984.

5. Robert A. Bennett, "Continental Loses Chicago Suitor," *New York Times,* 12 June 1984.

6. James L. Rowe, Jr., "Another Continental Suitor Drops Out," *Washington Post,* 13 June 1984.

7. Richard Ringer, "Thompson Signs Takeover Bill for Continental," *American Banker,* 27 June 1984.

8. Jeff Bailey and G. Christian Hill, "Continental Illinois Had 2nd-Period Loss of $1.16 Billion, Sees Possible Profit by '85," *Wall Street Journal,* 6 August 1984.

Chapter X / The Treasury Tiger

1. U.S. Department of Justice, Office of Legal Counsel, Memorandum for the Honorable Donald T. Regan, Secretary of the Treasury re proposed FDIC Assistance Package to Continental Illinois, 24 July 1984.

2. Wm. Roger Watson, Memorandum to the Board of Directors (FDIC) re Proposed Assistance transaction involving Continental Illinois Corporation (CIC) and Continental Illinois National Bank and Trust Company (CINB), 25 July 1984.

3. Kenneth B. Noble, "Continental Plan Set Despite Regan," *New York Times,* 26 July 1984.

4. Donald T. Regan, Memorandum for Messrs. Conover, Isaac and Volcker re: Continental Illinois Corporation Assistance Package, 25 July 1984.

5. Michael Bradfield, memorandum re Assistance Authority of the FDIC, 26 July 1984.

6. Margery Waxman, memorandum for Margaret L. Egginton, Subject: Continental Assistance Package, 25 July 1984.

Chapter XI / Choosing the Management

1. Board of Directors of the Federal Deposit Insurance Corporation, transcript of the meeting 26 July 1984.

2. "Reagan Calls Rescue of Bank No Bailout," *New York Times*, 29 July 1984.

3. James L. Rowe, Jr., "FDIC Hires Adviser on sale of Bank Stock," *Washington Post*, 22 May 1986.

Chapter XII / Liquidation

1. The ten Continental directors removed at FDIC direction were: James F. Beré, chairman and chief executive of Borg-Warner Corp.; William B. Johnson, chairman and chief executive of IC Industries, Inc.; Jewel S. Lafontant, a Chicago lawyer; Vernon R. Loucks, Jr., president and chief executive of Baxter Travenol Laboratories Inc.; Robert H. Malott, chairman and chief executive of FMC Corp.; Marvin G. Mitchell, retired chairman of CBI Industries Inc.; Paul J. Rizzo, vice-chairman of International Business Machines Corp.; Thomas H. Roberts, Jr., chairman and chief executive of DeKalb AgResearch Inc.; Blaine J. Yarrington, a retired executive vice-president of Indiana Standard Oil Company (Indiana); and Raymond C. Baumhart, president of Loyola University of Chicago.

2. Bill Neikirk and William Gruber, "10 Continental Directors Face Ouster," *Chicago Tribune*, 2 December 1984.

3. "Continental Director Beré Calls Leak a 'Cheap Shot,' " *Chicago Sun-Times*, 16 December 1984.

4. Steven Greenhouse, "The Humbling of Continental's Board," *New York Times*, 8 December 1984.

5. William Gruber, "Many Question FDIC's Purge of Continental," *Chicago Tribune*, 9 December 1984; Greenhouse, "The Humbling of Continental's Board."

6. "Viewpoint, Cont'l Directors Are to Blame," *Crain's Chicago Business*, 10 December 1984.

7. "Rolling Heads, Continental Directors Are Fired," *Time*, 17 December 1984, p. 69.

8. William Gruber, "Loss May Wipe Out Continental Holding; Bank's Loans Likely to Cost FDIC $800 Million," *Chicago Tribune*, 10 May 1985; Proxy statement of Continental Illinois Holding Company for 29 May 1985, annual meeting.

9. Continental Illinois Holding Corporation news release, 21 February 1986.

10. "U.S. Paid $50 Million to Private Firms," article in *The National Law Journal*, 4 February 1985.

11. Murphy, on reading the draft of this chapter, said he should get credit for the computerized system. Skillern told me he didn't care who got credit, so long as the system worked.

Lyndon Johnson should get the credit. Some time after Johnson ended his term as president, he invited me to his ranch on the Burton Alleys. It was a relaxed day—just the President, Mrs. Johnson, Lynda, and Lynda's baby daughter. After lunch, the President took me on a drive over the ranch, sometimes at speeds that caught my attention. We reminisced about many people and events. At one point, he told me that he had sent Joe Barr over to the FDIC as chairman in the 1960s to bring the FDIC into the Twentieth century, including installation of computers by Monday morning. This was on a Friday afternoon. Barr installed the computers, not on Monday morning, but expeditiously. So let's give Lyndon Johnson the credit.

Chapter XIII / Lessons Learned

1. Jesse H. Jones with Edward Angly, *Fifty Billion Dollars* (New York: Macmillan Company, 1951), p. 47.
2. Sanford Rose, "Random Thoughts," *American Banker,* 13 August 1985.
3. Hearings before the Committee on Banking, Housing, and Urban Affairs, United States Senate, September 16 and 19, 1977: incorporating *Study on Federal Regulation, Vol. V: Regulatory Reorganization,* from the Committee on Governmental Affairs, United States Senate, December 1977.
4. Arthur F. Burns, "Maintaining the Soundness of our Banking System," address to the American Bankers Association, Honolulu, Hawaii, 21 October 1974. Collected in *Reflections of an Economic Policy Maker: Speeches and Congressional Statements, 1969–78,* p. 365.
5. *Blueprint for Reform: The Report of the Task Group on Regulation of Financial Services* (Washington, D.C.: U.S. Government Printing Office, 1984).

Chapter XIV / The Public Policy Debate

1. "Rescue Operations Should Be Removed from FDIC," *Bank Letter,* 25 February 1985.
2. Martin Mayer, "Deposit Insurance Weakness Worst of All Banking Problems," *Financier,* August 1985, p. 64.
3. U.S. House of Representatives, Committee on Banking, Finance and Urban Affairs, 99th Congress, News Release For Release Mon, A.M.'s 5 August 1985.
4. House Committee on Banking, Finance and Urban Affairs, Continental Illinois National Bank: Report on an Inquiry into its Federal Supervision and Assistance, Staff report to the Subcommittee on Financial Institutions Supervision, Regulation and Insurance, 99th Congress, First Session, 1985, Committee Print 99-4, p. 185. The House Banking Committee Report summarized:

It may be that in its attempt to provide wide latitude and give greater flexibility to the regulators in such emergency situations, Congress may have sacrificed, to some degree, the *accountability* that such regulators should be called upon to provide. Admittedly, the Congress finds itself on the horns of a dilemma: It is absolutely necessary that the banking regulators be given certain powers (in some instances, extraordinary) not given to other governmental agencies, to provide immediate and broad assistance to troubled financial institutions, which if not provided, could have far-reaching and disastrous consequences for our national economy. However, these powers must in some way be offset by or balanced with equally necessary precautions which absolutely insure that such regulators are accountable for their actions and are subject to intensive Congressional review. There are no adequate procedures, at present, to accomplish this necessity. Hence, the decisions by the regulators to provide 13(c) assistance, to declare that the CINB was essential to provide the banking needs in the *community* in this case, and to do so without having done, apparently, a comprehensive cost analysis or evaluation, and without having to confer with any other authorities, raises substantial questions as to whether the regulators should continue to have such absolute authorities and whether such a momentous decision should be left to their "sole discretion." Perhaps, Section 13(c) should be left alone. Perhaps not. At the minimum, however, 13(c) should receive a thorough Congressional review. The issue is whether, in light of Continental, Section 13(c) assistance as it is now written is the most appropriate means to handle all sizes of troubled banks, whether the remedies provided therein are appropriate, whether they.truly serve the public interest, and whether, in its desire to provide flexibility, Congress may have also, inadvertently, relieved the regulators of accountability for their actions, or whether, unwittingly, it may have cast its blessings on banks "too big to fail," to the prejudice and detriment of smaller institutions.

5. "FDIC Set to Widen Aid Policy," *New York Times*, 14 March, 1986.

6. On April 3, my last day in office, we used a new approach for the first time, granting a $1.7 million six-year loan to the Talmage State Bank, Talmage, Kansas, a $10-million institution serving a farmer community of one hundred persons. The assistance was given on a finding that the bank was in danger of closing and keeping it open would be less costly to FDIC than a payoff.

On July 14 still another new approach was used as FDIC for the first time paid a negative premium; $73.3 million to First Interstate Bancorp of Los Angeles to take over the failed $1.6 billion First National Bank and Trust Co. of Oklahoma City. One factor necessitating the negative bid: there were no other viable bidders. Early estimates are that this may become one of the most expensive transactions in FDIC history, with losses possibly as high as $600 million. Desperate to do a deal, the FDIC board made a finding that the bank was in danger of failing and the transaction would be less costly than a payoff. Just to be sure, in case the numbers did not work out, the board added that the bank was essential. The deal was going to be legal, one way or another.

On August 15, again breaking new ground, the FDIC board approved in principle a transaction that would funnel $130 million into Bank of Oklahoma of Oklahoma City in a complicated deal that includes stock warrants, give-ups by bank creditors, and other innovative provisions. Again the FDIC board found that the bank was in danger of failing and this transaction would be less costly than a payoff, primarily because loss of this lead bank would threaten its parent, BancOklahoma Corp., a $2.7 billion eleven-bank holding company, the state's second largest.

By September Seidman was publicly advocating a change in FDIC policy to permit expanded use of open-bank assistance even if there is stockholder benefit, so long as the transaction is less costly than a payoff or sale.

INDEX